T0306172

Green Gentrification

Green Gentrification looks at the social consequences of urban "greening" from an environmental justice and sustainable development perspective. Through a comparative examination of five cases of urban greening in Brooklyn, New York, it demonstrates that such initiatives, while positive for the environment, tend to increase inequality and thus undermine the social pillar of sustainable development. Although greening is ostensibly intended to improve environmental conditions in neighborhoods, it generates green gentrification that pushes out the working class, and people of color, and attracts white, wealthier in-migrants. Simply put, urban greening "richens and whitens," remaking the city for the *sustainability class*. Without equity-oriented public policy intervention, urban greening is negatively redistributive in global cities.

This book argues that environmental injustice outcomes are not inevitable. Early public policy interventions aimed at neighborhood stabilization can create more just sustainability outcomes. It highlights the negative social consequences of green growth coalition efforts to green the global city, and suggests policy choices to address them.

The book applies the lessons learned from green gentrification in Brooklyn to urban greening initiatives globally. It offers comparisons with other greening global cities. This is a timely and original book for all those studying environmental justice, urban planning, environmental sociology, and sustainable development as well as urban environmental activists, city planners and policy makers interested in issues of urban greening and gentrification.

Kenneth A. Gould is Director of the Urban Sustainability Program and Professor of Sociology at the City University of New York/Brooklyn College and Professor at the CUNY Graduate Center in Sociology and Earth and Environmental Sciences, USA. He is Chair of the Environment and Technology Section of the American Sociological Association.

Tammy L. Lewis is Director of Brooklyn College's Macaulay Honors Program and Professor of Sociology at the City University of New York/Brooklyn College and Professor at the CUNY Graduate Center in Sociology and Earth and Environmental Sciences, USA. She is Chair-Elect of the Environment and Technology Section of the American Sociological Association.

Routledge Equity, Justice and the Sustainable City series
Series editors: Julian Agyeman, Zarina Patel,
Abdou Maliq Simone and Stephen Zavestoski

This series positions equity and justice as central elements of the transition toward sustainable cities. The series introduces critical perspectives and new approaches to the practice and theory of urban planning and policy that ask how the world's cities can become 'greener' while becoming more fair, equitable and just.

Routledge Equity Justice and the Sustainable City series addresses sustainable-city trends in the Global North and South and investigates them for their potential to ensure a transition to urban sustainability that is equitable and just for all. These trends include municipal climate action plans; resource scarcity as tipping points into a vortex of urban dysfunction; inclusive urbanization; 'complete streets' as a tool for realizing more 'livable cities'; the use of information and analytics toward the creation of 'smart cities.'

The series welcomes submissions for high-level cutting edge research books that push thinking about sustainability, cities, justice and equity in new directions by challenging current conceptualizations and developing new ones. The series offers theoretical, methodological, and empirical advances that can be used by professionals and as supplementary reading in courses in urban geography, urban sociology, urban policy, environment and sustainability, development studies, planning, and a wide range of academic disciplines.

Incomplete Streets
Processes, practices and possibilities
*Edited by Stephen Zavestoski
and Julian Agyeman*

**Planning Sustainable Cities and
Regions**
Towards more equitable
development
Karen Chapple

**The Urban Struggle for Economic,
Environmental and Social Justice**
Deepening their roots
Malo Hutson

**Bicycle Justice and Urban
Transformation**
Biking for all?
*Edited by Aaron Golub,
Melody L. Hoffmann,
Adonia E. Lugo and
Gerardo Sandoval*

Green Gentrification
Urban sustainability and the
struggle for environmental justice
*Kenneth A. Gould and
Tammy L. Lewis*

"*Green Gentrification* is a remarkable book. Gould and Lewis offer important insights for activists, policy-makers, and residents on one of the most central problems facing New York City today: how can cities 'go green' without triggering gentrification? This book should be required reading for those interested in urban life today."

Dr. Julie Sze, Professor and Chair of American Studies,
University of California, Davis, USA

"In this path-breaking book, Gould and Lewis demonstrate that social inequality and injustice are not inevitable outcomes of urban sustainability projects. When community leaders demand that social equity becomes a core component of these plans, and public policy initiatives embrace that vision, Gould and Lewis find that urban greening can facilitate just sustainabilities. *Green Gentrification* offers some of the most persuasive arguments and evidence I am aware of that urban sustainability projects will succeed only when they take social justice and equity seriously."

Dr. David N. Pellow, Dehlsen Chair and Professor
of Environmental Studies and Director of the Global
Environmental Justice Project, University of California,
Santa Barbara, USA

"This book provides a much needed analysis of the challenges of urban sustainability and equity issues from the field of urban sociology. Their work is applicable to cities around the world, where efforts to clean-up toxic environments often create economic hardship for low-income and working poor urban residents. The reality that 'greening whitens' socially diverse neighborhoods makes evident the persistent contradictions involved in how cities try to create just and livable places. These case studies offer historical accounts that provide insights into developing new strategies for equitable and ecologically vibrant places."

Dr. Sarah Dooling, Assistant Professor, University of Texas, USA

Green Gentrification

Urban sustainability and the struggle for
environmental justice

Kenneth A. Gould and Tammy L. Lewis

LONDON AND NEW YORK

from Routledge

First published 2017
by Routledge
2 Park Square, Milton Park, Abingdon, Oxon OX14 4RN

and by Routledge
711 Third Avenue, New York, NY 10017

First issued in paperback 2017

Routledge is an imprint of the Taylor & Francis Group, an informa business

British Library Cataloguing-in-Publication Data
A catalogue record for this book is available from the British Library

Library of Congress Cataloging-in-Publication Data
A catalog record for this book has been requested

ISBN 13: 978-1-138-30913-5 (pbk)
ISBN 13: 978-1-138-92016-3 (hbk)

Typeset in Sabon
by FiSH Books Ltd, Enfield

Contents

Illustrations

Figures

Tables

Acknowledgements

We are grateful to many people who have contributed to this work. We have been fortunate to work with a number of dedicated, smart students from Brooklyn College and the CUNY Graduate Center who assisted us with data collection and organization, copyediting, and bibliographic work. Thanks to Martyna Cieniewicz, Michael Jolley, Hamad Sindi, and Isabella Clark. Mike's work was supported by the CUNY Graduate Center, Hamad's by the Gittell Research Assistantship Program, and Isabella's by a Kurz Fellowship. Students in our Urban Sustainability classes and in Macaulay Honors College's Seminar on Science and Technology in New York City gave us valuable feedback as we developed the ideas for the book.

We are also grateful to our colleagues from the Center for the Study of Brooklyn at Brooklyn College, Lorna Mason and Ed Morlock, who assisted us with mapping our initial sites and who provided us with their expert knowledge on census data. Over the years, we have engaged in ongoing conversations with our colleagues at Brooklyn College about gentrification in the borough. A special thanks to Jerry Krase, Emily Molina, and Tim Shortell. Our colleague Judy DeSena at St. John's University has also inspired our work.

We would also like to thank the Tow Foundation for financial support, through a Tow Family Professorship, for the writing of this book. We would also like to acknowledge the cooperation and assistance of the NYC Rent Guidelines Board.

A thanks is also due to the editors Julian Agyeman, Zarina Patel, Abdoumaliq Simone, and Stephen Zavestoski for putting together this timely and pragmatic series to address Equity, Justice, and the Sustainable City. Thanks, too, to our editors, Khanam Virjee and Helen Bell, the production team at Routledge, and the anonymous reviewers.

Finally, thanks to our family: Anna, for first bringing us to Public Place on a school field trip, and Isabel, for getting us to tour the soccer and softball fields of Prospect Park, Brooklyn Bridge Park, and Sunset Park.

We dedicate this book to the community activists striving to make our cities just and our communities sustainable.

Brooklyn, New York, USA
February 2016

1 Urban greening and social sustainability in a global context

Urban greening is a global phenomenon

Cities and mayors are leading the way in responding to the global ecological crisis, especially in addressing threats stemming from climate change, by "going green." Resilience planning and adaptation plans are well underway in major urban areas. Environmental discourse has become a normal part of urban politics worldwide (Evans 2002; Isenhour et al. 2015; Sze 2015). This has the potential to have a tremendous impact given that in 2014, 54 percent of the world's population lived in cities and the United Nations (2014) projects that to grow to 66 percent by 2050. Greening includes, literally, increasing the amount of public green spaces, such as parks (Harnik 2010). Green initiatives also promote increasing the energy efficiency of buildings, developing public transportation, providing healthy, locally sourced food, and improving recycling programs, among other initiatives (Birch and Wachter 2008; Fitzgerald 2010).

A quick Internet search of green cities yields hundreds of green projects from around the world. Ecowatch's "Top Greenest Cities in the World" (Pantsios 2014) are praised for high rates of bicycling (Amsterdam), cleaning up industrial pollution (Singapore) and for setting a goal to become carbon neutral (Copenhagen). Tourists looking to visit green cities might look to Vancouver for its city parks and "clean-technology innovation like solar-powered garbage compactors" or to San Francisco, the first major U.S. city to ban the use of plastic bags (Green Uptown 2015). The Latin American Green City Index ranks the Brazilian city of Curitiba as the greenest city in the continent in part due to its history since the 1960s of integrated greening initiatives and the incorporation of environmentalism into public consciousness (Abruzzese 2010). Portland, Oregon is often ranked the greenest city in the U.S. (Karlenzig et al. 2007).

New York City is one of the leaders in creating adaptation and resiliency plans and establishing urban greening policies (Karlenzig et al. 2007; Birch and Wachter 2008). Under the administration of Mayor Michael Bloomberg (2002–2013), New York City created the Office of Long-Term Planning and Sustainability and PlaNYC 2030, the city's "sustainability and resiliency blueprint." Bloomberg's leadership resulted in a number of high-profile greening projects. For example, he helped bring to fruition two highly successful park projects: the High Line Park in Manhattan and Brooklyn Bridge Park in Brooklyn. Both parks, which were transformed from dilapidated industrial infrastructure sites, are funded through public-private partnerships, with city, state and developer funding. They are public green spaces that integrate sustainable practices. The High Line, which was transformed from an abandoned rail trestle, took an unwanted land use and turned it into an environmental amenity for the neighborhood (and visitors from far and wide). Brooklyn Bridge Park (BBP) was transformed from a 1.3-mile stretch of abandoned industrial piers into a public urban water-front amenity. Like the High Line, environmental sustainability is one of its main features. The park was constructed with recycled building materials, and its design incorporates sustainable environmental processes, including the collection of rainwater in large tanks for reuse, helping address a problem the city has with overflowing storm water. Funds from high-end residential and commercial spaces along BBP are used for the park's maintenance, thus promoting economic sustainability.

These projects are successful in literal greening, and in that they have some degree of fiscal security. They also laid the groundwork for nearby areas to gentrify, and in the case of BBP, created hyper-gentrification of an already wealthy neighborhood. We call this process – greening initiatives followed by gentrification – *green gentrification* to represent how green initiatives cause and/or enhance gentrification. Gentrification is a social equity problem because it pushes out low-income residents in favor of high-income in-migrants (Marcuse 1986). While greening initiatives such as New York's improve the environmental quality of neighborhoods and turn economically "wasted" spaces into productive spaces, they do not do so equitably. They contribute to environmental sustainability, and economic sustainability, but not social sustainability. The greening of neighborhoods prepares them for gentrification, which allows elites (politicians and real estate developers) to benefit (Bryson 2012). We call these elites the *green growth coalition* because they work together to advocate for greening. We elaborate on this in the next chapter.

Social equity matters

We assess urban greening initiatives in terms of whether they promote sustainability in a broad sense. The idea of sustainability grew out of the concept of "sustainable development," which was popularized in 1992 at the United Nations Conference on Environment and Development, also known as the Earth Summit. Up to that time, advocates for the "development" of poor nations promoted economic development that often came at the cost of environmental protection. For instance, agents of development promoted industrialization as a means of increasing a poor nation's income even if it increased pollution. The pollution was considered a cost of economic development. However, in 1987 the World Commission on Environment and Development (known as the Brundtland Commission) promoted the concept of "sustainable development" in their report *Our Common Future*. The simple idea behind it was that both economic development problems and environmental pollution problems could be solved by generating economic growth that did not spoil the environment: sustainable development. The Brundtland Commission defined sustainable development as "development that meets the needs of the present without compromising the ability of future generations to meet their own needs." At the time, this was a significant shift in thinking: poor countries could be lifted out of poverty without degrading their environment, thus sustaining opportunities for future generations. The report explicitly refers to inequality reduction as central to sustainability. Since that time, "sustainability" and "sustainable development" have been defined as having three pillars: environmental protection, economic growth, and social equity. The inclusion of the "social" pillar acknowledges the importance of power, decision-making, and distribution in development (Hess 2009; Pavel 2009; Manzi et al. 2010). Social equity has been interpreted in a number of ways, including its comprising at least two parts. One part of social equity focuses on process: who has a say about development? Who makes decisions? Who gets to participate? The second part is focused on outcome: the equitable distribution of environmental goods and bads. In other words, who bears the costs of development and who gets the benefits? Over time, the concept of sustainable development has been contested. For instance, what should be sustained? What should be developed? Is development the same as growth? Whose needs should be promoted? Which pillar should be prioritized? (Humphrey, Lewis and Buttel 2002: 223).

Governments around the world, from the national level down to local levels, incorporated sustainable development into their planning. For instance, in 1992 President Bill Clinton established the President's Council on Sustainable Development. The following is one of the fifteen principles the council established: "Economic growth, environmental protection, and social equity should be interdependent, mutually reinforcing national goals, and policies to achieve these goals should be integrated" (cited in Daly 1996: 13). Historically, in New York City's plans, sustainability has been defined largely by environmental and economic criteria. The social equity piece has not been well integrated. However, social equity – in terms of process and outcomes – is a key element of urban sustainability (Evans 2002; Manzi et al. 2010; Pavel 2009; Isenhour et al. 2015).

In terms of process, for a development trajectory to be sustained it must have buy-in from the community experiencing development. Development that is imposed upon neighborhoods by outside interests will be resisted or rejected by residents. Those residents then have an interest in derailing, rather than sustaining, a development trajectory. If the goal of urban sustainability is to improve the quality of life for residents, while providing rewarding livelihoods, and maintaining a healthy and clean environment, residents must participate in, agree to, and benefit from development plans. There must be process equity (Agyeman 2005). Communities must be key agents in establishing the livability of their urban spaces (Evans 2002; Harvey 2008). In terms of outcomes, when environmental goods and bads are inequitably distributed, separate environmentally rich and environmentally poor communities are created. When more powerful residents live in areas with greater amenities and vice versa, there is a severed feedback loop between the natural system and the social system. Specifically, when powerful decision makers live near beautiful parks with nature views, they are less concerned about environmental bads. Pollutions, toxics, and waste sites are out of sight and out of mind. This reduces environmental consciousness and incentives to improve the environment overall. Those living in environmentally poor areas suffer from ecological degradation, declining health, reduced livelihood capacities, and overall this reduces their capacity to make changes to the development trajectory. Thus, on both ends of the spectrum, but for different reasons, when social equity is not an outcome of development plans, environmental sustainability is diminished (Gould 2006).

There is no doubt that urban greening and sustainability initiatives are necessary to address environmental issues, especially climate change. However, without policies that are attentive to the social justice aspects of sustainability, greening leads to greater inequality, and adds credence to claims of environmentalism and environmentalists being elitist. But this does not need to be the case. For example, in New York City, Mayor Bill de Blasio, elected in 2013, promotes a higher percentage of "affordable" housing in new developments, which would lessen the widening income gap in gentrifying neighborhoods. Affordable housing in New York City used to mean public housing and rent control. In the neoliberal city, it now means that private developers negotiate with the city over what percentage of new multifamily developments will be set aside at below-market, "affordable," rates. These rates are based on the median income in the area where construction takes place. Affordable housing policies are one mechanism to address equity. De Blasio's "One NYC: The Plan for a Strong and Just City" explicitly adds equity as a component to earlier sustainability and resiliency plans. This sort of planning that places justice and equity at the center is closer to what some academics call "just sustainability," discussed below. Recall, however, that equity is one of the three pillars of "sustainable development," thus in some way adding justice to such plan names is redundant. De Blasio's plan won't stop the green growth coalition and the process of green gentrification in a city dominated by real-estate interests, but it might diminish the most severe inequities.

Finally, in New York City there is sometimes an irony to green gentrification. Green initiatives often take place along formerly industrial waterfronts. When green gentrification follows, it leads to increased concentrations of wealthy people living along the water. The result is that more wealthy people live in the areas most vulnerable to the very real consequences of climate change. For instance, despite the effects of Hurricane Sandy in New York City, real-estate development continues in Flood Zone 1, the evacuation zone. The premium placed on waterfront property simply overwhelms concern for the increased frequency of coastal flooding in the Anthropocene (Gould and Lewis 2016). Other major waterfront developments around the city, such as at Hudson Yards on Manhattan's west side, and in Brooklyn at the Domino Sugar site, along the Gowanus Canal, and on Coney Island, proceeded with only minor nods to increased flooding risk. While the logic of adaptation to ecological conditions argues for a staged retreat from coastal flood zones, the logic of capital argues for increased investment in real estate with water views.

The global trend in urban sustainability provided context for the green growth machine – the coalition of real-estate developers and political elites – to transform brownfields such as the abandoned docks under the Brooklyn Bridge and the polluted Gowanus Canal into environmental amenities (Greenberg 2014). Through real-estate development associated with the greening, the green growth machine turned a profit and demographically transformed neighborhoods through this process of green gentrification.

Why Brooklyn?

We focus on Brooklyn, one of the five boroughs of New York City, to examine the process of green gentrification. Brooklyn is an example of a global city, a green city, and a gentrifying city. As such, its analysis can shed light on other global, green, and gentrifying cities. Methodologically, it also makes sense to study multiple cases within one city in order to make controlled comparisons. By examining five cases of greening within a single city, we are able to hold a number of variables constant (such as economic changes and demographic shifts), which allows us to isolate the consequences of the creation of urban environmental amenities on environmental justice. Given Brooklyn's large size, there were numerous sites of green gentrification that could be analyzed.

While Brooklyn is one of the five boroughs of New York City, Brooklyn is, by itself, a *global city*, with 2.5 million residents (compared to Manhattan's 1.4 million). One third of Brooklyn's inhabitants were born outside of the United States, with a stunning array of national origins, making it one of the most diverse cities on the planet (Lobo and Salvo 2013). New York City is arguably the lead global city in what remains the dominant global nation-state (Sassen 1991, 2005). As a global city, New York has dynamic flows of people and high levels of diversity, making it ideal for studying the changing dynamics of neighborhoods (Mason et al. 2012).

In the first decade of the twenty-first century, New York City played a leading role in establishing urban *greening* policy and placing cities in the leadership role they now hold in responding to the global ecological crisis. Under Mayor Bloomberg, New York City was an early developer of a sustainability plan (2007) following smaller cities such as Seattle, but leading the way in terms of the U.S.'s large cities. "PlaNYC: A Greener, Greater New York" (2007) focused on thematic areas: land (housing, open spaces, and brownfields), water (quality and network), transportation (congestion and state of repair), energy, air quality, and climate change. Immodestly, the plan aims to be "a plan that can become a model for cities in the 21st century" (New York City 2007: 11). For each theme, specific and measurable goals were established. Many were focused on environmental quality, such as cleaning up waterways. Other goals had clear economic benefits, such as improving travel time. A few had equity components. For instance, in the land category a goal is to "ensure that all New Yorkers live within a 10-minute walk of a park" (2007: 12). The plan was forward-thinking. Perhaps most ambitiously, it set a goal to decrease greenhouse gas emissions in the city 30 percent by 2030. At the time of the 2014 progress report, emissions had already decreased by 19 percent (The City of New York 2014). Within New York City, Brooklyn serves as the epicenter of a new urban environmental consciousness. For instance, on city owned land, the Brooklyn Navy Yard Development Corporation "promote[s] local economic development and job creation" at the Navy Yard (Brooklyn Navy Yard 2016). A cornerstone of the development is sustainability. They have the following initiatives underway on-site: rooftop farms, construction of LEED (leadership in energy and environmental design) certified buildings, use of a hybrid low emission vehicle fleet, and use of eco-friendly cleaning products. They have a green business directory highlighting their green industry tenants. This includes a company that makes furniture from salvaged wood, a printing and packaging company certified by the Rainforest Alliance, and a dry cleaner that uses alternative cleaning methods and is a member of the Green Cleaners Council. In the neighborhoods of Brooklyn, there are numerous "sustainable food" restaurants promoting "farm to table" sustainability that draw hipsters and others who embrace the "artisanal" and sustainability labels (see Figure 1.1).

Brooklyn has become self-consciously "green" in the twenty-first century. An article in the *Brooklyn Daily Eagle* immediately following the 2014 People's Climate March was titled "When It Comes to Environmentalism, Brooklyn Leads The Way." In that article, Raanan Gerber opines: "a good case can be made that Brooklyn is way ahead of the country in sustainable building practices and conservation. Indeed, if municipalities around the nation all did what Brooklyn did, we'd be in much better shape" (*Brooklyn Daily Eagle* 2014). A number of recent high-profile LEED certified buildings (private and public), new bike routes, and ambitious greenways are highlighted, as well as the high ratings local

Figure 1.1 Superb sustainable Brooklyn

elected officials receive from environmental advocacy groups. Brooklynites, old and new, are not known for being particularly shy or self-effacing, but the environmental swagger is relatively new, quite evident, and increasingly integral to the borough's identity.

Finally, many areas of New York City, and Brooklyn in particular, are experiencing a wave of *gentrification* (DeSena 2009; DeSena and Shortell 2012; Rice 2015). A report by *Governing* magazine of all of the census tracts in the city shows that between 2000 and 2010, 30 percent of tracts in New York gentrified ("New York Gentrification Maps and Data"). Due in large part to foreign migrants, Brooklyn's population is increasing faster than the rest of the city, the state, and the country (Brooklyn Chamber of Commerce 2015: 1). Much of this growth is also due to internal migration (Mason et al. 2012). According to a recent assessment by the Brooklyn Chamber of Commerce (2015: 1), "During the last decade, Brooklyn has steadily evolved into an internationally recognized global brand as a destination for the creative class and a base for the innovative economy." In the chapters that follow, census data examining race, income, educational level, rents and housing prices for specific neighborhoods over time will show areas where gentrification has been most pronounced. We will examine the relationship between greening and gentrification in attempts to tease out what, if any, role greening plays in gentrification processes. As part of its gentrification process, Brooklyn became hip. In the early twenty-first century, "Brooklyn is the most talked about, trendsetting destination in the world" (DeSena and Krase 2015: 3). The following summary of an article by William Ferguson in the *New York Times Magazine,* titled "Where is the new Brooklyn?" suggests why studying gentrified Brooklyn can lead to insights into other cities:

> Philadelphia is the new Brooklyn. Oakland, too, is the new Brooklyn, as are Jersey City and Anaheim. And based on dozens of recent newspaper articles (and too many blog posts to count), please consider the following additional candidates: Montreal, Queens, Nashville, Richmond, Anchorage, Buffalo, Baton Rouge, Bangalore, Warsaw and Aurora, Colo. And Doha, Qatar. All potential new Brooklyns. Which is a little weird for a city that has spent most of its existence as an outer-borough punch line. But like the new black, the new-Brooklyn meme is curiously durable. The last time this sort of trope was so popular was with Seattle in the 1990s. But then, the meaning of "the new Seattle" was clear: any city with a surplus of guitar bands or coffee bars was a new Seattle. To be a new Brooklyn means – well, it depends. It can signify a "gritty arts enclave" (Philadelphia), a "surprisingly O.K. place without all those rich people" (Oakland), a "real-estate speculator's dream" (Queens). But for Richard Florida, author of "The Rise of the Creative Class," it's all the same thing. " 'Brooklyn' is a euphemism for 'gentrification'," Florida says.
>
> (Ferguson 2009: 54)

A very brief history of some of the major demographic shifts in Brooklyn over the postindustrial period sets the stage for understanding the current boom period and for the cases we explore.

Brooklyn: historical context for a dynamic city

Brooklyn has been a site of constant, often dramatic, economic and demographic change throughout its history. In the post-World War II era, Brooklyn experienced steady and dramatic deindustrialization, led by the shifting of port facilities to New Jersey and the closing of the Brooklyn Navy Yards. Like most of the northeastern United States, deindustrialization left abandoned waterfronts around the city. Most older Brooklynites mark the end of a romanticized era of working-class ethnic neighborhoods by the defection of the Brooklyn Dodgers to Los Angeles in 1957. Throughout the 1960s and 1970s the borough experienced a steady population decline, fueled by reduced economic opportunities, and white flight. Many of Brooklyn's white ethnic residents moved to the expanding suburbs of Long Island and New Jersey, or relocated to the borough of Staten Island, facilitated by the opening of the Verrazano Narrows Bridge in 1964. By 1981 Brooklyn's population began to rebound, largely due to a wave of immigration from the Caribbean that would eventually give Brooklyn the largest Caribbean population outside of the Caribbean itself.

As higher-wage manufacturing jobs gave way to lower wage service employment, the demographic profile of Brooklyn became poorer and less white. The well-known cycle of urban decay proceeded, with steady disinvestment following New York City's economic crisis of the 1970s, and steady increases in crime and aid dependency. The perception of most public officials was that Brooklyn was in "decline." That decline took its toll on Brooklyn's substantial environmental amenities as well, such as Prospect Park.

Of course, economic decline can be parlayed into economic opportunity, and gentrifiers were able to claim some of Brooklyn's high quality housing stock at relatively low costs while in disrepair (Osman 2011). However, major reinvestment in Brooklyn did not emerge until the 1990s, marked by the downtown construction of the MetroTech Center (in the corner of Brooklyn closest to Manhattan's financial district). Efforts to reinvigorate Brooklyn's economy and attract investment were not limited to office parks. For instance, investment in Brooklyn's premiere park – Prospect Park – was also part of the redevelopment push in an era in which urban environmental amenities were increasingly recognized as valuable. As real-estate prices in Manhattan pushed wealthy whites over the bridges into Brooklyn, and the attacks of 9/11 made lower Manhattan even less attractive, a wave of gentrification in Brooklyn ensued. By 2002 there were sufficient push-and-pull factors in place to set off a major wave of real-estate investment and a major redistribution of housing. In the first half of the first decade of the new century, unemployment in Brooklyn fell, the number of jobs increased, and so did wages (Brooklyn Chamber of Commerce 2006). Not only was existing housing stock increasingly colonized by in-migrants into formerly less wealthy neighborhoods, but some of that housing stock was purchased by developers for a wave of new construction. The number of new residential building permits issued for Brooklyn doubled from 2001 to 2005 (Brooklyn Chamber of Commerce 2006). By 2005, Brooklyn had more new residential units permitted for construction than did Manhattan (Brooklyn Chamber of Commerce 2006). According to a 2015 study for the Chamber of Commerce, new building peaked sometime between 2005 and 2008. During that time, almost 42,000 new permits were issued. New building slowed down during the recession, and has picked up in the last few years. "In 2013, Brooklyn experienced its largest one-year increase in the number of residential building permits issued in 14 years. In 2014, approximately 7,500 building permits were issued in Brooklyn, surpassing 2004 levels, but still significantly below the peak of 12,700 issued in 2008." (Chamber of Commerce 2015: 3) The same report notes that Brooklyn's rising rents and home prices are outpacing the rest of the city. From 2004 to 2014, median home prices rose 44 percent in Brooklyn but only 30 percent in Manhattan. Median rents from 2012 to 2015 rose 26 percent in Brooklyn and only 13 percent in Manhattan.

During this period, waterfront sites that had been abandoned by deindustrialization became attractive to real-estate developers not interested in shipping but in waterfront views for wealthy residents who worked in the city's service economy, specifically the banking and financial economy. The development "One Brooklyn Bridge Park" is emblematic of that type of development. Described prior to its opening in 2007 by *The Real Deal: New York Real Estate News* as "the largest industrial-to-residential conversion in Brooklyn's history" (Cutler 2007), the building had been a distribution center along the industrial piers in Brooklyn Heights that was converted into 449 luxury apartments (see Figure 1.2). Amenities listed on the building's website include a yoga studio, billiard room, children's art room and bike storage. Prices at the outset were half a million dollars for a studio apartment, and the highest priced penthouse was listed at $7 million. Developers bought the building from the Jehovah's Witnesses when the city announced that it would build the Brooklyn Bridge Park along the piers. The developer agreed to pay a portion of the park's maintenance costs through a public-private partnership. This building is a perfect example of how the use of the waterfront area shifted over time from industrial to abandoned to residential. As our economy shifted from industry to service,

Figure 1.2 One Brooklyn Bridge Park, with new park beach in foreground

our use of the waterfront shifted as well. Waterfront property was rezoned from manufacturing to residential. This wasn't unique to Brooklyn, but was a consequence of global shifts in manufacturing from the U.S. to other countries, and from the "developed" to "developing" world in general (Marshall 2004).

One Brooklyn Bridge Park is situated along Brooklyn's "Gold Coast," the northeast of Brooklyn that is closest to Manhattan. This is where the wealthiest Brooklynites reside, and the highest percentage of whites. Like other global cities, Brooklyn clearly manifests the geography of racial and class residential segregation, despite its remarkable diversity. While market forces in Brooklyn real estate serve to generate residential class segregation, overt and covert racism in the real-estate industry serve to generate greater residential racial segregation. The wave of gentrification and residential redevelopment in Brooklyn has redistributed housing along racial lines, and often quite intentionally. For example, from 2003 to 2006 the National Fair Housing Alliance (NFHA) conducted a study of housing segregation and racial discrimination in twelve cities. The NFHA found one of the largest real-estate firms operating in Brooklyn to be engaged in "discriminatory real estate sales practices, including limited service, lack of follow-up and withholding of housing information" in regard to its African-American clients (NFHA 2006: 4).

> In Brooklyn, NFHA's testing of the Corcoran Group Real Estate, a member of NRT, Inc., revealed that real-estate agents steered home-buyers by race and denied basic services to African-Americans. Throughout NFHA's investigations, NRT, Inc. has proven time and time again that it maintains a pattern and practice of discrimination based on race.
>
> (NFHA 2006: 4)

In the midst of Brooklyn's wave of gentrification, one of its largest real-estate firms was found to be deeply engaged in the intentional racial restructuring of the borough. Corcoran's red-lined map (discovered by NFHA in a sting operation) clearly marks neighborhoods adjacent to recently restored environmental amenities such as a rehabilitated Prospect Park, and green space redesignated piers (Brooklyn Bridge Park) as places to which white in-migrants should be resettled (Cohen 2006). Corcoran's racial steering illustrates the spatial relationship between redeveloped urban environmental amenities and the redevelopment of urban neighborhoods for new, white, residents.

To summarize: Brooklyn has had its ups and downs in terms of its demographics and real-estate swings. Since the 1990s, the population has been increasing, new housing has been built, and prices are going up at a faster rate than the rest of New York City. As the population becomes denser, and new areas are sought for development, remnants of Brooklyn's industrial past – especially those along the waterfront – are being converted to luxury residences. Market forces limit most people's access to those apartments, and institutionalized forms of racism limit who gets access to those (re)constructed environmental amenities.

Contributions to the analysis

We come to this topic as environmental sociologists who teach in departments of sociology, urban sustainability, and Earth and environmental sciences (within the geography subsection). We teach about the intersections of sustainability, urban issues, and justice issues. As is true of many subfields such as environmental sociology that are at the boundaries of their discipline, we read across disciplines. In the course of our research, we have found a handful of scholars discussing similar processes and aspects to what we are calling "green gentrification" but none from sociology. Geographers (Quastel 2009; Pearsall 2012), anthropologists (Checker 2011; Isenhour et al. 2015), urban planners (Dooling 2009; Anguelovski 2015), and economists (Banzhaf and McCormick 2007) discussing similar processes have used the terms "ecological gentrification" and "environmental gentrification." We use "green" gentrification to align with what the agents of these urban processes claim to be doing for cities: "greening." We bring these literatures together in a single analysis to stimulate cross-disciplinary discussion that contributes to a more general understanding of green gentrification, and especially to identify what responses have been most effective in integrating social justice concerns into greening initiatives.

A sociological perspective deepens the current understanding of green gentrification (and its variants). In particular, sociologists' work on environmental justice, inequality, gentrification and environmental sociology that we will discuss in greater detail in Chapter 2, contributes to analyzing the process of green gentrification. We situate this research squarely within the sociological research on environmental justice. This tradition of research has historically examined where landfills and toxics and other locally unwanted land uses (LULUs) are sited, with particular attention to who lives in those spaces. In urban areas, the environmental "bads" are disproportionately placed in poor and minority neighborhoods. Studies in environmental justice look to the contests over such distributions and their consequences. An excellent urban example of this is David Pellow's (2002) *Garbage Wars: The Struggle for Environmental Justice in Chicago*. Pellow examines neighborhood-level conflicts in Chicago regarding the sitings of waste disposal and processing facilities. Our work similarly examines the siting of green projects, the political conflicts and social movement actors that emerge (or fail to), and the consequences for communities.

Another example in the environmental justice framework that influenced our approach is Julie Sze's *Noxious New York: The Racial Politics of Urban Health and Environmental Justice* (2007). Sze focuses on struggles in four neighborhoods in NYC against the placement of noxious incinerators, power plants, and waste transfer stations. Our book begins where Sze's ends. We look at how efforts to improve the environment actually lead to environmental injustice. We look at what happens when communities are successful at getting environmental hazards remediated or environmental amenities constructed in their neighborhoods. We examine the often paradoxical situation of having the success of an environmental justice struggle lead to an environmental justice defeat as ecologically remediated and enhanced neighborhoods become attractive to developers and gentrifiers. Although gentrification processes have not typically been conceptualized as environmental justice issues (Bryson 2012), we believe the environmental justice frame is essential to understanding the social impacts of urban greening initiatives.

In this work, we flip the environmental injustice idea on its head to look at who gets the environmental "goods," – greening in the city. We are indebted to Lisa Sun-Hee Park and David Pellow's (2011) work, *The Slums of Aspen: Immigrants vs. the Environment in America's Eden,* that examines how environmental protection in the resort town of Aspen was used as a means to increase the access for the wealthy to environmental amenities while pushing immigrant laborers aside. They show the process of creating and reinforcing "environmental privilege" for certain classes and races over others. They explain:

> We argue that environmental privilege results from the exercise of economic, political, and cultural power that some groups enjoy, which enables them exclusive access to coveted environmental amenities such as forests, parks, mountains, rivers, coastal property, open lands, and elite neighborhoods. Environmental privilege is embodied in the fact that some groups can access spaces and resources, which are protected from the kinds of ecological harm that other groups are forced to contend with every day.
>
> (Park and Pellow 2011: 4)

In the US, proximity to and size of urban green space is negatively associated with both levels of poverty, and percentages of blacks and Hispanics (Wen et al. 2013). Green gentrification is a process of creating and reinforcing environmental privilege for elites in the city.

Studies of environmental injustice imply that there is some "justice." Our understanding of this is informed by Julian Agyeman's (2005, 2013) work on "just sustainability." He emphasizes the social equity pillar of the sustainable development concept in the urban context. With colleagues, he has defined just sustainability as "The need to ensure a better quality of life for all, now and into the future, in a just and equitable manner, whilst living within the limits of supporting ecosystems" (Agyeman, Bullard and Evans 2003: 5). For our analysis of green gentrification, this implies that a better quality of life is due to all city dwellers and it should be applied fairly. Just sustainability emphasizes the social equity pillar that is part of the characterization of sustainable development. If environmental amenities are justly distributed in the city, all should have equal access: rich and poor, dark- and light-skinned, Brooklyn-born and immigrant. Similarly, the process of greening should not displace communities. As the National Environmental Justice Advisory Council observed regarding the connection between ecological remediation and gentrification, "no population should consistently pay a disproportionate price for the cleanup and revitalization of neighborhoods in which they live" (National Environmental Justice Advisory Council 2006: 19).

Environmental sociologists are becoming more interested in cities. While environmental justice scholars have looked at urban issues, environmental sociologists, broadly speaking, have focused the majority of their attention elsewhere. New environmental sociology on food justice has highlighted some of the social equity issues around food distribution, especially in cities (Alkon and Agyeman 2011; Alkon 2012; Gottlieb and Joshi 2010; Myers and Sbicca 2015; Anguelovski 2015). Anguelovski's (2015) work examines the displacement of ethnic groceries by Whole Foods, what she calls "food gentrification," (Anguelovski 2016) a process that parallels green gentrification. Zavestoski and Agyeman's (2015) edited collection in this series, *Incomplete Streets: Processes, Practices and Possibilities* explicitly links city spaces to questions of justice and sustainability, and Lubitow and Miller (2013) look to how urban spaces are often depoliticized by sustainability rhetoric. Recent contributions of environmental sociologists to understanding climate change that examine resilience, adaptation, and mitigation have policy implications for cities (Carmen et al. 2015, Ehrhart-Martinez et al. 2015, O'Neill and Van Abs 2016, Shi et al. 2016). Environmental sociology grew out of rural sociology but we expect that as a greater percentage of our population moves to the cities, and the cities become contested sites around climate change, we will see even more work focused on the environment in urban areas. We hope this work contributes to that.

Overview of the book and research plan

Green Gentrification: Urban Sustainability and the Struggle for Environmental Justice looks at the social consequences of urban sustainability initiatives: what we call "greening." Through a comparative examination of five cases of greening in Brooklyn, New York, we demonstrate that the outcomes of such initiatives, while often positive for environmental sustainability, tend to be socially unsustainable. We emphasize how greening alters the demographics of neighborhoods, leading us to a thesis that "greening whitens." The irony is that though greening is often intended to improve environmental conditions in contaminated working-class, working-poor, and people-of-color neighborhoods, it has the simultaneous consequence of pushing out lower-income and minority residents and attracting wealthier white in-migrants. Thus greening benefits primarily accrue to those in positions of greater power. The ultimate result of greening, barring policy interventions, is a greater gap between the privileged and the marginalized in terms of access to environmental amenities. Simply put, the main point is that urban greening creates environmental inequality unless equity oriented public policies intervene, and increased inequality is incompatible with sustainable development. The next chapter lays out the theoretical argument, drawing upon literatures from environmental justice, gentrification, and environmental sociology.

The following four chapters present case studies that illustrate the dynamic relationship between green gentrification and environmental justice. The cases include the restoration of Prospect Park (Chapter 3), the construction of Brooklyn Bridge Park in Brooklyn Heights (Chapter 4), the remediation of the Gowanus Canal (Chapter 5), and two cases that we group together (Chapter 6): the redevelopment of the Greenpoint-Williamsburg waterfront around Bushwick Inlet Park and the redevelopment of the Sunset Park neighborhood waterfront around Bush Terminal Park (see Figure 1.3). Using data from field observations, media accounts, and the census, we trace each case historically from the inception of the greening idea through to its current state. The cases are at different stages of development, from early implementation (Greenpoint-Williamsburg) to the midpoint of remediation (Gowanus Canal), through to completion (Prospect Park) (see Table 1.1). Green gentrification is a process. Projects are sited, implemented, and completed. By examining the historical processes comparatively, we are able to assess causal relationships.

In the first three cases, an environmental amenity has been (or is being) (re)constructed, and the neighborhood composition has changed as a result. In Prospect Park and Brooklyn Bridge Park, no social justice policies, such as affordable housing, were built into the processes. These cases illustrate how green gentrification occurs. The final case chapter, illustrating the Greenpoint-Williamsburg waterfront and Sunset Park cases, provides counter examples to show what happens when communities contest green gentrification and make demands for social equity. These cases make a key point in the analysis: inequality and injustice may not be inevitable outcomes of greening. Early public policy interventions aimed at neighborhood stabilization may create more just sustainability outcomes. While the first three case chapters highlight some of the negative social consequences of movements to "green" the city, the final case chapter suggests that policy choices can be used to mitigate them.

While the substantive focus of the volume is on Brooklyn, the theoretical scope of the analysis is global. In the concluding chapter, we will examine the Brooklyn-specific findings and seek to understand which findings are relevant for other cities. Brooklyn is an exemplar of a global city under a neoliberal greening regime. It demonstrates how public policy can

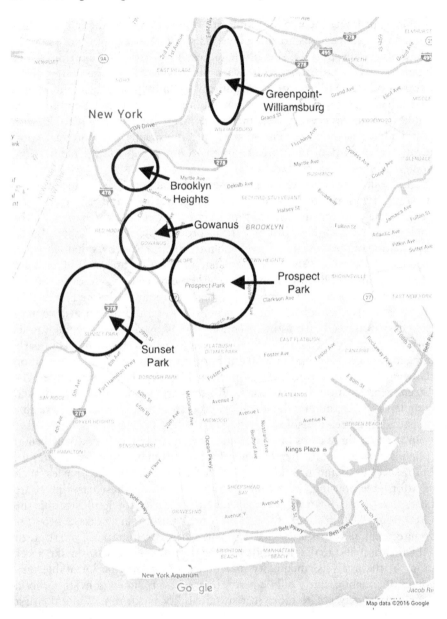

Figure 1.3 Green gentrification case study sites in Brooklyn

contribute to just sustainability. In our conclusion, we compare Brooklyn's initiatives with those of other global cities across the planet. We make comparisons with urban greening initiatives in Latin America (including São Paulo and Curitiba, Brazil), Asia (including Shanghai), Australia

Table 1.1 Cases in analysis

Case	Prospect Park	Brooklyn Bridge Park	Gowanus Canal	Greenpoint-Williamsburg Waterfront	Sunset Park
Type	Restoration of existing environmental amenity (park)	Rezoned from industrial to park and residential	Rezoned from industrial to residential; Superfund cleanup and brownfield restoration	Rezoned from industrial to residential, new green spaces promised	Limited rezoning for higher density; working waterfront remains; new park
Status	Completed	Nearing completion	In process	In process	Nearing completion
Community response	Supported restoration; no discussion of affordable housing	Supported park; resisted affordable housing	Supported cleanup and affordable housing	Demanding green space and affordable housing	Demanding green space, housing stability, and job retention
Gentrified?	Gentrified	Hyper-super-gentrified	Gentrifying	Gentrifying	Stable but threatened

(including Sydney), Africa (including Cape Town, South Africa), as well as in Europe (including Barcelona, Spain). We contrast global cities with smaller deindustrializing cities in the U.S., like Detroit, to consider why smaller cities might more easily incorporate social justice in greening initiatives to become "just green enough" (Curran and Hamilton 2012). We apply the lens developed by a deep analysis of urban greening in Brooklyn to urban greening initiatives globally.

Goals

Green Gentrification: Urban sustainability and the struggle for environmental justice is about the complicated goal of creating "sustainable" cities. In theory, sustainability has three pillars – environmental, economic, and social sustainability. In practice, however, sustainability has been equated with environmental improvements and/or protections. As a result, the social problems associated with environmental protection, namely unequal protection, are replicated in "sustainability" initiatives. Our book brings to light the social unsustainability of environmental sustainability initiatives and underscores the potential of public policy to create more socially sustainable cities.

Green Gentrification also aims to examine the role of urban greening as a catalyst for gentrification, rather than as a consequence. It does so in the largest borough of the largest global city in the U.S., which by itself would be the fourth largest city in the country, and which is both a major center of racial and ethnic diversity, and a major center of urban environmentalism. Brooklyn is arguably one of the "hottest" place names in the world at this moment. The five cases in various stages of greening initiatives provide a unique opportunity to examine the temporal variables in public policy intervention.

The book also aims to contribute to the understanding of urban public policy. Though the book's geographic focus is on Brooklyn, we compare and contrast it to other cities around the globe, with an emphasis on how public policies can be used to make greening more socially equitable. The findings are not unique to one city, but have implications for planning efforts generally.

Bibliography

Abruzzese, Leo. 2010. *Latin American Green City Index*. Siemens. Retrieved January 23, 2016 (www.siemens.com/press/pool/de/events/corporate/2010-11-lam/result-presentation.pdf).

Agyeman, Julian. 2005. *Sustainable Communities and the Challenge of Environmental Justice*. New York: New York University Press.

Agyeman, Julian. 2013. *Introducing Just Sustainabilities: Policy, Planning, and Practice*. New York: Zed Books.

Agyeman, Julian, Robert D. Bullard and Bob Evans. 2003. *Just Sustainabilities: Development in an Unequal World*. Cambridge, MA: The MIT Press.

Alkon, Alison H. 2012. *Black, White, and Green: Farmers Markets, Race, and the Green Economy*. Athens, GA: The University of Georgia Press.

Alkon, Alison H. and Julian Agyeman. 2011. *Cultivating Food Justice: Race, Class and Sustainability*. Cambridge, MA: The MIT Press.

Anguelovski, Isabelle. 2015. "Alternative Food Provision Conflicts in Cities: Contesting Food Privilege, Injustice, and Whiteness in Jamaica Plain, Boston." *Geoforum* 58: 184–194.

Anguelovski, Isabelle. 2016. "Healthy Food Stores, Greenlining and Food Gentrification: Contesting New Forms of Privilege, Displacement and Locally Unwanted Land Uses in Racially Mixed Neighborhoods." International Journal of Urban and Regional Research, DOI:10.1111/1468-2427.12299.

Banzhaf, H. Spencer and Eleanor McCormick. 2007. "Moving Beyond Cleanup: Identifying the Crucibles of Environmental Gentrification." Working Paper No. 07–29, Andrew Young School of Policy Studies Research Paper Series, Atlanta, GA: Georgia State University.

Birch, Eugenie L. and Susan M. Wachter. 2008. *Growing Greener Cities: Urban Sustainability in the Twenty-first Century*. Philadelphia, PA: University of Pennsylvania Press.

Brooklyn Chamber of Commerce. 2006. *Brooklyn Labor Market Review*. Spring 2006. Brooklyn, NY: Brooklyn Chamber of Commerce.

Brooklyn Chamber of Commerce. 2015. *Economic Assessment of the Brooklyn Economy – Baseline Study*. August 7. Submitted by Washington Square Partners.

Brooklyn Navy Yard. 2016. "Commitment to Sustainability." Retrieved January 14, 2016 (http://brooklynnavyyard.org/the-navy-yard/commitment-to-sustainability/).

Bryson, Jerome. 2012. "Brownfields Gentrification: Redevelopment Planning and Environmental Justice in Spokane, Washington." *Environmental Justice* 5(1): 26–31.

Carmen, JoAnn, Kathleen Tierney, Eric Chu, Lori M. Hunter, J. Timmons Roberts and Linda Shi. 2015. "Adaptation to Climate Change." In *Climate Change and Society: Sociological Perspectives*. Riley E. Dunlap and Robert J. Brulle. eds. New York: Oxford University Press, 164–198.

Checker, Melissa. 2011. "Wiped out by the 'Greenwave': Environmental Gentrification and the Paradoxical Politics of Urban Sustainability." *City & Society* 23(2): 210–29.

The City of New York. 2007. *PlaNYC: A Greener, Greater New York*. Mayor Michael R. Bloomberg.

The City of New York. 2014. *PlaNYC: Progress Report 2014: A Greener, Greater New York. A Stronger, More Resilient New York* (www.nyc.gov/html/plany c2030/downloads/pdf/140422_PlaNYCP-Report_FINAL_Web.pdf). Mayor Bill de Blasio.

Cohen, Ariella. 2006. "Corcoran Group Charged with Selling 'White' Nabes." *The Brooklyn Paper*, October 14.

Curran, Winifred and Trina Hamilton. 2012. "Just Green Enough: Contesting Environmental Gentrification in Greenpoint, Brooklyn." *Local Environment* 17(9): 1027–1042.

Cutler, Steve. 2007. "Brooklyn's Biggest Starts Selling." *The Real Deal: New York Real Estate News*, May 1.

Daly, Herman E. 1996. *Beyond Growth: The Economics of Sustainable Development*. Boston, MA: Beacon Press.

DeSena, Judith N. 2009. *Gentrification and Inequality in Brooklyn: The New Kids on the Block*. New York: Lexington Books.
DeSena, Judith N. and Jerome Krase. 2015. "Brooklyn Revisited: An Illustrated View from the Street 1970 to the Present." *Urbanities*, 5(2): 3–19.
DeSena, Judith N. and Timothy Shortell. 2012. *The World in Brooklyn: Gentrification, Immigration, and Ethnic Politics in a Global City*. Lanham, MD: Lexington Books.
Dooling, Sarah. 2009. "Ecological Gentrification: A Research Agenda Exploring Justice in the City." *International Journal of Urban and Regional Research* 33(3): 621–639.
Ehrhart-Martinez, Karen, Thomas K. Rudel, Kari Marie Norgaard, and Jeffrey Broadbent. 2015. "Mitigating Climate Change." In *Climate Change and Society: Sociological Perspectives*. Riley E. Dunlap and Robert J. Brulle. eds. New York: Oxford University Press, 199–234.
Evans, Peter. ed. 2002. *Livable Cities? Urban Struggles for Livelihood and Sustainability*. Berkeley, CA: University of California Press.
Ferguson, William. 2009. "Where is the New Brooklyn?" *New York Times Magazine*, March 15, p. 54.
Fitzgerald, Joan. 2010. *Emerald Cities: Urban Sustainability and Economic Development*. New York: Oxford University Press.
Gerberer, Raanan. 2014. "When It Comes to Environmentalism, Brooklyn Leads the Field." *Brooklyn Daily Eagle*, September 23.
Gottlieb, Robert, and Anupama Joshi. 2010. *Food Justice: Food, Health, and the Environment*. Cambridge, MA: The MIT Press.
Gould, Kenneth A. 2006. "Promoting Sustainability." In *Public Sociologies Reader*. Judith Blau and Keri Iyall Smith. eds. New York: Rowman and Littlefield, 213–230.
Gould, Kenneth A. and Tammy L. Lewis. 2016. "Green Gentrification and Superstorm Sandy: The Resilience of the Urban Redevelopment Treadmill in Brooklyn's Gowanus Canal." In *Taking Chances: The Coast After Hurricane Sandy*. Karen M. O'Neill and Daniel J. Van Abs. eds. New Brunswick, NJ: Rutgers University Press, 145–163.
Green Uptown. 2015. "Top Ten Greenest Cities in the World for 2015." Retrieved January 23, 2016 (www.greenuptown.com/top-ten-greenest-cities-world-2015/).
Greenberg, Miriam. 2014. "The Sustainability Edge: Competition, Crisis, and the Rise of Eco-City Branding in New York and New Orleans." In *Sustainability in the Global City: Myth and Practice*. Melissa Checker, Cindy Isenhour, and Gary McDonough. eds. Cambridge, UK: Cambridge University Press.
Harnik, Peter. 2010. *Urban Green: Innovative Parks for Resurgent Cities*. Washington, DC: Island Press.
Harvey, David. 2008. "The Right to the City." *New Left Review* 53: 23–40.
Hess, David J. 2009. *Localist Movements in a Global Economy: Sustainability, Justice, and Urban Development in the United States*. Cambridge, MA: The MIT Press.
Humphrey, Craig R., Tammy L. Lewis and Frederick H. Buttel. 2002. *Environment, Energy, and Society: A New Synthesis*. Belmont, CA: Wadsworth.
Isenhour, Cynthia, Gary McDonogh, and Melissa Checker. eds. 2015. *Sustainability as Myth and Practice in the Global City*. NY: Cambridge University Press.

Karlenzig, Warren, Frank Marquardt, Paula White, Rachel Yaseen, and Richard Young. 2007. *How Green Is Your City: The Sustainable US City Ranking.* Gabrioloa Island, BC: New Society Publishers.

Lobo, Arun Peter and Joseph J. Salvo. 2013. *The Newest New Yorkers: Characteristics of the City's Foreign-born Population, 2013 edition.* New York City Department of Planning. Retrieved January 24, 2016 (www.nyc.gov/html/dcp/pdf/census/nny2013/nny_2013.pdf).

Lubitow, Amy and Thaddeus R. Miller. 2013. "Contesting Sustainability: Bikes, Race, and Politics in Portlandia." *Environmental Justice* 6(4): 121–126.

Manzi, Tony, Karen Lucas, Tony Lloyd Jones, and Judith Allen. 2010. *Social Sustainability in Urban Areas: Communities, Connectivity, and the Urban Fabric.* London: Earthscan.

Marcuse, Peter. 1986. "Abandonment, Gentrification, and Displacement: The Linkages in New York City." In *Gentrification of the City.* Neil Smith and Peter Williams. eds. New York: Allen and Unwin, Inc., 153–157.

Marshall, Richard. ed. 2004. *Waterfronts in Post-Industrial Cities.* New York: Taylor & Francis.

Mason, Lorna, Ed Morlock, and Christina Pisano. 2012. "Mapping a Changing Brooklyn, Mapping a Changing World: Gentrification and Immigration, 2000–2008." In *The World in Brooklyn: Gentrification, Immigration, and Ethnic Politics in a Global City.* Judith N. DeSena and Timothy Shortell. eds. Lanham, MD: Lexington Books, 7–50.

National Environmental Justice Advisory Council. 2006. *Unintended Impacts of Redevelopment and Revitalization Efforts in Five Environmental Justice Communities.* National Environmental Justice Advisory Council. August.

National Fair Housing Alliance. 2006. *Housing Segregation Background Report: Brooklyn, NY.* Washington, DC: NFHA.

"New York City Gentrification Maps and Data." Retrieved January 14, 2016. *Governing* (www.governing.com/gov-data/new-york-gentrification-maps-demographic-data.html#citieslist).

O'Neill, Karen M. and Daniel J. Van Abs. eds. 2016. *Taking Chances: The Coast After Hurricane Sandy.* New Brunswick, NJ: Rutgers University Press.

Osman, Suleiman. 2011. *The Invention of Brownstone Brooklyn: Gentrification and the Search for Authenticity in Postwar New York.* New York: Oxford University Press.

Pantsios, Anastasia. 2014. "Top 10 Greenest Cities in the World." *EcoWatch,* October 24. Retrieved January 23, 2016 (http://ecowatch.com/2014/10/24/top-ten-greenest-cities-world/).

Park, Lisa Sun-Hee and David Naguib Pellow. 2011. *The Slums of Aspen: Immigrants vs. The Environment in America's Eden.* New York: NYU Press.

Pavel, M. Paloma. ed. 2009. *Breakthrough Communities: Sustainability and Justice in the Next American Metropolis.* Cambridge, MA: The MIT Press.

Pearsall, Hamil. 2012. "Moving out or Moving in? Resilience to Environmental Gentrification in New York City." *Local Environment* 17(9): 1013–1026.

Pellow, David Naguib. 2002. *Garbage Wars: The Struggle for Environmental Justice in Chicago.* Cambridge, Massachusetts, MA: The MIT Press.

Quastel, Noah 2009. "Political Ecologies of Gentrification." *Urban Geography* 30(7): 694–725.

Rice, Andrew. 2015. "The Red Hot Rubble of East New York: How Brooklyn's Gentrification Profiteers Are Expanding their Boundaries." *New York Magazine*, January 26, p. 9.

Sassen, Saskia. 1991. *The Global City: New York, London, Tokyo*. Princeton, NJ: Princeton University Press.

Sassen, Saskia. 2005. "The Global City: Introducing a Concept." *The Brown Journal of World Affairs* XI(2): 27–43.

Shi, Linda, Eric Chu, Isabelle Anguelovski, Alexander Aylett, Jessica Debats, Kian Goh, Todd Schenk, Karen C. Seto, David Dodman, Debra Roberts, J. Timmons Roberts and Stacy D. VanDeveer. 2016. "Roadmap Towards Justice in Urban Climate Adaptation Research." *Nature Climate Change* 6: 131–137.

Sze, Julie. 2006. *Noxious New York: The Racial Politics of Urban Health and Environmental Justice*. Cambridge, MA: The MIT Press.

Sze, Julie. 2015. *Fantasy Islands: Chinese Dreams and Ecological Fears in an Age of Climate Crisis*. Oakland, CA: University of California Press.

United Nations. 2014. "World's Population Increasingly Urban with More than Half Living in Urban Areas." Retrieved January 23, 2016 (www.un.org/development/desa/en/news/population/world-urbanization-prospects.html).

Wen, Ming, Xingyou Zhang, Carmen D. Harris, James B. Holt, and Janet B. Croft. 2013. "Spatial Disparities in the Distribution of Parks and Green Spaces in the USA." *Annals of Behavioral Medicine* 45(1): S18–S27.

World Commission on Environment and Development. 1987. *Our Common Future*. Oxford University.

Zavestoski, Stephen and Julian Agyeman. eds. 2015. *Incomplete Streets: Processes, Practices and Possibilities*. London: Routledge.

2 Conceptualizing green gentrification

This chapter defines "green gentrification." We draw on the sociological literature focused on environmental justice, inequality, gentrification, urban sociology and environmental sociology. We situate the concept of green gentrification within broad social processes that produce and reproduce inequality in society.

Real estate markets that reproduce race and class inequalities in capitalist societies in general also reproduce them in greening urban communities. Similarly, coalitions of elites that promote (and are rewarded by) economic growth initiatives, are rewarded in the same way by green growth initiatives. Thus, while greening may appear to be a benefit to society, as sociologists we persistently ask the question: for whom? Green initiatives tend to reproduce current structures of inequality, benefit those at the top of those structures, and hurt those at the bottom. These processes, however, are not inevitable. Other stakeholders (community groups and social movement actors) can resist these processes, but they are in structurally less powerful positions.

Defining green gentrification

We use the term green gentrification to describe a subset of urban gentrification. The process of green gentrification is started by greening initiatives that create or restore environmental amenities. Environmental amenities draw in wealthier groups of residents and push out lower-income residents, thus creating gentrification.

Rather than cases in which already gentrified neighborhoods develop constituencies for local environmental amenities (where gentrification leads to greening), our focus is primarily on cases in which a significant greening event leads to gentrification. In cases in which the gentrification process *may* be in the earliest stage, it is often difficult to tease out the causal direction (i.e. whether gentrification leads to greening or greening to gentrification). We do not doubt that gentrification can lead to greening. In the 1980s, the Park Slope neighborhood adjacent to Prospect Park showed early signs of gentrification (in terms of shifting constituencies) at the same time the city and a nonprofit organization were starting to raise funds for redevelopment of Prospect Park. The neighborhood gentrification and the park redevelopment contributed to each other, i.e. the nascent gentrification created a local constituency for greening and the greening increased the gentrification, though it is not clear which came first. In addition to this iterative growth process, we argue that greening has an independent and direct effect on gentrification. In other words, a "greening event" on its own can generate gentrification. Nevertheless, both causal directions have distributional implications. They both have the effect of providing greater access to environmental amenities to richer, more powerful groups.

In green gentrification, existing and potential environmental amenities price out the current group of residents and draw in a wealthier group. The displaced become a new form of "environmental refugee" who are forced to flee from enhanced environmental improvements which increase quality of life and property values simultaneously. In many instances, such green-led redevelopment is intentional, as investors and public officials create new or renewed green spaces as a means to raise property values and tax revenues.

For example, as we discuss later, the original idea for Prospect Park emerged as a gentrification scheme where the establishment of a green amenity would attract wealthy residents and boost real estate values in Brooklyn. The success of the park generated high-quality housing stock that would later provide the infrastructure for subsequent waves of gentrification. Clearly, there are many causes of gentrification. Historical architecture, proximity to transportation, public policies, and cycles of investment are some of these (see Zukin 1982, 1987; Abu-Lughod 1994; Smith 1996). Our purpose here is to show the impacts and implications of "greening" as an element of gentrification.

The concept of green gentrification builds on the idea of gentrification. Marcuse defines gentrification as "the movement into a previously working-class area by upper-income households, generally professionals, managers, technicians, the new gentry, resulting in the displacement of the former lower-income residents" (Marcuse 1999: 790–791, cited in Curran 2007). His focus on displacement is a key part of the process of green gentrification. A second definition we find useful for its emphasis on the distributional impacts is the one Tom Angotti (2008) uses in his book about New York City real estate processes, *New York for Sale*:

> Throughout the city's history, working people without wealth have been shunted from one city tenement to another, especially after they make improvements to their housing and neighborhood. As tenants and small business owners invest their time and money to gradually upgrade their neighborhoods, real estate investors become attracted to these areas and anxious to capitalize on the improvements. As investors large and small move in, they effectively appropriate the value generated by

others. This is the essence of what is now known as *gentrification*. It is not simply a change in demographics. It is *the appropriation of economic value by one class from another.*

(Angotti 2008: 108, italics in original)

"Green" gentrification is different than the gentrification that Angotti describes in that the greening of the amenity is not necessarily due to the actions of "tenants and small business owners," rather the greening often comes primarily from outside investors (public and private) who appropriate the value of an un-revitalized environmental resource. In this sense it is the *appropriation of the economic values of* an environmental resource *by one class from another.* As we will illustrate with the cases of Prospect Park, Brooklyn Bridge Park, and the Gowanus Canal, calls for environmental restoration draw state resources aimed at producing an urban environmental amenity, which is then appropriated by extra-local capital interests (both developers and in-migrants). This process has been documented in environmental justice struggles elsewhere in New York City (Sze 2007).

Environmental injustice

The concept of green gentrification also grows out of the literature on environmental injustice. This literature provides ample evidence to show that the environmental "bads" in society, such as toxic pollutants and "locally

Figure 2.1 The High Line Park green gentrification site in Manhattan

unwanted land uses" (LULUs) and their consequent public health hazards, are disproportionately found in politically disenfranchised minority- and poor- neighborhoods (United Church of Christ 1987; Bullard 1990, 1993, 1994; Bryant and Mohai 1992; Bryant 1995; Szasz and Meuser 1997; Pulido 2000; Roberts and Toffolon-Weiss 2001; Pellow 2002; Sze 2007; Bullard et al. 2007; Taylor 2009). The term "environmental racism" was coined specifically to describe race-based discrimination in the siting of hazardous facilities and the remediation of environmental hazards in the United States. Numerous studies have indicated that in the United States, race is a strong predictor of where environmentally hazardous facilities will be located (Bryant and Mohai 1992; Bullard 1994; Brulle and Pellow 2006; Mohai and Saha 2007, 2015).

The flip side of environmental injustice looks at who gets the environmental "goods," such as parks, clean air and water, and access to waterfront resources (Lewis 2011; Park and Pellow 2011). Historical processes matter in the siting of both environmental hazards and amenities. At each end of the spectrum, the consequences for communities of such sitings tend to exacerbate social and economic inequality. Inequitable distribution of environmental goods and bads occurs, in part, because of segregation in housing (Bullard, Grigsby, and Lee 1994; Cole and Foster 2001; Gould 2006).

Figure 2.2 LULUs clustered in Gowanus, Brooklyn

Residential racial segregation and its institutional reproduction

Residential neighborhoods in the United States are segregated by race and class (Massey and Denton 1993). This is especially true in Brooklyn. Racism in real estate markets, lending institutions, and employment generates extreme levels of racial segregation in residential patterns (Massey and Denton 1993). Well-documented social phenomena such as "white flight" allow real estate companies to "block bust" and "flip" entire neighborhoods. Race-based differences in access to credit due to lending discrimination in mortgage and home improvement loans, and lending institutions' redlining of neighborhoods, restrict housing markets for people of color and slate neighborhoods for decay and devaluation. Real estate companies similarly redline neighborhoods to use racial animosity and unease to manipulate the relative value of housing stock in order to maximize profits on sales and investments. As discussed in Chapter 1, this is not an abstract hypothesis. The National Fair Housing Alliance (NFHA) found that one of Brooklyn's largest real estate companies discriminated on the basis of race (NFHA 2007). The NFHA noted regarding Corcoran Group Real Estate's actions in Brooklyn that "During its sixteen-year history of existence, the NFHA has never uncovered such a literal and blatant example of sales steering" (NFHA 2007: 7).

Segregation by race (and class) exacerbates inequality on a number of levels through key social institutions. Take education, for example. In the United States, public education is promoted as a means of giving everyone equal access to opportunity. However, the reliance of funding for public education on property values (and fundraising by local parent-teacher associations in urban neighborhoods) reinforces neighborhood inequalities. Neighborhoods of color and lower-class neighborhoods receive lower levels of funding, lower-quality education, and worse educational outcomes (Kozol 1992; MacLeod 1995). This reduces long-term purchasing power and creditworthiness, and restricts access to more expensive and extensive housing options and locations. All of this feeds into larger sociocultural and social structural patterns of racial discrimination in employment and promotion, again limiting access to the income, wealth and credit that could facilitate better and wider housing horizons for people of color (Cole and Foster 2001).

These multifaceted systems of racial inequality produce the landscape of "residential apartheid" that is a key factor in allowing the owners of and investors in production and disposal facilities to target communities of color for a disproportionate share of the environmental and public health costs of production (Bullard et al. 1994; Cole and Foster 2001).[1] At the same time, the existence of racially segregated housing patterns allows for the environmental protection of white communities, which reap a greater share of the economic benefits of production while shifting the ecological and health costs to communities of color. Underlying the race-based systems of housing distribution is an economic structure that routinely and regularly distributes environmental hazards socioeconomically downward, and environmental amenities socioeconomically upward (Gould 2006).

Real estate markets reproduce class inequalities

Housing market dynamics are key to understanding how it is that environmental hazards can be placed among the poorest and least powerful, while environmental amenities can be afforded by the richest and most powerful. The class-based segregation of housing is a normal outcome of the functioning of a capitalist economy in which housing is distributed on the basis of wealth. Housing costs near hazardous sites such as industrial plants, waste dumps, and sewage treatment plants will be lower; those near environmental amenities, higher. In general, the higher the known and obvious environmental risks in an area, the lower the cost of housing. Housing in environmentally safe areas at greater distances from hazardous facilities tends to command higher prices. Housing abutting well-maintained parks, greenways, and clean waterfronts comes at a premium, especially in congested urban areas. As a result, the poor and working class are constrained in their choice of housing location and restricted to living in those areas with greater environmental and health risks and lower access to environmental amenities (Wen et al. 2013). Those earning higher wages or receiving their income from investments have greater freedom to choose among more, and less, desirable housing locations. With the option to do so, wealthy individuals will tend to choose to live where environmental risks are lower and environmental amenities are greater. The structure of housing markets functions to reinforce class-based distributions of environmental bads and goods.

Housing markets also shape responses to real or perceived changes in neighborhood environments. If an area believed to be free of environmental hazards is found to be contaminated, those with greater wealth will be able to move to a less hazardous location. Those with less wealth will be forced to remain in the contaminated area (Szasz 1994). In this way the structure of housing markets functions to continually reinforce and deepen the class-based distribution of exposure to environmental hazards, as the wealthy exercise an exposure "exit option" that is unavailable to the lower classes (see Figure 2.3). Because of the restricted housing markets for people of color, even wealthier people of color have more limited exit options to avoid environmental risks and to gain access to environmental goods (Pulido 2000; Cole and Foster 2001).

Conversely, if environmental amenities are created or restored in a previously poor or working-class community, the value of that real estate increases. As demand for housing next to the environmental amenity increases, housing prices are pushed upward. Existing residents (without

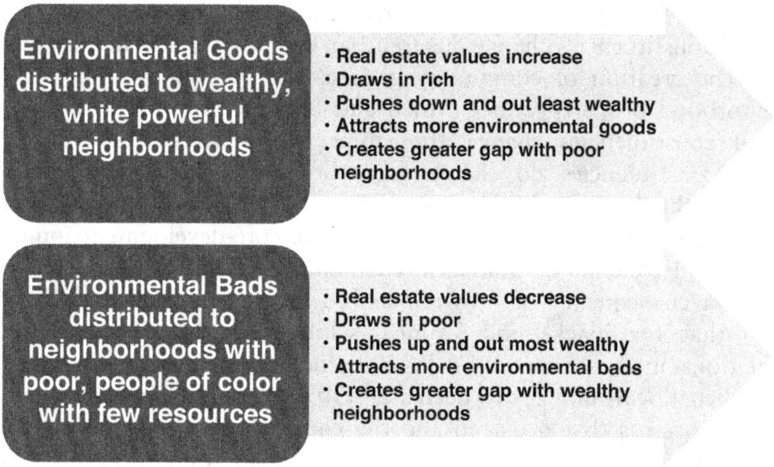

Environmental Goods distributed to wealthy, white powerful neighborhoods
- Real estate values increase
- Draws in rich
- Pushes down and out least wealthy
- Attracts more environmental goods
- Creates greater gap with poor neighborhoods

Environmental Bads distributed to neighborhoods with poor, people of color with few resources
- Real estate values decrease
- Draws in poor
- Pushes up and out most wealthy
- Attracts more environmental bads
- Creates greater gap with wealthy neighborhoods

Figure 2.3 Distribution of mobile environmental goods/bads creates increasing gap between affluent and poor neighborhoods

the means to increase the share of their incomes spent on rent) are forced to abandon their neighborhoods to make room for new, wealthier residents. For homeowners, as the market values of homes near a restored environmental amenity rise, the incentive to sell increases, further increasing the likelihood that houses and neighborhoods will be "flipped." The higher the home value relative to the owner's wealth, the greater the incentive to sell. Real estate market forces tend to respond to greening by redistributing access away from existing poor, working-class, and middle-class residents to wealthier in-migrants able to afford the higher housing costs that the environmental improvements have generated (Bryson 2012). This process exacerbates the gap between the haves and the have-nots (see Figure 2.4).

IMMOBILE RESOURCE — Environmental site with low value, yet potential, is remediated with funds via state, developers, NGOs, etc.

RESOURCE TRANSFORMED — Environmental bad (or environmental neutral) becomes environmental good and site with high value

POPULATIONS SHIFT — Wealthy, white powerful in-migrants

Poor, people of color with less resources displaced

Figure 2.4 Changes in distribution of benefits of immobile environmental resource when it changes from an environmental bad (or environmental neutral) to an environmental good via remediation/restoration

There are few published accounts that empirically examine how neighborhood constituencies change due to urban ecological restoration in global cities. The creation of community gardens has been shown to increase neighborhood property values (Voicu and Been 2008), although it is not clear if constituencies change after these events. According to Essoka (2010), constituencies do change after brownfield redevelopment. His analysis of the demographic changes that took place at sixty-one brownfield redevelopment sites comparing census data from pre-development and post-development concludes: "Statistical techniques revealed that gentrification is often a consequence of brownfields redevelopment. The data demonstrates that for Blacks and Latinos, while their overall metropolitan populations increase or stay the same, local brownfields revitalization forces their [local] number to decrease" (309). Though he does not examine the processes that occurred and the changes to real estate, his study documents racial demographic shifts as a result of restoration or "greening." In contrast, Banzhaf and McCormick (2007) find little evidence of racial transition following LULU remediation. Case studies, such as that of a Superfund cleanup in Spokane, Washington, show how some of these processes occur and are tied into the speculative real estate market (Bryson 2012). An analysis of housing values within one kilometer of Superfund site cleanups found that they increased after cleanup by 18 percent (Gamper-Rabindran, Mastromonaco and Timmins 2011). When sites are removed from the Superfund list, nearby demographics change: mean household income increases, as does the percentage of college graduates (Gamper-Rabindran and Timmins 2011). In the cases that we study, we examine demographic changes in the neighborhood throughout the greening process.

Intersectional disempowerment and environmental equity

If residential patterns were not segregated by race and class, environmental hazards and their negative public health impacts would by necessity tend to be distributed more evenly across the stratification system. Similarly, access to neighborhood environmental amenities could not be easily reserved for the wealthy. As noted above, a combination of racial discrimination in lending and real estate practices (rooted in exploiting racism to boost profitability) limits the housing market for people of color. The structure of the economy limits the ability of the poor and working class to avoid exposure to environmental hazards; and institutional and cultural racism serves to limit the ability of people of color to avoid exposure to environmental hazards. Since poor people of color experience both forms of restriction both independently and synergistically (in terms of racism reducing access to the means by which to increase class status – most notably education, employment, and credit), it is they who have the least capacity to avoid exposure to environmental hazards, and the least capacity to exercise an "exit option" when hazards are identified.

Conversely, these same synergistic and independent processes of racial and class discrimination in housing options make it less possible for people of color (especially poor, working-class, and middle-class people of color) to move into neighborhoods which offer easy access to environmental amenities, or to remain in neighborhoods in which environmental amenities have been added or restored. Ecological remediation of potential environmental amenities is therefore likely to not only redistribute access to the amenity through residential access to those with greater wealth, but in doing so, such environmental improvements are likely to redistribute access to the amenity and surrounding residential spaces from people of color to white in-migrants (National Environmental Justice Advisory Council 2006).

Real estate markets reproduce power inequalities and structure the degree to which communities can resist

Markets, left to function on their own without state intervention, will normally distribute goods and services on the basis of wealth. In capitalist societies, wealth is a primary component of power. Those with greater economic power have a greater ability to influence the state, even in ostensibly democratic political systems (Domhoff 1998). People of color are systematically excluded from mechanisms of capital accumulation. Power to control patterns of capital investment, to control the creation and distribution of employment, to finance electoral campaigns, and to purchase mass media time and space provides the wealthy with greater access to, and influence over, public policy decision-makers. While greater political power accrues to those with greater wealth, greater wealth also accrues to those with greater political power. Residential segregation concentrates the politically powerful in specific communities (Domhoff 1998), while simultaneously concentrating the politically less powerful in other communities. The distribution of political power and the distribution of housing location synergistically generate a spatial distribution of power (Zukin 1991). In theory, it should be possible to map this distribution as a social geography of political power.

The distribution of distinct spatial locations of political power within and between various neighborhoods is a normal outgrowth of the functioning of a market economy. These market functions intersect with systems of racial discrimination. This produces neighborhoods with limited capacities to reject the imposition of environmental hazards and to effect the restoration of environmental amenities, while simultaneously creating neighborhoods with enormous capacity to control their own environmental trajectories (Cole and Foster 2001). The more powerful neighborhoods will be home to politicians, lawyers, doctors, real estate developers, and other professionals whom may be mobilized as a political resource in efforts to repel the siting of a LULU or to locally initiate the remediation of a degraded environmental resource. The less powerful, less wealthy neighborhoods are less likely to have such human capital resources immediately at their disposal (Pastor, Sadd and Hipp 2001). This lack of professional human capital resources makes those neighborhoods more vulnerable to state and industry efforts to site LULUs in close proximity to their residential locations.

This unequal spatial distribution of power operates in two ways. First, those seeking to locate a hazardous facility can apply their sense of the spatial geography of power to choose siting locations where low levels of effective political resistance are likely (Cerrell Associates and Powell 1984; Mohai and Saha 2015). In this way, the existence of potentially mobilizable power is sufficient to keep environmental hazards out of wealthier neighborhoods. The environmental trajectory of gentrified urban neighborhoods is therefore "greener." Poorer, less powerful neighborhoods are, conversely, more likely to be targeted for hazardous facility siting as decision-makers anticipate the political resistance of more powerful neighborhoods (Lake 1996; Pulido 1996). The neighborhoods to which those displaced by gentrification are forced to relocate are therefore likely to have "browner" environmental trajectories.

Second, more powerful neighborhoods, if chosen as the preferred location for the siting of a LULU, can mobilize their economic and political resources to effectively defeat the siting effort. Less powerful poor communities, lacking the economic resources, political connections, and professional human capital resources which may bolster an effort to prevent a facility siting, will often be less able to mount a successful rejection campaign. The outcome of the unequal spatial distribution of political power is a further reinforcement of the economic tendency to distribute environmental and public health risks to poor, working-class, and minority populations.

Less wealthy and less powerful communities of color will clearly find it difficult to effectively fight for the ecological restoration of environmental amenities in their urban neighborhoods (Bullard 1994). Poor and working-class communities of color possess limited resources, and greater policy attention will be focused on the environmental demands of wealthier neighborhoods. Additionally, policymakers have an incentive to retain the important functions that environmentally degraded neighborhoods play in the greater metropolis as spaces to which the environmental risks that are unwanted by wealthier communities may be distributed (Pellow 2002). Therefore, community-based grassroots struggles for green space or waterfront restoration in poor neighborhoods face a daunting uphill battle. Environmentally motivated community activists from wealthier neighborhoods may be enlisted to join the battle to restore urban environments, but arguments resting on purely ecological and quality of life grounds may fall short in a policy arena that responds to power, profit and economic growth. However, with the potential profit to be realized from environmental restoration for real estate investors and developers, efforts for the rehabilitation of environmental amenities may attract other external allies. Ecological remediation can make entire neighborhoods more attractive and more valuable, thus holding out the promise for fusing economic growth priorities with environmental values. However, from its conception, the social trajectory of such ecological renewal is to combine the improvement of the environment with the dislocation of the urban residents who inhabit it. Neighborhoods may be environmentally rehabilitated, but for newcomers with resources, not for those who currently live with the degraded amenity. As the National Environmental Justice Advisory Council noted in 2006, "environmental cleanup of these formerly industrial, now residential, communities can be a powerful displacing force" (National Environmental Justice Advisory Council 2006: 2).

Resisting injustice; seeking just sustainability

Community struggles that seek environmental justice (Čapek 1993; Cole and Foster 2001; Pellow 2002; Bullard et al. 2007; Sze 2007), just sustainability (Agyeman, Bullard, and Evans 2003; Agyeman 2005, 2013; Alkon 2012), enhanced quality of urban life (Zavestoski and Agyeman 2015), and those that resist gentrification broadly speaking (Smith 1996; Muñiz 1998; Newman and Wyly 2006), run parallel to the grassroots movements in neighborhoods that resist the negative consequences of green gentrification. While there is a relatively new and growing literature that examines variants of green gentrification (Banzhaf and McCormick 2007; Dale and Newman 2009; Dooling 2009; Quastel 2009; Pearsall 2010; Checker 2011; Eckerd 2011; Gould and Lewis 2012, 2016), only a small subset of that research explores whether and how communities respond to gentrification caused by greening (Curran and Hamilton 2012; Pearsall 2012; Hamilton and Curran 2013; Pearsall 2013).

We contribute to these studies of resistance through the cases in Sunset Park (Bush Terminal Park) and the Greenpoint-Williamsburg waterfront (Bushwick Inlet Park). Of the five cases we examine, these two cases stand apart because the communities are organized to fight against the injustices associated with greening initiatives. In two of our cases (Prospect Park and Brooklyn Bridge Park), the communities made no equity demands and no official actions were taken to ensure equitable distribution of the environmental goods. In the case of Gowanus, community groups demanded some affordable housing, and that's what they got – some. In Sunset Park and Greenpoint-Williamsburg, the communities are more engaged and more demanding to ensure that the existing communities benefit from the new and proposed environmental amenities. By comparing cases with and without community engagement and strong resistance to displacement, we can better understand the results of such engagement.

The treadmill of production, the green growth machine, and the urban greening treadmill

The logic of growth that is at the center of the political economy underlies all of these processes. In environmental sociology, the "treadmill of production" (TOP) frames our understanding of the dialectical relationship between social systems and ecological systems (Schnaiberg 1980; Schnaiberg and Gould 2000; Gould, Pellow and Schnaiberg 2008). In short, the TOP theory argues that key actors in the social system (states, corporations, and citizen-workers) all have an interest in economic growth. States benefit from growth because it enables them to collect taxes, which funds their work and increases their power. Corporations promote growth because it generates profit, their primary goal. Citizen-workers favor growth because it provides them with jobs. However, economic growth in postindustrial capitalist societies tends to: 1) create environmental problems, and 2) create social problems, especially those associated with the unequal distribution of economic resources. Social responses to these problems paradoxically call for increased economic growth, because growth promises to generate revenues for environmental improvements, economic opportunities for upward social mobility, and the revenues for social welfare relief. Growth is not recognized as the inherent cause of the problems of growing inequality and growing environmental disorganization. Calls to solve the problems generated by growth, through yet more growth, benefit treadmill elites (government and corporate leaders), while those lower in the social structure bear the costs. The nature of the "treadmill" is that with each cycle of growth, the problems are exacerbated but the response to the problem – growth – deepens the problems. In this model, change comes from social movement actors seeking ways to slow the treadmill, demanding greater equity and environmental protection without growth – often through redistribution (Gould, Schnaiberg, and Weinberg 1996; Lewis 2016).

The treadmill of production generates both economic benefits and environmental hazards. The economic benefits of production tend to be distributed upward in the stratification system. Owners, managers and investors reap a greater share of the economic benefits generated by the production of goods and services than do workers. Conversely, the environmental hazards generated by the production of goods and services tend to be distributed downward in the stratification system (Gould et al. 2008). The contamination of water, land and air by toxic industrial effluents and their consequent negative impacts on human health disproportionately impact workers and the unemployed, while owners, managers and investors are able to use the wealth gained from production to purchase housing in environmentally safe areas (Gould 2006). Those who cannot afford to move to such areas are forced to live with environmental hazards. In this way, each round of economic growth tends to increase the gap between rich and poor, as well as increase the gap between environmentally safe and environmentally hazardous residential spaces (Schnaiberg and Gould 2000).

Similarly, the best jobs in the production process tend to be awarded to the already wealthier individuals, while the dirtiest and most hazardous jobs are reserved for the poor and people of color (Hurley 1995; Pellow 2002). The poor and working class therefore find themselves at the greatest environmental risk both on the job and at home, while the wealthy remain relatively protected in both locations (Szasz 1994). Managers tend to live at some distance from potentially hazardous production facilities, and usually upwind and upstream from industrial effluent flows. Workers tend to live close to production facilities, and downwind and downstream from effluent flows (Mumford 1934; Hurley 1995). Workers and their families are thereby exposed to carcinogens and other toxins resulting from production, while managers, owners and investors are not.

The greening of urban areas also follows the logic of the treadmill of production. In cases of urban greening, *green growth coalitions* operate along the logic of an *urban greening treadmill*. Local and state government (states), real estate developers (corporations), and residents (citizen-workers) favor greening (a form of growth, or improvement). Local governments and real estate developers see economic benefits in the form of taxes and profits respectively, and local residents seek improvements to their quality of life. This is especially true as urban environmental consciousness has grown. Local politicians and developers (treadmill elites), what we call *green growth coalitions,* create plans to add green amenities to otherwise "brown" spaces. Unlike the treadmill of production model, these plans actually benefit the environment (at least locally). However, they create the social problem of gentrification, which especially hurts those with lower incomes and people of color (National Environmental Justice Advisory Council 2006). Elites win big economically, while lower classes are displaced, often to neighborhoods with worse environments. Unless the working class, working poor, and communities of color are able to actively resist or demand that the greening include affordable housing for the local population, the process continues.

The concept of a green growth machine/green growth coalition builds on Molotch's (1976), and Logan and Molotch's (1987) urban growth machine model. That model argues that developers lobby and otherwise manipulate municipal governments to make public investments that will raise property values, thus generating profits for themselves with the consequence of the displacement of local populations. With a green growth machine, greening forms the basis for a local growth coalition to initiate site-specific green urban redevelopment. In the drive to extract increased value from real estate, elites harness environmental concerns to generate publicly funded environmental amenities and restoration (Schnaiberg 1980; Schnaiberg and Gould 2000). Those environmental improvements raise the value of real estate investments, enable investors to quickly resell properties at a profit, and thus promote gentrification, increasing capital gains to private developers and tax revenues for the state. The green growth machine is thus part of an urban greening treadmill (drawing on the TOP model) in which neighborhoods are destroyed by sustainability initiatives and recreated in ways that benefit nonresidents.

Summary

Due to the intersection of processes reproducing environmental injustice and housing segregation, and the operation of markets and elite actors, the creation or restoration of an environmental good – greening – will tend to increase racial and class inequality and housing segregation, and will decrease environmental justice (National Environmental Justice Advisory Council 2006). As Bryson (2012: 31) notes: "Without a deliberate approach to mitigating the negative ripple effects of contemporary urban environmental management strategies, … social and environmental equity both tend to decrease as middle-class [and upper-class] quality of life increases." As equity is one of the three pillars of sustainability, such urban greening schemes are misrepresented when they are characterized as urban sustainability initiatives. This type of greening makes cities less sustainable. This, however, is not an inevitable result. Social movement actors can resist and insist that equitable policies, such as affordable housing, be integrated into greening initiatives and direct them to outcomes that are more just. Simply put, urban greening increases environmental inequality in the absence of social movements and/or policy interventions to do otherwise through the process we refer to as *green gentrification*.

Note

1   In terms of the siting of new potentially hazardous facilities, similar processes operate. Production facilities will tend to locate where land values are lowest in order to reduce construction costs. Lower land values will be found in precisely those locations where the poor and working class can afford to live. Higher land values will be found where the upper and upper-middle class can afford to live in relatively environmentally sound locations. New environmental hazards are therefore likely to be placed in close proximity to the residential areas inhabited by those near the bottom of the stratification system. Those areas that are attractive as residential locations for those with the wealth to avoid environmental hazards are likely to be the least attractive locations for installation of new production facilities that are associated with increased environmental and public health costs. So, as environmental restoration proceeds, it shifts people of color and the poor and middle class out, draws wealthier whites in, then serves as a bulwark to protect the new residents from exposure to potential future environmental risks. The same real estate value-based processes that fuel urban gentrification of an environmentally restored neighborhood act to distribute future environmental hazards away from the gentrified area and toward those locations where the less wealthy and people of color live.

The poor and working class are concentrated in areas typified by high levels of environmental risk and low levels of wealth, and people of color are disproportionately represented among this socioeconomic group. Poor communities face limited economic options in terms of type of employment and remuneration from that employment. Concentrating the unemployed and underemployed in specific locations creates communities of economic desperation. Under such conditions, poor and working-class communities are structurally coerced into accepting any economic development initiative promising an increase in local employment (Pellow 2002). As a result, poor communities are less free to reject specific proposals for the siting of production or disposal facilities within their communities than are wealthier communities where new employment opportunities are a less pressing concern. The less wealthy a community, the more likely it is to be accepting of new environmental hazards where those hazards come with the promise of economic benefit (Pellow 2002). It is not that poor communities are less concerned about the protection of their health and environment but rather that they have less structural freedom to act on their environmental and health concerns when faced with the consequences of absolute poverty. Conversely, wealthy communities are no more environmental or health-conscious than poor communities but with little need for additional local economic development, they are more structurally free to prioritize their environmental and health values under conditions where their basic needs are already being met. Segregated residential housing patterns generate a spatial distribution of economic development need. Environmentally hazardous facilities will be most attractive to communities with the highest level of economic desperation (Gould 1991, Pellow 2002). The ability of wealthy communities to reject hazardous facilities due to low economic need (and greater political resources), combined with the desperation of poor communities for any increase in employment opportunity, reinforces both the downward distribution of environmental hazards, and the upward distribution of environmental amenities, increasing both the environmental protection of the rich and the environmental degradation of the poor.

Bibliography

Abu-Lughod, Janet. 1994. *From Urban Village to East Village: The Battle for New York's Lower East Side.* Cambridge, MA: Blackwell.

Agyeman, Julian. 2005. *Sustainable Communities and the Challenge of Environmental Justice.* New York: New York University Press.

Agyeman, Julian. 2013. *Introducing Just Sustainabilities: Policy, Planning, and Practice.* New York: Zed Books.

Agyeman, Julian, Robert D. Bullard and Bob Evans. 2003. *Just Sustainabilities: Development in an Unequal World.* Cambridge, MA: The MIT Press.

Alkon, Alison Hope. 2012. *Black, White, and Green: Farmers Markets, Race, and the Green Economy.* Athens, GA: University of Georgia Press.

Angotti, Tom. 2008. *New York For Sale: Community Planning Confronts Global Real Estate.* Cambridge, MA: The MIT Press.

Banzhaf, H. Spencer and Eleanor McCormick. 2007. "Moving Beyond Cleanup: Identifying the Crucibles of Environmental Gentrification." Working Paper No.

07–29, Andrew Young School of Policy Studies Research Paper Series, Atlanta, GA: Georgia State University.

Brulle, Robert J. and David Naguib Pellow. 2006. "Environmental Justice: Human Health and Environmental Inequalities." *Annual Review of Public Health* 27: 103–124.

Bryant, Bunyan. ed. 1995. *Environmental Justice: Issues, Policies and Solutions.* Washington, DC: Island Press.

Bryant, Bunyan and Paul Mohai. eds. 1992. *Race and the Incidence of Environmental Hazards: A Time for Discourse.* San Francisco, CA: Westview Press.

Bryson, Jerome. 2012. "Brownfields Gentrification: Redevelopment Planning and Environmental Justice in Spokane, Washington." *Environmental Justice* 5(1): 26–31.

Bullard, Robert D. 1990. *Dumping in Dixie: Race, Class and Environmental Quality.* San Francisco, CA: Westview Press.

Bullard, Robert D. ed. 1993. *Confronting Environmental Racism: Voices from the Grassroots.* Boston, MA: South End Press.

Bullard, Robert D. ed. 1994. *Unequal Protection: Environmental Justice and Communities of Color.* San Francisco, CA: Sierra Club Books.

Bullard, Robert D., Carl Anthony and Don Chen. 2007. *Growing Smarter: Achieving Livable Communities, Environmental Justice, and Regional Equity.* Cambridge, MA: The MIT Press.

Bullard, Robert D., J. Eugene Grigsby and Charles Lee. eds. 1994. *Residential Apartheid: The American Legacy.* Los Angeles, CA: CASS Publications.

Bullard, Robert D., Paul Mohai, Robin Saha and Beverly Wright. 2007. *Toxic Waste and Race at Twenty 1987–2007.* United Church of Christ.

Čapek, Stella. 1993. "The 'Environmental Justice' Frame: A Conceptual Discussion and an Application." *Social Problems* 40(1): 5–24.

Cerrell Associates and J.S. Powell. 1984. *Political Difficulties Facing Waste-to-Energy Conversion Plant Siting.* Sacramento, CA: California Waste Management Board.

Checker, Melissa. 2011. "Wiped out by the 'Greenwave': Environmental Gentrification and the Paradoxical Politics of Urban Sustainability." *City & Society* 23(2): 210–229.

Cole, Luke W. and Sheila R. Foster. 2001. *From the Ground Up: Environmental Racism and the Rise of the Environmental Justice Movement.* New York: NYU Press.

Curran, Winifred. 2007. "'From the Frying Pan to the Oven': Gentrification and the Experience of Industrial Displacement in Williamsburg, Brooklyn." *Urban Studies* 44(8): 1427–1440.

Curran, Winifred and Trina Hamilton. 2012. "Just Green Enough: Contesting Environmental Gentrification in Greenpoint, Brooklyn." *Local Environment* 17(9): 1027–1042.

Dale, Ann and Lenore L. Newman. 2009. "Sustainable Development for Some: Green Urban Development and Affordability." *Local Environment* 14(7): 669–681.

Domhoff, G. William. 1998. *Who Rules America?: Power and Politics in the Year 2000.* Mountain View, CA: Mayfield Publishing Company.

Dooling, Sarah. 2009. "Ecological Gentrification: A Research Agenda Exploring Justice in the City." *International Journal of Urban and Regional Research* 33(3): 621–639.

Eckerd, Adam. 2011. "Cleaning Up Without Clearing Out? A Special Assessment of Environmental Gentrification." *Urban Affairs Review* 47(1): 31–59.

Essoka, Jonathan D. 2010. "The Gentrifying Effects of Brownfield Redevelopment." *Western Journal of Black Studies* 34(3): 299–315.

Gamper-Rabindran, Shanti, Ralph Mastromonaco and Christopher Timmins. 2011. "Valuing the Benefits of Superfund Site Remediation: Three Approaches to Measuring Localized Externalities." Working Paper No. 16655, National Bureau of Economic Research.

Gamper-Rabindran, Shanti and Christopher Timmins. 2011. "Hazardous Waste Cleanup, Neighborhood Gentrification, and Environmental Justice: Evidence from Restricted Access Census Block Data." *American Economic Review* 101(3): 620–624.

Gould, Kenneth A. 1991. "The Sweet Smell of Money: Economic Dependency and Local Environmental Political Mobilization." *Society and Natural Resources: An International Journal.* 4(2): 133–150.

Gould, Kenneth A. 2006. "Promoting Sustainability." In *Public Sociologies Reader.* Judith Blau and Keri Iyall Smith. eds. New York: Rowman and Littlefield, 289–316

Gould, Kenneth A. and Tammy L. Lewis. 2012. "The Environmental Injustice of Green Gentrification." In *The World in Brooklyn: Gentrification, Immigration, and Ethnic Politics in a Global City.* Judith DeSena and Timothy Shortell. eds. Lanham, MD: Lexington Books, 113–146.

Gould, Kenneth A. and Tammy L. Lewis. 2016. "Green Gentrification and Superstorm Sandy: The Resilience of the Urban Redevelopment Treadmill in Brooklyn's Gowanus Canal." In *Taking Chances: The Coast After Hurricane Sandy.* Karen M. O'Neill and Daniel J. Van Abs. eds. New Brunswick, NJ: Rutgers University Press, 145–163.

Gould, Kenneth A., David Naguib Pellow and Allan Schnaiberg. 2008. *The Treadmill of Production: Injustice and Unsustainability in a Global Economy.* Boulder, CO: Paradigm Press.

Gould, Kenneth A., Allan Schnaiberg, and Adam S. Weinberg. 1996. *Local Environmental Struggles: Citizen Activism in the Treadmill of Production.* Cambridge: Cambridge University Press.

Hamilton, Trina and Winifred Curran. 2013. "From 'Five Angry Women' to 'Kickass Community': Gentrification and Environmental Activism in Brooklyn and Beyond." *Urban Studies* 50(8): 1557–1574.

Hurley, Andrew. 1995. *Environmental Inequalities: Race, Class, and Industrial Pollution in Gary, Indiana, 1945–1980.* Chapel Hill, NC: University of North Carolina Press.

Kozol, Jonathan. 1992. *Savage Inequalities: Children in America's Schools.* New York: Harper Perennial.

Lake, Robert W. 1996. "Vounteers, NIMBYs, and Environmental Justice: Dilemmas of Democratic Practice." *Antipode* 28(2): 160–174.

Lewis, Tammy L. 2011. "Global Civil Society and the Distribution of Environmental Goods: Funding for Environmental NGOs in Ecuador." In *Environmental Justice Beyond Borders: Local Perspectives on Global Inequities.* Julian Agyeman and JoAnn Carmin. eds. Cambridge, MA: The MIT Press, 87–104.

Lewis, Tammy L. 2016. *Ecuador's Environmental Revolutions: Ecoimperialists, Ecodependents, and Ecoresisters.* Cambridge, MA: The MIT Press.

Logan, John R. and Harvey L. Molotch. 1987. *Urban Fortunes: The Political Economy of Place.* Berkeley, CA: University of California Press.

MacLeod, Jay. 1995. *Ain't No Makin' It: Aspirations & Attainment in a Low-income Neighborhood.* Boulder, CO: Westview Press.

Massey, Douglass S. and Nancy A. Denton. 1993. *American Apartheid: Segregation and the Making of the Underclass.* Cambridge, MA: Harvard University Press.

Mohai, Paul and Robin Saha. 2007. "Racial Inequality in the Distribution of Hazardous Waste: A National-Level Reassessment." *Social Problems* 54(3): 343–370.

Mohai, Paul and Robin Saha. 2015. "Which Came First, People or Pollution? A Review of Theory and Evidence From Longitudinal Environmental Justice Studies." *Environmental Research Letters* 10(12): 125011.

Molotch, Harvey. 1976. "The City as a Growth Machine: Toward a Political Economy of Place." *The American Journal of Sociology* 82(2): 309–332.

Mumford, Lewis 1934. *Technics and Civilization.* New York: Harcourt Brace Jovanovich.

Muñiz, Vicky. 1998. *Resisting Gentrification and Displacement: Voices of Puerto Rican Women of the Barrio.* New York: Routledge.

National Fair Housing Alliance. 2007. *The Crisis of Housing Segregation: 2007 Fair Housing Trends Report.* Washington, DC: National Fair Housing Alliance.

National Environmental Justice Advisory Council. 2006. *Unintended Impacts of Redevelopment and Revitalization Efforts in Five Environmental Justice Communities.* National Environmental Justice Advisory Council.

Newman, K. and E.K. Wyly. 2006. "The Right to Stay Put, Revisited: Gentrification and Resistance to Displacement in New York City." *Urban Studies* 43: 23–57.

Park, Lisa Sun-Hee and David Naguib Pellow. 2011. *The Slums of Aspen: Immigrants vs. The Environment in America's Eden.* New York: NYU Press.

Pastor, Manuel, Jim Sadd and John Hipp. 2001. "Which Came First? Toxic Facilities, Minority Move-In, and Environmental Justice." *Journal of Urban Affairs* 23: 1–21.

Pearsall, Hamil. 2010. "From Brown to Green? Assessing Social Vulnerability to Environmental Gentrification in New York City." *Environment and Planning C: Government & Policy* 28(5): 872–886.

Pearsall, Hamil. 2012. "Moving Out or Moving In? Resilience to Environmental Gentrification in New York City." *Local Environment* 17(9): 1013–1026.

Pearsall, Hamil. 2013. "Superfund Me: A Study of Resistance to Gentrification in New York City." *Urban Studies* 50(11): 2293–2310.

Pellow, David Naguib. 2002. *Garbage Wars: The Struggle for Environmental Justice in Chicago.* Cambridge, MA: The MIT Press.

Pulido, Laura. 1996. "A Critical Review of the Methodology of Environmental Racism Research." *Antipode* 28: 142–159.

Pulido, Laura. 2000. "Rethinking Environmental Racism: White Privilege and Urban Development in Southern California." *Annals of the Association of American Geographers* 90(1): 12–40.

Quastel, Noah. 2009. "Political Ecologies of Gentrification." *Urban Geography* 30(7): 694–725.

Roberts, J. Timmons and Melissa Toffolon-Weiss. 2001. *Chronicles from the Environmental Justice Frontline.* Cambridge, MA: Cambridge University Press.

Schnaiberg, Allan. 1980. *The Environment: From Surplus to Scarcity.* New York: Oxford University Press.

Schnaiberg, Allan and Kenneth A. Gould. 2000. *Environment and Society: The Enduring Conflict.* Caldwell, NJ: Blackburn Press.

Smith, Neil. 1996. *The New Urban Frontier: Gentrification and the Revanchist City.* London, UK: Routledge.

Szasz, Andrew. 1994. *EcoPopulism: Toxic Waste and the Movement for Environmental Justice.* Minneapolis, MN: University of Minnesota Press.

Szasz, Andrew and Michael Meuser. 1997. "Environmental Inequalities: Literature Review and Proposals for New Directions in Research and Theory." *Current Sociology* 45(3): 99–120.

Sze, Julie. 2007. *Noxious New York: The Racial Politics of Urban Health and Environmental Justice.* Cambridge, MA: The MIT Press.

Taylor, Dorceta E. 2009. *The Environment and the People in American Cities, 1600s–1900s: Disorder, Inequality, and Social Change.* Durham, NC: Duke University Press.

United Church of Christ. 1987. *Toxic Waste and Race in the United States.* United Church of Christ Commission for Racial Justice.

Voicu, Ioan and Vicki Been. 2008. "The Effect of Community Gardens on Neighboring Property Values." *Real Estate Economics* 36 (2): 241–283.

Wen, Ming, Xingyou Zhang, Carmen D. Harris, James B. Holt and Janet B. Croft. 2013. "Spatial Disparities in the Distribution of Parks and Green Spaces in the USA." *Annals of Behavioral Medicine* 45(1): S18–S27.

Zavestoski, Stephen and Julian Agyeman. eds. 2015. *Incomplete Streets: Processes, Practices and Possibilities.* London: Routledge.

Zukin, Sharon. 1982. *Loft Living.* Baltimore, MD: Johns Hopkins University Press.

Zukin, Sharon. 1987. "Gentrification: Culture and Capital in the Urban Core." *Annual Review of Sociology* 13: 129–147.

Zukin, Sharon. 1991. *Landscapes of Power: from Detroit to Disney World.* Berkeley, CA: University of California Press.

3 Prospect Park

From social hazard to environmental amenity[1]

Watching hundreds of carefree families romp through the bucolic splendor of Prospect Park on a sunny weekend afternoon, it is hard to imagine that thirty-five years ago this patch of forest and meadow in the heart of Brooklyn was regarded as a feared social hazard. The case of Prospect Park – the example that has the longest history, with the remediation intervention beginning in 1980 – proceeded without any policy interventions that addressed distributional outcomes. It is an example of the restoration of an existing environmental amenity. Prospect Park's creation is arguably Brooklyn's oldest and earliest example of the coalescence of a green growth machine to generate an urban environmental amenity for the purpose of raising property values and attracting wealthy gentrifiers. Our focus here is on its second incarnation as a green gentrifying engine, more than 100 years later.

History: from real estate scheme to social hazard to environmental amenity

The idea of Prospect Park was conceived in the 1850s and construction began in 1866.[2] At the time, Brooklyn was a separate city from Manhattan, and leaders in the two cities competed on all fronts. A builder and railroad constructor (aka early developer), James Stranahan, wanted Brooklyn to have a park that rivaled Manhattan's new Central Park, to draw the wealthy and to increase property values (Alexiou 2015). He wanted the park to "hold out strong inducements to the affluent to remain in our city, who are now too often induced to change their residences by the seductive influences of the New York [Central] park" (Berenson and deMause 2001). Stranahan recruited Calvert Vaux in the planning process, who in turn recruited Frederick Law Olmsted, both designers of New York's Central Park. The original motivation for the park's creation was clearly tied to creating wealth in Brooklyn via housing distribution around a green amenity.

Prospect Park was a success. By 1871 property values around the park had been raised by $77 million (Berenson and deMause 2001). In the years that followed park construction, a row of mansions emerged on Prospect

Park West (Brooklyn's "Gold Coast"), and the areas surrounding the park became residential wealth centers (Jackson 1998; Low, Taplin and Scheld 2005). Starting in the 1930s, with Robert Moses as Parks Commissioner, modifications to Olmstead and Vaux's original park design were made, including the addition of the Bandshell, a skating rink, and ball fields.[3]

By the 1950s, many of the wealthiest park side residents had left for wealthy suburban enclaves, and the neighborhoods surrounding the park became more white ethnic and working class (Snyder-Grenier 1996). In the 1960s and 70s, African-American and Puerto Rican communities expanded near the park, and clashed with the largely Italian-American and Irish-American populations (Osman 2011). Racial conflict and white flight further depressed housing values, and many homes continued to be subdivided into multifamily units and rooming houses. By the early 1970s, high-quality housing stock and greatly depressed housing prices combined to attract an early wave of young, white professionals ("brownstoners") to the increasingly crime-ridden neighborhood of Park Slope (Krase 1982, Osman 2011). In 1973, both the Park Slope Historic District and the Park Slope Food Coop were established.

By the time of Prospect Park's 100th anniversary, the park's infrastructure had been neglected and as a result, visits to the park dropped in the late 1970s to the lowest in its history (fewer than 2 million visitors per year). The park had developed a reputation as a crime-ridden haven for drug dealing and homeless encampments, a dangerous place that people tried to avoid. In the 1970s and 80s, reportage on the park was distinctly negative. Local papers routinely reported on murders, bicycle thefts, muggings, and purse snatching in the park, deepening the park's image as a social hazard rather than an environmental amenity. In October 1980, the *New York Times* ran a series of articles addressing the decay of New York's parks, bemoaning the fact that "these once glorious urban oases are now unsightly and dangerous dumps" ("Losing Ground in the Parks" 1980: A30).

In response to concerns raised by local citizens, the city, under Mayor Ed Koch, committed $10 million "to preserve and rehabilitate Prospect Park" as the first phase of a long-term effort. The *New York Times* announced the start of Prospect Park restoration with the headline "For Prospect Park, $10 Million to Recapture What It Was." That article further noted that "The project also seeks to alleviate neighborhood concerns about the park ... which has also become known in recent years as a haunt for vandals and muggers" (Quindlen 1980: B1). According to the Prospect Park Alliance, this is when the Park's renaissance officially began. By 1985, police had established anti-graffiti stakeouts in Prospect Park to thwart highly visible signs of neglect and decay (Carmody 1985: B3), nearly thirteen years after Mayor Lindsay had publicly denounced graffiti in a speech at the Prospect Park boathouse ("Lindsay Assails Graffiti Vandals" 1972: 30). Throughout the following three decades, the ecological restoration and social transformation of the park picked up steam.

In 1987, the Prospect Park Alliance (PPA) was formed to "restore and maintain Prospect Park after a long period of steady deterioration and decline" (Prospect Park Alliance 2010). Based on the neoliberal model of public-private partnership in green space management pioneered by the Central Park Conservancy (Taylor 2009), the PPA quickly became a key actor of the green growth machine. The PPA harnessed private donations and foundation funding to restore the park in line with its original purpose of raising property values and attracting wealthy residents. In a city where public resources are never sufficient for green space maintenance, let alone restoration, public-private partnerships fuse public funds and land with the private capital of developers, real estate brokers, and wealthy local residents in pursuit of greening that serves the interests of political and economic elites. For Prospect Park, the PPA "plays a significant role in funding the operating budget that keeps the Park clean, safe and beautiful, and employs three-quarters of the staff that take care of the Park" (Prospect Park Alliance 2010).

The work of the PPA has been successful, and the park has been restored as an environmental amenity. The ecological restoration of the park has included a meticulous reconstruction of Olmsted and Vaux's original design specifications, increased focus on restoring native species and controlling invasive and non-native species, reducing soil compaction by limiting visitors' off-path access to forested areas, and restoring understory and herbaceous plants (again by limiting visitors' off-path access) (DiCicco 2014). The ecological and social renewal and redirection of the park have come hand in hand. "Prospect Park has successfully overcome its 1970s reputation as an unsavory place. Today more than 10 million annual visitors enjoy a variety of activities and destinations, from in-line skating to nature walks, from baseball games to zoo visits, and from picnicking to volunteer projects" (Prospect Park Alliance 2010). Park programming also seeks ways to embrace the cultural diversity of Brooklyn's residents. Numerous racial/ethnic groups use the park for a variety of activities (Low et al. 2005), although some must travel further to get there than others. Today the park is operated by the PPA in partnership with New York City. The park reached its low point in the late 1970s, and since that time, has been transformed from an *in situ* socio-environmental bad with potential, to an important socio-environmental amenity.

The ecological restoration of Prospect Park helped transform the image of the park from an urban liability to an urban amenity. Park features such as the Third Street Playground became attractions for white, wealthy parents and children who in an earlier era would have avoided the park. The late twentieth-century image of the park as a social liability contrasts starkly with the image of the park presented by Brooklyn's booming real estate industry in the early twenty-first century. The Corcoran Group uses proximity to Prospect Park to sell real estate in Park Slope, Prospect Heights, and Prospect Park South, listing the park as one of the neighborhood's "most wonderful amenities" (Corcoran Group 2010). Fillmore Real Estate proclaims the virtues of the park's "majestic 585 acres" noting that it "includes a forest, [and] a meadow," to sell real estate in the Crown Heights and Lefferts Gardens neighborhoods (Fillmore Real Estate 2010). Other real estate agencies describe Windsor Terrace as "tucked between the rolling hills and vast green spaces of Prospect Park and Green-Wood Cemetery," and Prospect Park as "home to green lawns, lakes, a tennis center and endless recreational opportunities," an "urban oasis" (Prudential Douglas Elliman Real Estate 2010, Rapid Realty 2010). And Corcoran marketed the 2006 Richard Meier building as "the borough's premier address, gracing the heart of Brooklyn at One Grand Army Plaza. Steps away from over 500 acres of natural parkland" (see Figure 3.1) (Corcoran Group 2010).

Indeed, Prospect Park has been transformed. Meticulous restoration to much of its original beauty has proceeded effectively, and continues with the completion of new ice skating facilities to replace those that blighted Olmstead and Vaux's original design. Park restoration largely proceeded from north to south and from west to east, beginning near the highest value real estate in Park Slope and working toward the lower value properties in Lefferts Gardens, raising values in its wake. No longer perceived as a place

Figure 3.1 One Grand Army Plaza; Richard Meier on Prospect Park

one goes to get mugged, the park is vibrant with runners, bikers, skaters, baby strollers, picnickers, and others (see Figure 3.2). Park users can be seen sporting thousands of dollars' worth of outdoor recreation equipment, seemingly without serious security concerns. Clearly, it is not the 1970s in the park anymore.

As Prospect Park was transformed from a perceived social hazard into a quality of life-enhancing environmental amenity, it attracted both urban gentrifiers and those who would profit from them. In her book, *Landscapes of Power*, Sharon Zukin notes small-scale real estate developers as a primary category of gentrifiers. She quotes one such gentrifier in Brooklyn who explains the strategy: "You find it [a building to upscale] in a neighborhood that still has problems but is close to a park ... something that will bring in the middle class. And almost by the time you are through other buildings around it will have started to be fixed up" (Zukin 1991: 193). In addition to rehabilitating existing structures, the restoration of the park set off a wave of new construction. Brooklyn's new housing construction boom was, and is, focused on a number of specific neighborhoods. The social re-taming, and ecological rewilding, of Prospect Park made many of the neighborhoods surrounding it prime targets for developers. The onset of the new construction boom is captured in the five community districts that border Prospect Park, which had an almost 1,800 percent increase in new

Figure 3.2 Riders and runners in Prospect Park

residential construction building permits in the span of five years, increasing from thirty-five in 1997 to 653 in 2002 (Brooklyn Community District Profiles 2009). As the purchase and rental costs of new construction in Brooklyn have approached (and sometimes exceeded) those of Manhattan, the class and racial profile of the neighborhoods into which such construction has been thrust has necessarily shifted up the stratification scale.

Neighborhood demographics

To evaluate the degree to which green gentrification has occurred around Prospect Park, we use census data to examine three propositions. If green gentrification is occurring we expect that over time: 1) people of color will be displaced from the area surrounding the park (*greening whitens hypothesis*), 2) poor people will be displaced (*greening richens hypothesis*), and 3) rents and property values will rise (*greening raises rents hypothesis*).

In Gould and Lewis (2012) we provide detailed data for each of the five neighborhoods surrounding the park (see Figure 3.3). These neighborhoods include Park Slope, Prospect Heights, Lefferts Gardens, Prospect Park South, and Windsor Terrace. Neighborhood boundaries are fluid and shift according to the desirability of the neighborhood. For instance, as Park Slope – the gentrified neighborhood on the west side of Prospect Park – has commanded higher and higher rents and sales prices, its "real estate borders" grew westward and southward. In this context, it can be tricky to define the borders of the neighborhoods around the park. In order to define the neighborhoods, we used five types of sources: 1) maps in print and online (see, for example, Jackson 1998); 2) real estate agency borders; 3) geographic boundaries; 4) census tracts; and 5) residents' self-identification. As the map in Figure 3.3 illustrates, this resulted in an examination of five neighborhoods in the area around the park, within about two census tracts from the park boundary. The proximity of these neighborhoods makes them most likely to experience a "park effect." We use this same method of defining neighborhoods to examine the effects of greening in the other four cases.

In Gould and Lewis (2012) we evaluated the demographic changes from 1990 to the present to see if "greening" the park also "gentrified" the neighborhoods by way of "whitening," "richening," and raising rents. We compiled census data from the U.S. Census Bureau with regard to race, class, social power, and housing for each neighborhood to evaluate the trends and we considered how Brooklyn changed over the same period to tease out broader borough-wide changes from local changes.

Before discussing the quantitative changes we found, it is worth providing some qualitative background for each of these neighborhoods. Park Slope, the original focus of upscale development following park construction, on the west side of the park, is once again one of the most sought-after places to live in Brooklyn. It features restored brownstones (see Figure 3.4),

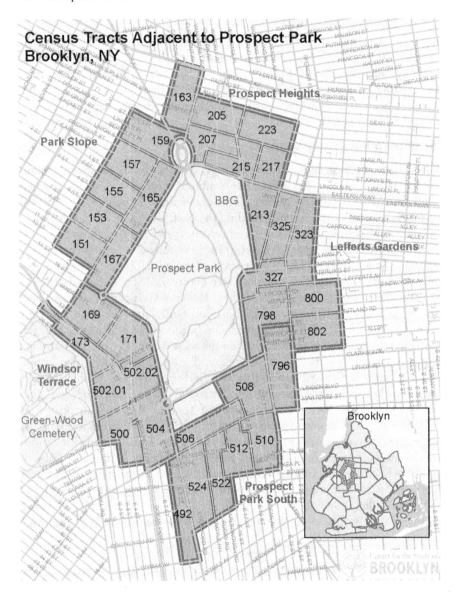

Figure 3.3 Census tracts adjacent to Prospect Park, Brooklyn, NY

trendy coffee shops, Brooklyn's oldest natural food co-op, and numerous children's clothing boutiques. Park Slope is famously the butt of "stroller jokes," a center for yoga classes, and a vortex of permissive parenting. The park is its most important amenity, with multiple entrances to the neighborhood along Prospect Park West. This side of the park has three renovated playgrounds, the Bandshell (which hosts free summer concerts),

Figure 3.4 Park Slope, brownstone Brooklyn

the Picnic House, a New York City landmark (Litchfield's Villa), in addition to being close to Grand Army Plaza, which is the focal point of the park.

Prospect Heights (the highest elevation of the park) sits at the north end of the park surrounding Grand Army Plaza, where the weekly farmers' market draws thousands of visitors to buy local produce just across from the main branch of the Brooklyn Public Library (Figure 3.5). Though there are multiple entrances around the park, this is the "main" entry into the park's famous "long meadow." The entry at Grand Army Plaza also serves as the venue for community events, such as Brooklyn's New Year's Eve party where elected officials speak, local bands play, and families gather to watch the fireworks on the long meadow. Real estate agents have been aggressively expanding the boundaries of the neighborhood east, to associate more housing stock with the park. As a result, Prospect Heights has absorbed a large swath of Crown Heights, a neighborhood name associated with ethnic conflict, not green amenities. Prospect Heights was developed in the 1870s following park construction, and was primarily middle class, white ethnic in composition (Jewish, Italian, Irish) until the post-World War II era, when it became increasingly poor and African-American.

Lefferts Gardens (sometimes called Prospect-Lefferts Gardens) runs along the east side of the park. In 1894, in response to the increased property values resulting from the construction of Prospect Park, Leffert Pietersen van Haughwout subdivided his farm into 600 building lots.

Figure 3.5 Farmers' market at Grand Army Plaza

Restrictive covenants kept the housing development single-family and costly (Jackson 1998). Limestone row houses (see Figure 3.6) were followed by apartment buildings in the 1920s and 30s. Originally intended as luxury

Figure 3.6 Lefferts Gardens row houses across the street from Prospect Park

units, by the 1950s these apartments became middle-class and working-class housing (Krase 1982). In the 1970s, in an attempt at neighborhood revitalization and redefinition, a community group named the area Prospect-Lefferts-Gardens (Prospect for Prospect Park, Lefferts for the historic Lefferts homestead, and Gardens for the Brooklyn Botanical Gardens) (Krase 1979, 2016). The neighborhood name was shortened to "Lefferts Gardens" for many years, but more recently the association with the park has returned in common reference to the neighborhood. There are numerous attractions along this side of the park, such as the carousel, the Prospect Park Zoo and the historic Lefferts House; however, access to the park from Lefferts Gardens is limited in two ways. First, on the northern end, the park and the neighborhood are separated by a swath of green space that contains the Brooklyn Botanic Garden (BBG). While the BBG is certainly a green amenity, it is fenced in and charges an entry fee. Residents of Lefferts Gardens cannot walk across the BBG to enter the park, they must walk to the north, to Grand Army Plaza, or to the south, to the entry located in the center of the park's east side, near the carousel. Secondly, if residents were able to cross the BBG, they would find that when they do reach the border of the park, because of the location of the zoo, this area of the park is fenced. Thus, despite the proximity of Lefferts Gardens residents to the park, access is difficult. Recently, illegal breaks in the fence on the

Lefferts Gardens side of the park have been informally legitimated, as the trails leading from them into the parks have been paved. In this way increased access has followed increased property values as the park greens and the neighborhood whitens.

Prospect Park South abuts the park at the narrow south end. The Parade Grounds, which include soccer and football fields, and the tennis center, are in Prospect Park South. It was not until 1899 when Dean Alvord established an enclave of large, stately single-family houses on forty acres purchased from the Dutch Reformed Church that this end of the park was developed (Jackson 1998). Streets with anglophile names and houses with English gardens made this an attractive neighborhood for turn-of-the-century executives. Apartment buildings came later, along with white flight to suburbia. The park's lake is at the south end, and in the southeast corner is the "Drummer's Grove." According to the Prospect Park website:

> In 1968, the Congo Square Drummers began gathering here informally. Since then, the circle has expanded to include an ever-evolving mix of musicians, dancers, and vendors. The growing popularity of this area as a site for a weekly drumming circle inspired the Prospect Park Alliance to add seating and officially name the site. Anyone is free to bring their drums and participate, or just stop and listen while passing by on the East Drive. The Drummer's Grove was a part of a $1 million renovation of the Parkside Avenue/Ocean Avenue entrance to the Park that occurred in 1997.
>
> (Prospect Park Alliance 2010)

Finally, Windsor Terrace sits to the southwest of the park, between Prospect Park South and Park Slope, and is near the park's ball fields. Green-Wood Cemetery, Brooklyn's second largest green space, borders the other side of Windsor Terrace. At its northern corner is a large entryway to the park with subway access. This neighborhood was developed before Prospect Park was created. Row houses appeared along Prospect Park Southwest at the turn of the century, and apartment buildings followed in the 1930s and 40s. Windsor Terrace has a reputation as a stable residential neighborhood where houses rarely go on the market because homes are bought among mostly Irish-American family members, neighbors, and friends.

The five neighborhoods adjoining Prospect Park each responded to the restoration of the green space as an environmental amenity. The extent to which greening whitened, richened, and raised rents in Prospect Park neighborhoods varied, in part due to the variations in ease of park access, the extent and pace of park restoration, and preexisting demographics noted above. We examine the changing demographics from 1990 – the first census after the founding of the Prospect Park Alliance in 1987 – through to the period just after the opening of the 2006 Richard Meier building at

Grand Army Plaza, to examine how the demographics of the park changed in roughly a fifteen-year period following greening. We report the raw data in Gould and Lewis (2012). Here, we highlight the percentages of change from 1990 to 2009 (Table 3.1) in three neighborhoods of interest.

Does greening whiten? In the period from the 1990 census until the American Community Survey estimates in 2009, the population of Brooklyn became less "white" and less "black." In 1990, almost 47 percent of the Brooklyn population was white and in 2009 the figure was 44 percent. For blacks, the percentages are 38 percent and 35 percent, respectively. These figures probably reflect changes in the data collection method, since now respondents must respond "white only" and "black only" in an effort to identify the increasing biracial population. Also, the Hispanic and Asian populations of Brooklyn increased during this time. Despite the borough-wide decreases in whites (a 2.5 percent drop from 1990 to 2009), around the Park the percentage of whites increased in three of the five neighborhoods (Prospect Heights, Lefferts Gardens, and Prospect Park South). The population of whites in these neighborhoods increased by 19.9 percent, 4.6 percent, and 4.3 percent respectively. These neighborhoods had relatively small percentages of whites in 1990 (18 percent, 4 percent, and 14 percent). The two neighborhoods whose white population percentage

Table 3.1 Comparative percent change in Brooklyn and selected neighborhoods around Prospect Park, 1990–2009

		Brooklyn	Park Slope	Prospect Heights	Lefferts Gardens
	Population change	10.3%	7.6%	7.6%	−8.3%
Race	White (%)	−2.5%	−0.3%	19.9%	4.6%
	Black (%)	−3.2%	−2.8%	−27.8%	−8.8%
Class	Median household income 1999 ($)	−3.5%	38.6%	24.1%	−13.7%
	Families below poverty line (%)	−0.9%	−2.1%	−5.4%	−0.2%
Social power	Bachelor's degree or higher (%)	11.8%	16.4%	19.8%	8.3%
Housing	Owner-occupied housing units (%)	4.7%	13.8%	9.1%	−2.6%
	Median single-family owner-occupied home value 1999 ($)	71.3%	19.0%	4.9%	102.2%
	Median rent 1999 ($)	24.8%	51.7%	40.9%	20.0%

Sources: 2000 U.S. Census Bureau, Social Explorer
2005/09 American Community Survey, Social Explorer, 5-year estimates

decreased (Park Slope and Windsor Terrace) already had high percentages of whites in 1990 (82 percent and 80 percent). The decline was very small for Park Slope (from 81.9 percent to 81.6 percent), but larger for Windsor Terrace (from 80 to 74 percent). In short, the overwhelmingly white neighborhoods around the park became slightly less white between 1990 and 2009, while the non-white neighborhoods became substantially whiter. The whitening of Prospect Heights was particularly dramatic in this period.

In terms of the change in black population around the park, all of the five neighborhoods showed losses. The percentage decrease in black population in the borough overall was 3.2 percent; the neighborhoods surrounding Prospect Park had a higher percentage decrease overall. The three blackest neighborhoods in 1990 decreased by large percentages. Prospect Heights was 74 percent black in 1990 and by 2009 this percentage had decreased to 46 percent, a percentage decrease of 28 percent. Lefferts Gardens went from 92 percent black to 83 percent black, almost a nine percent decrease. Prospect Park South's black population also declined: from 74 percent to 65 percent, a 9 percent decline from 1990. The very white neighborhoods (Park Slope and Windsor Terrace), which already had small percentages of blacks, both had around 3 percent decreases in the percentage of blacks, similar to Brooklyn overall. In sum, even though the percentage of blacks declined across the borough, collectively, the neighborhoods around Prospect Park lost blacks at a far greater rate. By the end of the period of major Prospect Park restoration, Prospect Heights was no longer a majority black neighborhood. In the case of the restoration of Prospect Park as an urban environmental amenity, the census data support the claim that greening whitens. If we stretch this out over a longer time frame, from 1990 to 2014, this trend continues. Gentrification continues to curve around the northeast of the park moving from Prospect Heights into Lefferts Gardens. In Brooklyn overall from 1990 to 2014, the percentage of the population that is black decreased by 4 percent (see Table 3.2); in Lefferts Gardens that percentage declined 14.5 percent. For whites in Brooklyn, the population declined by 3 percent; in Lefferts Gardens, it increased by 10.5 percent.

Does greening richen? In Brooklyn, the median household income declined from $34 thousand to $33 thousand over the 1990 to 2009 period (adjusted to 1999-era dollars). A pattern emerges around the park (Table 3.1). The two whitest neighborhoods (Park Slope and Windsor Terrace) and the neighborhood experiencing the greatest whitening (Prospect Heights) have income increases, while the two blackest neighborhoods show income decreases (Lefferts Gardens and Prospect Park South). The median incomes of Lefferts Gardens and Prospect Park South are very close to that of Brooklyn's overall median. Park Slope, which started with the highest median income ($60 thousand), had the highest percentage increase (39 percent) and the highest ending income in 2009 ($83 thousand). Windsor Terrace, which started with the second-highest median income (around $45 thousand), increased 24 percent to almost $56 thousand. Prospect Heights

Table 3.2 Demographic changes in Brooklyn, 1990–2014

		1990	2000	2014	Change over time, 2000–2014	Change over time, 1990–2014
	Population change	2,300,664	2,465,326	2,570,801	4%	12%
Race	White (%)	46.9%	41.2%	43.6%	2%	−3%
	Black (%)	37.9%	36.4%	33.9%	−3%	−4%
Class	Median household income 2013 ($)	$46,588	$44,926	$46,188	3%	−1%
	Families below poverty line (%)	19.5%	22.0%	19.8%	−2%	0%
Social power	Bachelor's degree or higher (%)	16.6%	21.9%	31.6%	10%	15%
Housing	Owner occupied housing units (%)	26.1%	27.1%	29.5%	2%	3%
	Median single family owner occupied home value 2013 ($)	$336,226	$310,041	$557,500	80%	66%
	Median rent 2013 ($)	$824	$909	$1,189	31%	44%

Sources: 1990 U.S. Census Bureau, Social Explorer
2000 U.S. Census Bureau, Social Explorer
2014 American Community Survey, Social Explorer, 5-year estimates

and Lefferts Gardens started similarly (around $37–$38 thousand) but they diverged over this period: Prospect Heights increased 24 percent to end at $47 thousand (well above Brooklyn's median), but Lefferts Gardens dropped 14 percent to end just below the borough median. Prospect Park South also declined by 9 percent over the period. This pattern of median income-change reflects growing inequality and a declining middle class nationally. The richest neighborhoods became richer, the poorest neighborhoods became poorer, and the neighborhood experiencing the most dramatic whitening also became much wealthier. In terms of poverty, nearly 19 percent of the families in Brooklyn had incomes below the poverty line in 2009. With the exception of Prospect Park South (22 percent below poverty), all of the neighborhoods around the park are below that rate, with Park Slope having the lowest level (2.5 percent).

Greening appears to have richened three of the neighborhoods: Park Slope, Windsor Terrace and Prospect Heights. It did not richen Lefferts Gardens or Prospect Park South. Prospect Heights is an interesting case to explore. Why did it richen while Lefferts Gardens and Prospect Park South did not? Here the relationship between race and class would appear to be quite evident. Of the three majority black neighborhoods, the one that most dramatically lost black population (Prospect Heights), leaving it no longer majority black at the end of the 1990–2009 period, became substantially richer. The neighborhood adjacent to Prospect Park with the highest percentage of blacks in the 1990 to 2009 time period, Lefferts Gardens, had the largest decrease in median income in the same period.

Does greening raise rents (and home values)? The impact of urban environmental amenities on the trajectory of home values and rents is a primary engine of the redistribution of environmental goods. Across the borough, controlling for inflation, median home values increased by 71 percent from 1990 to 2009. In 2009, the median home value was $429,931 (in 1999-era dollars). Values also increased around the park. The largest percentage gains were in Lefferts Gardens and Windsor Terrace, which outpaced the increases in Brooklyn, both at least doubling the 1990 median value. The percentage changes were smaller in Park Slope, which already had very high values in 1990. In 2009, Lefferts Gardens exceeded Brooklyn's median value by over $100 thousand and Park Slope exceeded it by over a quarter million dollars. Windsor Terrace exceeded the borough median by $50 thousand and Prospect Heights and Prospect Park South were around Brooklyn's median. The percentage of owner-occupied housing units in Brooklyn increased over the period from 27 percent to 31 percent. All of the park neighborhoods also increased in percentage of owner-occupied housing, with very high ownership rates in Park Slope and Windsor Terrace (both 49 percent). Lefferts Gardens and Prospect Park South were well below the Brooklyn average (11 percent and 10 percent respectively).

Another important indicator of housing value is median rent. In Brooklyn, rents increased 25 percent over the 1990–2009 period. Lefferts Gardens and Prospect Park South track closely to Brooklyn's changes in median gross rent in terms of both actual dollar amounts and changes over time. Brooklyn's median in 2009 was $759 (in 1999-era dollars). Bigger increases and higher rents are seen in Windsor Terrace (30 percent increase), Prospect Heights (41 percent increase) and Park Slope (52 percent increase). In 2009, the median rent in Park Slope was $1,274 (in 1999-era dollars). In the case of Prospect Park restoration, urban greening appears to have raised rents. Rents continued to rise as gentrification continued around the park.

No civil society/public policy interventions for social equity

During the period of major Prospect Park restoration as an urban environmental amenity, community organizations did not demand public housing, Access to housing near that park became increasingly restricted to those situated higher on the socio-economic stratification pyramid, contributing to their environmental privilege. Although increases in median gross rent in Lefferts Gardens from 1990 to 2009 were similar to Brooklyn as a whole, the simultaneous decline in income in the blackest neighborhood surrounding Prospect Park during the same period indicates that it became increasingly difficult for Lefferts Gardens residents to remain in their neighborhood (as rising rents ate larger and larger shares of declining incomes). Given that changes were coming later to Lefferts Gardens, as park improvements started on the west side and moved to the east side of Prospect Park, we analyzed data in that neighborhood from 2000 to 2014 and compared it again to changes in Brooklyn during that period. Indeed, we see that Lefferts Gardens is gentrifying (Table 3.3). It got whiter, less black, slightly wealthier, more educated, with higher rents and much higher home values; all at a faster rate than Brooklyn overall (compare to Table 3.2).

As the green gentrification pressures on Lefferts Gardens continued to build, so did community resistance. Things came to a head with the construction of a 23-story tower overlooking Prospect Park. Although the

Table 3.3 Demographic changes in Lefferts Gardens, 2000–2014

		2000	2014	*Change over time, 2000–2014*
Race	Population change	36,842	35,180	–5%
	White (%)	3.6%	14.2%	11%
	Black (%)	89.3%	77.8%	–12%
Class	Median household income 2013 ($)	$42,932	$44,910	5%
	Families below poverty line (%)	20.9%	17.8%	–3%
Social power	Bachelors degree or higher (%)	15.7%	30.3%	15%
Housing	Owner occupied housing units (%)	13.5%	14.3%	1%
	Median single family owner occupied home value 2013 ($)	$303,864	$644,702	112%
	Median rent 2013 ($)	$883	$1,173	33%

Sources: 2000 U.S. Census Bureau, Social Explorer
2014 American Community Survey, Social Explorer, 5-year estimates

tower would include 20 percent affordable units, Lefferts does not lack affordable housing. Residents' concern, in addition to the towers' architectural incongruousness with the surrounding neighborhood, is the "seemingly inevitable wave of gentrification that would push out longtime residents" that this tower represents (Budin 2015). Citizens organized the Movement To Protect the People (MTOPP) to defend this mostly Afro-Caribbean neighborhood from the green gentrification that has worked its way around the park as environmental restoration progressed. As one journalist noted, "Once a drug-filled, crime-ridden area in the 1970s and 1980s, Prospect Park's rehabilitation is said to be the reason for a sharp rise in interest and property prices in Lefferts Gardens" (Cantú 2015). A local real estate developer indicated that proximity to "Prospect Park was a major selling point for newcomers priced out of Manhattan and hip areas of Brooklyn. They want to be in a desirable neighborhood along the park" (Cantú 2015: 6). To defend against green gentrification, MTOPP is pushing to downzone Lefferts Gardens, reducing the allowable height for new construction. They are actively opposing inclusionary zoning which would allow high-rise densification of the neighborhood while adding affordable units. The community board approves of the new development, and has been charged with racism in its enthusiasm for the appropriation of Lefferts Gardens and the park for gentrifiers (Budin 2015).

As our model of green gentrification would predict, many former near-Prospect Park residents experienced reduced access to Brooklyn's premier green space as a result of park renewal efforts, and many who remain are threatened with being displaced and losing their access. As working-class and minority residents are progressively priced further back from environmental amenities like Prospect Park, it becomes evident that urban greening and the reclaiming and renewal of urban environmental amenities can be a broadly negatively redistributive policy. If not by intent, then by effect, urban greening tends to increase environmental inequality, reduce the access of poor and working-class communities and communities of color to environmental amenities, and dissolve communities to make way for new, wealthier residents. The combination of market forces in urban real estate, institutional and cultural racism, and urban environmental policy can be a powerful tool of urban renewal and urban removal, with the "greening" of urban areas becoming code for the "whitening" of neighborhoods. This is not to say that outcomes could not be different with appropriate policy interventions.

As calls for environmental justice expand from the focus on the distribution of environmental hazards to include demands for more equitable distribution of environmental amenities (Park and Pellow 2011), processes of green gentrification have clear implications for community-based urban environmental justice groups seeking to generate more local environmental goods. The success of activists in poor and working-class communities of color in achieving remediation of parks, waterfronts, or other local environmental amenities, or in gaining the establishment of new green spaces in urban environments, is likely to be followed by green gentrification processes similar to those around Prospect Park. Efforts at achieving community quality of life improvements may thus be converted into community disintegration outcomes, as urban growth machines seize upon greening as an opportunity for profit. Under such conditions, the restoration of urban environmental amenities might be properly viewed as an environmental bad, posing a greater threat to community stability than the siting of some locally unwanted land uses (LULUs). Environmental justice activists therefore need to be vigilant to prevent green gentrification processes from turning their efforts on their heads.

Policy that responds to public intervention can make a difference in the outcomes of green gentrification. In 2005, the Greenpoint-Williamsburg development on the northeast Brooklyn waterfront was approved by the zoning commission (see DeSena 2009). It is an important case to examine because

> The zoning text change adopted by the Commission and the City Council includes a groundbreaking Inclusionary Housing program, reflecting recommendations made during the public review process. The program promotes affordable units in both rental and condominium developments, encourages preservation of existing affordable units, and targets affordable housing to a range of income levels.
> (New York City Department of City Planning 2011)[4]

We will explore such local activist-inspired public policy interventions in Chapter 6 to illustrate how organized communities are attempting to push the social equity pillar back into urban sustainability planning in contested spaces.

Unfortunately, no such policy interventions were put in place in regard to the restoration of Prospect Park in the 1980s, 1990s and 2000s, and the trajectory of near-park neighborhoods indicates that affordable housing near Brooklyn's largest environmental amenity has rapidly waned. The renewal of Prospect Park, which used public and private funds, involved no redesignation of existing land uses (i.e. from industrial to residential or to public green space). As an existing island of newly attractive green space, the restoration project was less available to public intervention to preserve existing patterns of distribution of access to the amenity, and the fate of surrounding neighborhoods was left to (notoriously racist) real estate market forces. Although the park is under the jurisdiction of the city's Parks and Recreation Department, it is managed by the Prospect Park Alliance, which can make decisions about the park without public input (O'Neill 2011). The lessons from the distributional consequences of the restoration of Prospect Park may be utilized by other communities, as environmental restoration plans are proposed and implemented in their neighborhoods.

Alternatively, the real estate profitability consequences of the restoration of Prospect Park serve as a model of, and incentive for, residential displacement and upward distribution of access to urban environmental amenities, illustrating the viability of using urban greening as a method of attack on the urban poor, working class, and communities of color.

Often presented to the public as urban sustainability projects, the restoration of urban environmental amenities may, in effect, be just the opposite. The concept of sustainability rests on the three pillars of ecological integrity, economic development, and social equity. If urban greening initiatives tend to decrease social equity, then they may be properly conceived as antithetical to the pursuit of urban sustainability. As the case of Prospect Park restoration illustrates, urban greening may whiten and richen as it redistributes environmental amenities upward. Such an approach to urban greening contributes to environmental improvement and economic growth, but it does not enhance urban sustainability from a social equity perspective.

Notes

1   Excepts from the following chapter are republished with permission of Lexington Books, from Gould, Kenneth A. and Lewis, Tammy L. 2012. "The Environmental Injustice of Green Gentrification: The Case of Brooklyn's Prospect Park." In *The World in Brooklyn: Gentrification, Immigration, and Ethnic Politics in a Global City.* Judith DeSena and Shortell, Timothy (eds). Lanham, MD: Lexington Books, 113–46; permission conveyed through Copyright Clearance Center, Inc.
2   This brief history is compiled from *The Complete Illustrated Guidebook to Prospect Park and the Brooklyn Botanic Garden,* 2001, New York: Silver Lining Books, and the Prospect Park Alliance's website (www.prospectpark.org).
3   Many of Moses's modifications would be the target of later restoration efforts.
4   The New York City Department of Housing guidelines defined low-income housing (in 2005) as a maximum income of $37, 675 for a one-bedroom apartment, at a rent of $877 per month. To qualify for a one-bedroom moderate-income unit, the maximum income is $58,875, with a rent of $1,407 per month.

Bibliography

Alexiou, Joseph. 2015. *Gowanus: Brooklyn's Curious Canal.* New York: NYU Press.
Berenson, Richard J. and Neil deMause. 2001. *The Complete Illustrated Guidebook to Prospect Park and the Brooklyn Botanic Garden.* New York: Silver Lining Books.
Brooklyn Community District Profiles. 2009. Retrieved December 12, 2009 (http://home2.nyc.gov/html/acs/downloads/pdf/cd_snapshots/brooklyn_cd6.pdf).
Budin, Jeremiah. 2015. "Prospect-Lefferts Gardens Tower Clears Last Legal Hurdle." Curbed NY, February 6. Retrieved January 27, 2016 (http://ny.curbed.com/archives/2015/02/06/prospectlefferts_gardens_tower_clears_last_legal_hurdle.php).

Cantú, Aaron Miguel. 2015. "'Progressive' Gentrification: One Community's Struggle Against Affordable Housing." Truthout, February 5. Retrieved January 27, 2016 (http://truth-out.org/news/item/28934-progressive-gentrification-one-community-s-struggle-against-affordable-housing).

Carmody, Deirdre. 1985. "Staking Out Parks to Stop Graffiti." *The New York Times*, February 18, B3.

Corcoran Group. 2010. "Prospect Park South Real Estate." Retrieved October 10, 2010 (www.corcoran.com/nyc/Neighborhoods/Display/71).

DeSena, Judith. 2009. *Gentrification and Inequality in Brooklyn: The New Kids on the Block*. Lanham, MD: Lexington Books.

DiCicco, Jessica M. 2014. "Long-Term Urban Park Ecological Restoration: A Case of Prospect Park, Brooklyn, NY." *Ecological Restoration* 32(3): 314–326.

Fillmore Real Estate. 2010. "Crown Heights." Retrieved October 20, 2010 (www.fillmore.com/neighborhoods/crown-heights).

Gould, Kenneth A. and Tammy L. Lewis. 2012. "The Environmental Injustice of Green Gentrification: The Case of Brooklyn's Prospect Park." In *The World in Brooklyn: Gentrification, Immigration, and Ethnic Politics in a Global City*. Judith DeSena and Timothy Shortell. eds. Lanham, MD: Lexington Books, 113–146.

Jackson, Kenneth T. 1998. *The Neighborhoods of Brooklyn, 2nd Edition*. New Haven, CT: Yale University Press.

Krase, Jerome. 1979. "Stigmatized Places, Stigmatized People: Crown Heights and Prospect-Lefferts-Gardens." In *Brooklyn U.S.A.: The Fourth Largest City in America*. Rita Seiden Miller. ed. New York: Brooklyn College and Columbia University Press, 251–62.

Krase, Jerome. 1982. *Self and Community in the City*. New York: University Press of America. Online edition. Retrieved October 20, 2010 www.brooklynsoc.org/PLG/selfandcommunity/index.html

Krase, Jerome. 2016. Personal communication. February 1, 2016.

"Lindsay Assails Graffiti Vandals." 1972. *The New York Times*, August 25, p. 30.

"Losing Ground in the Parks." 1980. *The New York Times*, October 15, A30.

Low, Setha, Dana Taplin, and Suzanne Scheld. 2005. *Rethinking Urban Parks: Public Space and Cultural Diversity*. Austin, TX: University of Texas Press.

New York City Department of City Planning. 2011. "Greenpoint-Williamsburg Land Use and Waterfront Plan." Retrieved March 6, 2011 (www.nyc.gov/html/dcp/html/greenpointwill/greenoverview.shtml).

O'Neill, Natalie. 2011. "Prospect Park Alliance Slashes Budget, Killing Macy's Contest and Other Programs." *The Brooklyn Paper*, May 25.

Osman, Suleiman. 2011. *The Invention of Brownstone Brooklyn: Gentrification and the Search for Authenticity in Postwar New York*. New York: Oxford University Press.

Park, Lisa Sun-Hee and David Naguib Pellow. 2011. *The Slums of Aspen: Immigrants vs. The Environment in America's Eden*. New York: NYU Press.

Prospect Park Alliance. 2010. Retrieved October 30 (www.prospectpark.org/).

Prospect Park Alliance. 2016. Retrieved January 28 (www.prospectpark.org/).

Prudential Douglas Elliman Real Estate. 2010. "Windsor Terrace Real Estate." Retrieved October 10, 2010 (www.elliman.com/new-york-city/brooklyn/windsor-terrace/2-92).

Quindlen, Anna. 1980. "For Prospect Park, $10 Million to Recapture What It Was." *The New York Times,* January 4, B1.

Rapid Realty. 2010. Retrieved October 10, 2010 (www.rapidnyc.com/living/neighborhood/35/Windsor-Terrace-Brooklyn-Neighborhood-Information).

Snyder-Grenier, Ellen M. 1996. *Brooklyn! An Illustrated History.* Philadelphia, PA: Temple University Press.

Taylor, Dorceta E. 2009. *The Environment and the People in American Cities, 1600s–1900s: Disorder, Inequality, and Social Change.* Durham, NC: Duke University Press.

Zukin, Sharon. 1991. *Landscapes of Power: From Detroit to Disney World.* Berkeley, CA: University of California Press.

4 Brooklyn Bridge Park

From abandoned docks to destination park

Playing soccer on Brooklyn Bridge Park's Pier 5, looking out into the New York Harbor toward the Manhattan skyline, it is hard to believe that fifteen years ago this was the site of abandoned warehouses. The case of Brooklyn Bridge Park is a fairly recent one. Its creation was conceived in the 1980s and park construction started in 2008 and continues as we write in 2016. Its transformation from brownfield to park started two years before the Gowanus Canal was added to the Superfund cleanup list and Brooklyn Bridge Park will be completed long before the Gowanus Canal is declared safe. The park sits on an area that had been warehouses and shipping piers, with tremendous views of Lower Manhattan. It is an example of an industrial site that had been abandoned and has been renewed through re-zoning for the park and residences.

In some ways, the case of Brooklyn Bridge Park may seem different from Prospect Park and the other cases. Its construction did not create a vast wave of green gentrification. We use it to show how green growth coalitions are able to maintain and increase the quality of life for wealthy and powerful residents. The distribution of environmental amenities is not by chance. Brooklyn Bridge Park is being constructed in an already "super-gentrified" (Lees 2003) neighborhood, thus keeping property values high, and likely leading to increasing values. The construction of Brooklyn Bridge Park maintains and deepens spatial stratification. The abandoned piers and warehouses along the river could have become many things. The local residents used their social capital to lobby the city, which owned the land, to ensure that it would be transformed into an environmental amenity rather than a locally unwanted land use. They used their social capital to maintain and improve their local quality of life.

Distributional problems with New York's City's commitment to parks

Throughout the United States, urban parks are not equitably distributed (Wen et al. 2013). It is no surprise that in one of the most unequal cities in one of the most unequal countries of the world, parks are not equitably distributed or maintained in New York City. Inequality in the distribution of green spaces mimics economic inequality. Mayor Bloomberg addressed this problem in PlaNYC 2030. One of the goals of that plan is for all New Yorkers to live within a ten-minute walk of a park. This inspired "New York's third great era of park building" (The City of New York 2007), following the nineteenth century's great parks (Central and Prospect) and the doubling of park space under Robert Moses as City Parks Commissioner. In this third era, a major initiative was to "target high-impact projects in neighborhoods underserved by parks" (The City of New York 2007). This included opening school yards so they could be used when schools were closed. It also encouraged urban gardening in schools and public housing projects. At the end of Bloomberg's term, a quarter million of the two million New Yorkers who had not had access, gained ten-minute walking access through those efforts (Green NYC 2016). This aspect of PlaNYC 2030 contributed to the social equity pillar of sustainability. This was a first step: access. A second equity issue that remained unresolved was the differences in the quality of the parks that people had in their neighborhoods.

Another key parks initiative in PlaNYC is to "create destination-level spaces for all types of recreation" (2007). Former Mayor Michael Bloomberg counts the construction of Brooklyn Bridge Park among his city greening accomplishments in this category (Green NYC 2016).[1] The 2011 PlaNYC follow-up report calls Brooklyn Bridge Park, "the most significant major park to be built in that borough since Prospect Park was built 135 years ago" (The City of New York 2011: 38). The destination spaces, however, did not contribute to social equity in terms of being placed in areas most in need. Being able to go to a schoolyard that opens its gates after school hours is not the same as going to a park with numerous recreational facilities that has just been injected with $355 million for playgrounds, soccer fields, exercise equipment, etc. Brooklyn Bridge Park is an example of how elites can use urban greening to increase their property values and their quality of life and demonstrates how urban greening can be a vehicle for reproducing and intensifying inequality.

History: from industrial piers to destination parkland

The area that is now home to Brooklyn Bridge Park was described by *The New York Times* in 1985 as "87 neglected acres" (Lyons 1985). The area along the Brooklyn side of the East River, roughly a mile and a half south from the Brooklyn Bridge to Atlantic Avenue, thrived in the early part of the twentieth century. However, like the story of other New York City working waterfronts, numerous factors came together to decrease the area's economic viability: container shipping, the building of highways such as the Brooklyn-Queens Expressway and the Gowanus Expressway, and deindustrialization of the U.S. due to economic globalization.

Historically, this area had been home to Dutch settlers. Ferries between Manhattan and Brooklyn arrived at what is now the northern end of the park, Fulton's Ferry Landing. In the early 1800s, local landowner Hezekiah Beers Pierrepont laid out a grid pattern in Brooklyn Heights and brothers John Middagh Hicks and Jacob Middagh Hicks started developing land on streets they named after fruits (Pineapple, Orange, Cranberry) to attract wealthy Manhattanites. Together, they created "the suburban commuter" (Nevius 2015). Pierrepont enlisted his friend Robert Fulton to launch a commuter boat that ran from 1814 until forty-one years after the 1883 opening of the Brooklyn Bridge. Since the opening of Brooklyn Bridge Park, a ferry service has returned to Fulton's Landing.

The Port Authority of New York and New Jersey owned six piers and the shoreline, which by the late 1970s included underutilized and empty warehouses. The last cargo ship arrived at the piers in 1983 (Brooklyn Bridge Park 2006: 4). At that time the Port Authority looked to sell the piers and conducted a study as to what should be done. "Suggested options include[d] public housing, parkland, a resort hotel, condominiums, athletic fields, exhibition halls, marinas and manufacturing plants" (Lyons 1985). Community organizations took notice. The adjacent neighborhood of Brooklyn Heights had become an historic district (recognized by the city and nationally) in 1965. Due to this status, it had some legal protections; most notably the protection of their views of downtown Manhattan. At the time, *The New York Times* reported the development preferences of the former president of the Brooklyn Heights Association, an investment banker:

> One of the things that has occurred to me is a hotel and executive training center, a low-rise with gardens, athletic fields and a swimming pool, a whole resort of the type we see in Beverly Hills and Florida, a type of community that would cater predominantly to the Wall Street market … it would be unrealistic to put 87 acres out as public parkland … We also need to avoid family-oriented housing because of the infrastructure that it would entail, that is schools, stores and the like.
>
> (Lyons 1985)

City planners from Brooklyn, however, argued that public access to the waterfront was an important goal. The strain between the local community's goals and the broader goals of public access would be ongoing throughout the process.

The Brooklyn Heights Association (BHA), an existing community organization, mobilized to create their own vision, which included the idea of a "Harbor Park" and set up a Piers Committee to focus on the issue (Hand and Pearsall 2014). The group consisted of residents from Brooklyn Heights, which consistently ranks among the wealthiest and whitest neighborhoods of Brooklyn. Later, the Piers Committee morphed into the

Brooklyn Bridge Park Coalition and now the Brooklyn Bridge Park Conservancy. This community wielded tremendous power at the time the Port Authority was considering selling Piers 1–6 to developers, and they used it. Two of the lead actors in this history, in a remarkable ninety-page report titled "The Origins of Brooklyn Bridge Park, 1986–1988," chronicle how the Brooklyn Heights Association was able to turn the Port Authority away from housing and office developments (an "International City") to the idea of a Harbor Park. Along with the rich historical data presented in the report, what is noteworthy is the detailed account of the way a community with social, cultural, economic, and political capital is able to deploy its assets. Though the report opens by calling the history a David and Goliath tale against Goliath's attempt to "monetize Brooklyn Piers 1–6" (the BHA versus the Port Authority and the Koch Administration, respectively), it reads as a tale of powerful people using their resources to make the state change its course. The BHA advocated "its bold concept of a grand 'Harbor Park'" and won (Hand and Pearsall 2014: 1). The organization fought against "Powerful public authorities intent on reaping major financial reward" (Hand and Pearsall 2014: 2). In this case, the residential elites defeated democratically elected officials.

In 1998 the Downtown Brooklyn Waterfront Local Development Corporation was created to develop a conceptual framework for the park, which they completed in 2000 (New York State Urban Development Corp 2006: 4). In 2002 the state and city, under Governor George Pataki (R) and Mayor Michael Bloomberg, signed an agreement to create the Brooklyn Bridge Park Development Corporation with the charge of planning, designing, and building the Brooklyn Bridge Park. Funding was secured through city and state and the project was required to be economically self-sufficient following its construction. "The cost of operation, maintenance and upkeep would be paid out of the revenues received from appropriate commercial activities and residential projects located within the Project" (Brooklyn Bridge Park 2006: 3). There were debates leading up to the park's construction about how the revenue would be generated. In 2005, neighbors argued against a design that put luxury condos on the site as a means of revenue. Locals argued against the proposal:

> We want a park we can use, not just look at … It is not a park – it is an exclusive luxury condo development that is publicly inaccessible, but with award-winning landscape! … Why is there this rush to build housing first? … The process caters to residential real estate developers, which is in conflict with the public park values.
>
> (Wisloski 2005)

In the end, the residential buildings were included. One Brooklyn Bridge Park, a warehouse that was converted into luxury condominiums, opened in 2008.

Construction of the park began in 2008 and in 2010 the first section of the park opened. In 2016, construction continues with new areas opening as they become completed. Brooklyn Bridge Park runs along the East River, spanning from just north of the Brooklyn Bridge south, along the waterfront, down through former shipping Piers 1 through 6, ending at the working piers of the Columbia Waterfront on Atlantic Avenue (see Figure 4.1). The park is adjacent to the neighborhoods of DUMBO (Down Under

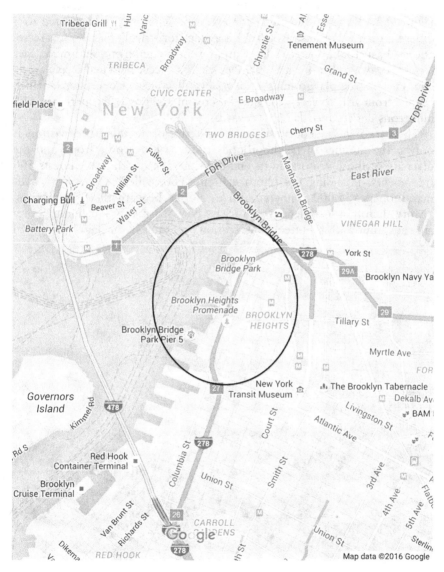

Figure 4.1 Map of Brooklyn Heights

the Manhattan Bridge Overpass) and Brooklyn Heights. It spans 1.3 miles of the waterfront and covers eighty-five acres.

The park is self-consciously green. As noted in Chapter 1, the architects integrated sustainability features into the design, including using salvaged materials, native species, recycling storm water, composting, using green roofs, and much more. The park, like The High Line, has a website dedicated to explaining its sustainable (mostly environmentally sustainable) practices (Brooklyn Bridge Park 2016b).

It is truly an astounding park. In addition to its views of Manhattan (see Figure 4.2), there is something for everyone. Each pier is dedicated to a different theme. For instance, Pier 1 is a place for a stroll; Pier 2 offers recreation – basketball, bocce, roller skating, fitness equipment, and more; Pier 3 is a greenway; Pier 4 is a beach; Pier 5 has a soccer field and picnic areas, and Pier 6 has playgrounds and volleyball courts. Concessions, which change from year to year, sell wine, ice cream, and pizza. The park has won numerous design awards (Park Awards 2016).

The park is outrageously successful in terms of the number of visitors it draws, the number of neighborhoods those visitors come from, and the diversity of those visitors. In its end-of-year wrap up, the park boasts 500 free events, including the photo exhibit "Photoville," a party for half-marathoners (25,000 runners), and its Books Beneath the Bridge series. "More than 8,000 students from across New York City – including every zip code in Brooklyn – attended education programs in the park" (Brooklyn

Figure 4.2 View of Manhattan from Brooklyn Bridge Park

Bridge Park 2014). It has become a tourist destination. It is common to see visitors walking around with guidebooks written in French, German, and Japanese, among others. Park officials estimate that an average Saturday and Sunday in the summer bring 119,000 visitors and a weekday brings just under 25,000 (Brooklyn Bridge Park 2014).

Park programming is diverse. Brooklyn Bridge Park Conservancy hosts music, outdoor movies and waterfront workouts in the summer. You can take a free tour or kayak ride or go for a swim in the "pop-up" pool. Arts events are designed to cater to Brooklyn's multicultural constituency. For example, 2015's "dance party" line up included Latin Jazz, Classic Soul Funk, and Gypsy Punk. These events draw from all of Brooklyn and other boroughs. The park is less than fifteen minutes walk away from seven subway lines.

Though public funding provided capital for the park, the maintenance and operations of the park are mandated to come from revenues generated by development on the site, namely concessions, residences and commercial spaces. The park's maintenance cost is $16 million per year. Currently, one renovated warehouse with condominiums is completed (One Brooklyn Bridge Park). Its first floor has retail space. The first shop to open was the Wag Club, a luxury dog spa, whose amenities include "an air-purification system, rubber flooring that's gentle on paws, bedding that repels dirt and liquids, filtered water, and all-natural treats" (Briquelet 2011a). The second space to open was a wine retailer. This building is expected to contribute $3 million per year to maintenance costs.

At the north part of the site, a LEED (Leadership in Energy and Environmental Design)-certified hotel and new residential building are under construction (Figure 4.3). These are also expected to contribute to park maintenance and operations. Toll Brothers and the Starwood Capital group are developing the area. According to signs posted at the construction site, the residential townhomes start in "the low $2 millions." The most expensive unit is listed at $10.49 million (Carlson 2016). There are just over one hundred of these luxury condos with amenities in addition to park access, including concierge service, fitness centers, a children's playroom, a meditation center, and a pet washing station (Pierhouse at Brooklyn Bridge Park 2016). Seventy-eight of these luxury units were in contract by January 2016 (Carlson 2016). These sites are also expected to contribute over $3 million per year (Gregor 2013). Like One Brooklyn Bridge Park, all property taxes go to the park through what is known as "payment in lieu of taxes." Though the area was out of price-reach for most Brooklynites even before the park was built (in large part due to its close proximity to Manhattan and for the views), it is even further out of reach now.

Brooklyn Bridge Park is the only park in New York City where you can live. This unique "solution" for how to deal with diminishing public funds is an extreme version of earlier neoliberal, public-private partnerships. Conservancies such as the Prospect Park Alliance and the Central Park

Figure 4.3 Construction of residences at Brooklyn Bridge Park

Alliance, raise private funds for public parks. In One Brooklyn Bridge Park – and the other residences that will be put in the park – the city is literally charging those with private resources who can afford to live within a public park in order to finance the park. Both of Mayor Bloomberg's high-profile park additions, his legacy parks – the Highline and Brooklyn Bridge Park – use local housing maintenance fees to provide part of the maintenance funding for parks. While in theory this concept sounds like an innovative solution to a lack of government funding, in practice its consequences disadvantage poor neighborhoods, as will be examined later in the chapter.

Neighborhood demographics

Brooklyn Heights has long been a wealthy, white, educated neighborhood along Brooklyn's "Gold Coast." Its close proximity to Manhattan has made it an attractive place to live. In Loretta Lees' (2003) work on "super-gentrification," she describes Brooklyn Heights: "Brooklyn Heights was one of the first neighborhoods in the US to gentrify … in [the] early 19th century by wealthy business, shipping and tradespeople drawn across the East River from Lower Manhattan by the availability of the Fulton Street steam ferry service" (2492). Throughout that century it was "one of the wealthiest communities in the U.S." (2493). The neighborhood's status slipped when the subway opened and commuters moved into subdivided brownstones and boarding houses. It gentrified again after World War II.

After this, its second gentrification, the Brooklyn Heights Association (BHA) took on Robert Moses and his plan to put the Brooklyn-Queens Expressway (BQE) through the neighborhood. The BHA had been in existence since 1910. According to Lees, they handed Moses his first defeat. The BQE was instead built on the perimeter of Brooklyn Heights. To protect the community from the site and noise of the expressway, the now iconic Promenade walkway was built over it – forming a walkway with views of the water and the Manhattan skyline. This wasn't the BHA's only success in keeping out "locally unwanted land uses" (LULUs). In the early 1960s, they also successfully fought off low-income housing in the neighborhood. James Nevius (2015) reports that the BHA president stated, "The city is trying to put over public housing on us and overexploit the neighborhood." Nevius (2015) adds, "another resident succinctly put it: 'Heights residents don't want poor people and they don't want Negroes and Puerto Ricans.'" The residents were organized through the BHA and effective at keeping their neighborhood as they wanted it.

Investments were made in the 1960s following historic district designation, and home prices rose in the 1970s through to what Lees call "a more corporatized" gentrification in the 1990s (a third gentrification). State-led improvements to nearby downtown assisted the gentrification. Lees argues that whites replaced white ethnics in the already high-percentage white neighborhood. The neighborhood became more wealthy, educated, and involved in financial services. Brooklyn Heights was a suburb of Wall Street.

Lees uses Brooklyn Heights as a case study to define "super-gentrification" as "the transformation of already gentrified, prosperous and solidly upper-middle-class neighborhoods into much more exclusive and expensive enclaves" (2003: 2487). She argues that this happens in global cities "like London and New York that have become the focus of intense investment and conspicuous consumption by a new generation of super-rich 'financiers' fed by fortunes from the global finance and corporate service industries" (2003: 2487). An important point that she makes is that this sort of gentrification "is now also increasingly state-led with national and local governmental policy tied up in supporting gentrification initiatives" (Lees 2003: 2490). We see this in support of greening initiatives. Lees argues that super-gentrification is indeed what happened in Brooklyn Heights. We argue that what is happening now with the greening of Brooklyn Bridge Park and the consequences on the neighborhood is a form of *hyper-super-gentrification*: part of an upward spiral.

This hyper-super-gentrification is part of a feedback loop whereby nicer places become nicer, not through some natural consequence, but by concerted actions of determined actors. The Brooklyn Heights Association played a key role in the development of their Harbor Park. They had a number of interests in mind, including keeping others out and keeping their views of lower Manhattan in. When the question arose as to what would happen with the dilapidated piers along the waterfront, they had resources in line to get what they wanted. Their leaders were experienced professionals: lawyers, architects, CEOs, investment bankers. They had considerable experience among them, including having done the work to add the Fulton Ferry Historic District to the Landmarks Preservation list. They were able to commission their own study of the piers to investigate alternatives to the Port Authority's study (Hand and Pearsall 2014: 9), they recruited their influential neighbors (including Norman Mailer) to serve on committees (Hand and Pearsall 2014: 10), and in short order they raised $130,000 (Hand and Pearsall 2014: 11). From there, the BHA conceived the Harbor Park and had it put to paper by a landscape architect. The plan "could hardly help but fire the imagination" (Hand and Pearsall 2014: 13). The park "concept would best serve the BHA's goals of protecting the views and providing the needed recreational facilities" (Hand and Pearsall 2014: 12–13). During the battle, Scott Hand likened losing the scenic view to Brooklyn losing the Brooklyn Dodgers (Hand and Pearsall 2014: 41).

Data in Table 4.1 paints a picture of a neighborhood that through the decades has been whiter and wealthier than Brooklyn as a whole (compare this to Table 3.2).[2] Through all of the three moments in time (1990, 2000, and 2014), Brooklyn Height's median income has been far above Brooklyn's. In 2000 and 2014, the median income in the Heights was more than double Brooklyn's overall, with significantly lower percentages of families living in poverty (2.6 percent in 2014). The Heights is also consistently higher overall in terms of education. In 1990, it had double the rate of college graduates that Brooklyn, as a whole, has today. Presently, over 77 percent of the residents have bachelor's degrees or higher. The rate of home ownership is likewise consistently higher (46 percent compared to 30 percent in Brooklyn in 2014). Housing values and rents are also higher than Brooklyn's, with rents in the area rising much faster than Brooklyn's. Home values have not risen in the period from 1990 to 2014. Anecdotally, this seems very surprising and may be a result of the measure that is being used (median rather than mean). It may also be due to the fact that 2014 data is from the American Community Survey (ACS). Unlike the census, which counts every housing unit, the ACS only collects a sample of housing units, and in tracts like this can have very large margins of error. A 2015 *Daily News* story with the headline, "Brooklyn's Most Expensive Home: Brooklyn Heights brownstone listed for record $40M" reports, "Sales of Brooklyn townhouses priced at $3 million or more jumped by a jaw-dropping 579 percent in the brownstone and north Brooklyn [where Brooklyn Heights is located] markets over the last five years, and almost doubled over the past year, according to a recent report by Ideal Properties" (Clarke 2015). Reports like this, and our experience in the neighborhood, suggest that the ACS data may not be picking up the recent changes. Unfortunately, this information was not collected in the 2010 census.

Table 4.1 Demographic changes in Brooklyn Heights, 1990–2014

		1990	2000	2014	Change over time, 2000–2014	Change over time, 1990–2014
	Population change	18,320	20,416	19,369	–5%	6%
Race	White (%)	87.7%	81.9%	78.5%	–3%	–9%
	Black (%)	7.2%	7.6%	5.8%	–2%	–1%
Class	Median household income 2013 ($)	$88,340	$95,334	$100,317	5%	14%
	Families below poverty line (%)	1.2%	2.7%	2.6%	0%	1%
Social power	Bachelors degree or higher (%)	63.6%	70.8%	77.3%	7%	14%
Housing	Owner occupied housing units (%)	38.0%	41.7%	46.4%	5%	8%
	Median single family owner occupied home value 2013 ($)	$863,891	$361,667	$695,595	92%	–19%
	Median rent 2013 ($)	$1,059	$1,250	$1,896	52%	79%

Sources: 1990 U.S. Census Bureau, Social Explorer
2000 U.S. Census Bureau, Social Explorer
2014 American Community Survey, Social Explorer, 5-year estimates

The greening of the park has made Brooklyn Heights an even more desirable and even less attainable address for most New Yorkers. It is a bedroom community for Wall Street financiers who send their children to its highly coveted private schools (Packer and St. Ann's whose 2015–16 tuition for high schoolers is over $40k). The gentrification that has continued since the park was built has increased the neighborhood's already high prices, and has displaced both residential renters and small businesses. For instance, the *Brooklyn Paper* reported on a small restaurant, Siggy's, that had been in the neighborhood for ten years, since before the park was built. The owner argued that rents in the neighborhood are higher than in Manhattan and blamed the park for leading her landlord to raise the rent beyond her reach. "Now with the development of the park, landlords think they can charge higher-than-Manhattan prices" (Perlman 2015). Ironically, in the online comments section of the paper, a lawyer, who was also pushed out of Brooklyn Heights, invites Siggy's to move where he moved – to Lefferts Gardens, the newly green gentrifying area on the east side of Prospect Heights. This is the story of gentrifying Brooklyn: the 0.1 percent push out the 1 percent who push out the 5 percent and so on.

What we can learn from Brooklyn Heights is that neighborhoods with economic and social capital are able to resist unwanted development and attract environmental amenities. When neighborhoods are stratified by capital, this creates a dynamic where the rich get richer amenities and the poor get poorer amenities and the distance between the top and the bottom increases. Hyper-super-gentrification is not an accident. As Chapter 6 will illustrate, community organizations resisting unwanted developments in Greenpoint, Williamsburg, and Sunset Park did not have this level of resources, nor this level of self-perpetuating success.

Social equity for the rich?

There are currently two controversies in Brooklyn Bridge Park. The first is on Pier 1. Residents are arguing that the residential and hotel developments are too tall and are blocking their view. These buildings are currently being constructed. The continuation of existing sight lines was promised as part of the original park plan. Residents filed a lawsuit to stop work on the hotel and condos. In fact, the buildings are taller than originally approved, but only by about a meter, and developers argue that it is due to new flood maps and building codes that were enacted after Superstorm Sandy, which required elevation of the building and relocating some vulnerable systems to the roof.

The second controversy is on Pier 6 with regard to development in general. The original plan suggests that housing could be built on the site. Indeed, that is what the Brooklyn Bridge Park Development Corporation proposed: two condo towers to generate revenue. Residents have resisted this and other residential development in the area (Figure 4.4). However, Mayor de Blasio had made increasing affordable housing in the city one of his major goals (specifically adding 80,000 units in ten years) (Glen 2015). He has called for the new towers to include 30 percent affordable moderate- and middle-income housing.[3] Affordable housing in New York City is distributed by lottery and the odds of getting in are very slim. An online newspaper's analysis of sixty housing lotteries found that there were 2.9 million applications for 3,400 apartments, which is 843 applicants per unit (Zimmer and Chiwaya 2015), which is just slightly higher than a 0.01 percent chance. Current residents oppose the development, in general,

Figure 4.4 Sign near Brooklyn Bridge Park against new residences in the area

based on two lines of argumentation: 1) density and open space, and 2) they say the park already has enough revenue for maintenance. Densification and inclusionary zoning are central elements of de Blasio's strategy to accommodate a growing population and expand affordable housing.

An anti-development group, People for Green Space, filed a suit against the development. They cite data from the city that shows that the density is high and there is not enough green space in the neighborhood. They called for a new environmental review and for the new plan to go through an application process. Density is a salient argument in this neighborhood. The neighborhood adjacent to the south, Cobble Hill, also a very wealthy brownstoner area, recently lost its battle to keep the Long Island College Hospital open. The site of the former hospital is being developed into thirty- and forty-story luxury condominium towers, increasing density dramati- cally. Also, the loss of the hospital is not an insignificant hit in these battles as public services are being replaced by private real estate development (Figure 4.5). Regarding the Pier 6 developments, local officials take up this cause arguing that there are not enough public services in the area. For instance, there are already wait lists for the local elementary schools. State Senator Daniel Squadron argued, "The neighborhood's changes are not

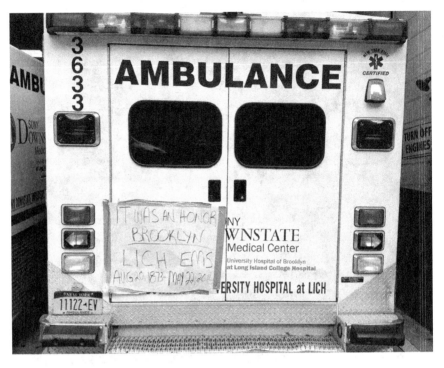

Figure 4.5 Hospital closing to make way for new condo development

being driven by thoughtful urban planning, but rather by real estate values"
(Hurowitz 2015). Lawmakers have asked de Blasio to dismiss Bloomberg's
funding plan and find alternative funding for the park (Foderaro 2014). The
courts denied the environmental review, but will require formal amendment
to the plan.

The second argument against the housing development is that the
revenue is unnecessary. The Brooklyn Bridge Park Corporation (BBP)
reported that due to rising real estate values that "had soared along with
park use, the park was in better financial shape than projected" and could
thus afford to move ahead with affordable housing (Robbins 2014). There
have been numerous arguments over funding for the park and actual
revenues collected over the years. According to the *Brooklyn Paper,* the BBP
Corporation, because it is not a public agency, does not follow the same
transparency rules. The BBP Corporation does post their annual audit information online, but only through 2013. The audits provide overall numbers,
but are not broken down by concession/buildings, etc. (Brooklyn Bridge
Park 2016a). In 2011 there were reports that – although the One Brooklyn
Bridge Park development in the park is supposed to pay $3 million per year
in payments in lieu of taxes that are used directly for the maintenance of the
park – the city's Department of Finance had reduced the fees through a deal

with the developer (Briquelet 2011b). This raises significant issues around the neoliberal public-private program that many of these sorts of new projects are dependent upon for funding: they are not transparent and special deals for special groups can be made without public constituencies being informed. Presently, however, BBP Corporation argues the "Pier 6 development is essential to Brooklyn Bridge Park's long term financial stability" (Brooklyn Bridge Development Corporation 2016). They argue that it is needed both for ongoing revenue and for a one-time payment needed to shore up piers. They also argue that the development of the approximately four-hundred-unit building will not adversely affect school overcrowding.

The development on Pier 6 is also opposed specifically because the plan has called for affordable housing. Locals oppose the affordable housing because they say that it will not generate enough revenue. A widely reported sentiment voiced by a resident at one of the public hearings about the Pier 6 condo development sums up the "Not in my back yard" (Nimby) perspective: "Why does it have to be in Brooklyn Heights? Why not build it in Williamsburg?" (Hurowitz 2015). This Nimby statement was echoed by a One Brooklyn Bridge Park resident who posted online, "With the mayor's new agenda, not only did the current owners of one Brooklyn get a bait and switch, but we would probably never have made the purchase had we known there would be 100 percent subsidized housing immediately next door." The writer followed up in an interview noting, "By no means am I looking to come across as an elitist" (Robbins 2014). The president of the Brooklyn Bridge Park Defense fund, which is opposed to housing in the park in general, argued, "Affordable housing is a noble and fine thing. But a park that has to pay for itself is not supposed to pay for the ills of society" (Robbins 2014). A mayor's representative from the housing department argues, "We are able to maintain this park and advance the public good" (Robbins 2014). De Blasio's administration sees the development as a win-win for park revenue and affordable housing.

Other developments in the area are using the park as an amenity to promote sales, much like the Richard Meier building did in Prospect Heights around Prospect Park. An interesting site is a nearby development at 60 Water Street. This building is notable for its lack of amenities. It is outside the park and does not offer fitness centers or children's lounges. Its developer notes that "the neighborhood [steps from the park] is really the amenity" (Kaysen 2015).

Mayor Bloomberg's other high-profile park addition – The High Line – which opened in 2009, gentrified the area around it. A 2012 *New York Times* opinion piece critical of that development, argues "The High Line has become a tourist-clogged catwalk and a catalyst for some of the most rapid gentrification in the city's history" (Moss 2012). Moss goes on to argue that the park "is destroying neighborhoods as it goes." The park "became a tool for the Bloomberg administration's creation of a new, upscale, corporatized stretch ..." Real estate prices doubled and the working class and light industry moved out of the area. The High Line's effect more closely resembles what is happening around the Gowanus Canal, where light industry is giving way to residential development. The case of Brooklyn Bridge Park differs from these green gentrification areas in that Brooklyn Bridge Park made an already beautiful and gentrified neighborhood more beautiful and hyper-super-gentrified (see Figure 4.6).

In terms of city-wide equity, siting a park in one of the richest neighborhoods was not equitable. Nevertheless, that is what the city did. Once the city, state and community worked to develop plans, agreements were made, including preserving the neighborhoods' sight lines and allowing residences within the park to fund the park. Brooklyn Heights residents were involved in the discussions; there was process justice. The residents wanted their sight lines and they wanted a park. They were reluctantly willing to trade some condo development for that.

In terms of the outcomes, residents felt like there was no justice: they would be sacrificing some of their sight lines, and they would be living in a denser neighborhood. The changes to the sight lines were arguably slight. The real loss to this community will be the increasing density of the area. The quality of life will be diminished. On this count, the Brooklyn Heights

Figure 4.6 Brooklyn Bridge Park amenities

Association lost to the green growth coalition. Real estate interests have been more powerful than even this very wealthy and powerful community association. Residents, however, need not be concerned that their real estate values will decline, even if de Blasio's affordable housing is developed on Pier 6. Housing prices in the area will stay high and likely go higher. The issue of equity for this wealthy enclave is different than in areas where poor people are being displaced. In this case, the 1 percent is pushing out the 5 percent. The 5 percent have more options than less affluent residents and business owners from Sunset Park, Greenpoint, and Gowanus.

The real estate heat is on in Brooklyn Heights and in the neighboring areas. In Cobble Hill, just to the south, an already gentrified area is rushing to turn all available space into luxury condos. As noted, Cobble Hill has lost its hospital to real estate development, thus trading public services for private profit. The set of piers that lie just to the south of the park's Pier 6, currently working piers, will undoubtedly be turned over to real estate when the lease expires, and densification will continue. When Pier 7, currently a beer distributor, was leased in 2009, it was hailed by Borough President Marty Markowitz as bringing good jobs to Brooklyn and the New York City Economic Development President praised the development for its environmental qualities – water being "the most environmentally efficient means of getting goods and products into and out of the New York City region" (NYCEDC 2009). However, since that time, and with the green gentrification that has taken place around the park, the Citizens Budget Commission produced a report that recommends that the Port Authority sell these terminals. Specifically, they note, "Building housing at the ports in Brooklyn, where the median sale price of condominiums, co-ops and single-family homes climbed to a record of almost $590,000 last year, may be a better use for the Brooklyn-Port Authority Marine Terminal in Cobble Hill and the Red Hook Container Terminal" (Braun 2015). Thus, the march of green hyper-super-gentrification continues its spread around Brooklyn Bridge Park, shoring up values for homeowners, pushing out the 5 percent, and eliminating social services (Long Island College Hospital) and the few remaining working-class, waterfront jobs.

Next phase of parks: the city government as an agent for creating social equity

While wealthy and powerful residents seek park amenities for their own benefit, the city, pressed by public officials, has remained attentive to its public mission and the broader issues of equity. As discussed above, aspects of PlaNYC increased equity of access to parks: today more people have a ten-minute walk to the park than before the plan. That modest policy proposal made a difference. However, the quality of those parks is in question. Access to poorly maintained parks with few amenities versus destination-grade parks matters. The election of progressive mayor Bill de

Blasio enabled questions of equity not just around park access, but about the quality of parks and the quantity of funding, to come to the fore.

The funding of New York City's parks has been affected by two trends: 1) the decline of funding overall, and 2) the privatization of funding. In the 1960s, approximately 1.5 percent of the city's budget went to parks; today, even with increased acreage under the Parks Department, that number is less than half of 1 percent (Shakarian 2014). A strategy that has been used quite successfully to deal with declining public dollars has been to create nonprofit conservancies that privately raise funds, and through agreements with the Parks Department, manage and operate parks. The Prospect Park Alliance and the Central Park Alliance are two prominent examples of this (Taylor 2009). In 2012 the Central Park Alliance received a record-setting $100 million gift. The consequence of this type of funding is what some politicians, including de Blasio, call a "two tiered" funding system (Levine 2014). Large parks in affluent areas are able to fundraise to maintain and improve their parks whereas less wealthy parks, in less wealthy areas, that rely on diminishing public funds, likewise diminish. In this way, richer neighborhoods become nicer places to live and poorer neighborhoods become worse places to live, reinforcing environmental injustices.

To deal with these disparities, local politicians have made a number of proposals: increase overall public funding, distribute a portion of conservancies' private donations to other parks, and/or make the park's budget and its distributions transparent. There are pros and cons to each. There are a variety of opponents against the conservancy proposal. Existing conservancies, as we would expect, argue against that model because they believe it would hurt their ability to fundraise. Donors don't want to give to their local park if they think the funds will end up in parks far from where they live. Some politicians, however, have a broader critique of the problem of private funding for public goods in general.[4] For instance, New York City council member Mark Levine argues against the conservancy model because, "The most insidious effect of the rise of conservancies is that it dampens the political will of the city's most influential citizens for robust public funding of the Parks Department, mostly because such high-income individuals live adjacent to parks benefitting from private donations" (Levine 2014). When you're rich and you live next to a privately well-funded park, increases in the park budget seem unnecessary. When you're poor and live next to a dilapidated park, you want the public budget to increase. Due to the inequality in the spatial distribution of parks, the rich can isolate themselves from poor neighborhoods and poor parks, and argue that funding them is not necessary. If poor people want the benefits of destination-level parks, they need to get on the subway or bus to visit them.

Local politicians made park equity a "hot topic" and the de Blasio administration responded. In April 2014, there was a city council hearing: Equity in Parks: Do Disparities Exist in the Care of the City's Open Space? (Shakarian 2014). In fall of 2014, de Blasio's administration came out with

"NYC Parks: Framework for an Equitable Future" outlining the city's plans to deal with city parks in a more equitable way, especially related to funding. The plan includes $130 million for capital improvements in neighborhoods "with higher-than-average concentrations of poverty" and growing populations (called Community Parks Initiative neighborhoods) (New York City Department of Parks and Recreation 2014). A year later, two additional strategies were added. In 2015, a law was passed that requires the Parks Department to report how much it spends on each city park, thus addressing the transparency facet. Later, eight major conservancies committed $15 million to parks in Community Parks Initiative neighborhoods. These are voluntary contributions that range from assistance with waste management, gardener training, and teen programs, to sister park partnerships, and other in-kind contributions (OneNYC 2015). The Mayor's office calls its Community Parks Initiative "NYC Parks' first major equity initiative and part of OneNYC, the Mayor's plan for a strong and just New York City" (OneNYC 2015).

These actions by the city government are an attempt to distribute funds in a transparent and equitable way. The Community Parks Initiative focuses its funds on poor neighborhoods with young people in areas without easy access to destination parks. In addition to addressing access equity, it also addresses quality equity. It puts resources into creating and upgrading the quality of these sites. It draws on private conservancies to assist, but does not rely on their largess. The partnerships that are created, such as the sister park partnerships, also have the advantage of breaking down physical barriers between rich park conservancies and the realities of most of the city's parks. People involved with the parks can see the real differences between these two types of parks and advocate for greater parks budgets, across the city. Finally, it is key to note that the impetus for these changes came from elected officials. The public sector has a role to play in ensuring that greening initiatives embrace the social pillar of sustainability.

Conclusion

The city's actions related to greening need not be inherently negative in terms of their distributional aspects. While the creation of Brooklyn Bridge Park served to increase environmental injustice by promoting environmental privilege in Brooklyn Heights, city policies that integrate greening and social equity can have positive outcomes for a larger number of New Yorkers across the socio-economic spectrum.

The case of Brooklyn Bridge Park demonstrates how organized community associations with wealth and social power can collaborate with government partners to attract green amenities to their neighborhoods, thus making nice, rich neighborhoods green, and intensifying environmental privilege. However, in this instance, the community traded-off density. The low-rise brownstone neighborhood is increasingly becoming denser and more crowded, and will become even more so in the coming years as developers purchase sites in the periphery of this area to build tower condominiums. Brooklyn Heights homeowners' home values will likely rise, but the quality of this brownstoner neighborhood will be diminished. The difference between this case and others where there is involuntary displacement lies in the options that the residents of this community have that others do not. White, wealthy homeowners in rich neighborhoods have a world of housing options to choose from. Their choices of new location have consequences for others with restricted access to housing markets.

Notes

1   Bushwick Inlet Park (Greenpoint-Williamsburg) and Bush Terminal Piers Park (Sunset Park) are both on Bloomberg's destination-park upgrades list.
2   For 1990 and 2000, we analyzed census tracts 1, 3.01, 3.02, 5, and 7. The lines were shifted, but contained the same area for the 2010 census. For the 2014 data, we analyzed tracts 1, 3.01, 5.01, 5.02 and 7.
3   For a four-person household, the income range included in this category is from $67,121 to $138,435 (Glen 2015).
4   This argument parallels the problem of private funding for national parks (Lewis 2000).

Bibliography

Braun, Martin Z. 2015. "Port Authority Should Sell Brooklyn Marine Terminals, Group Says." *Bloomberg Business,* January 13. Retrieved February 5, 2016 (www.bloomberg.com/news/articles/2015-01-13/port-authority-should-sell-brooklyn-marine-terminals-group-says).
Briquelet, Kate. 2011a. "Brooklyn Bridge Bark! New Dog Spa Opens at Pier 6 Condo." *Brooklyn Paper,* November 3.
Briquelet, Kate. 2011b. "The Fix is in! City Cuts Big Developer's Taxes in Brooklyn Bridge Park." *Brooklyn Paper,* June 15.
Brooklyn Bridge Development Corporation. 2016. "Details on Pier 6 Development Site." Retrieved February 5, 2016 (www.brooklynbridgepark.org/pages/pier-6-development-facts).
Brooklyn Bridge Park. 2014. "2014 Season Wrap Up." Retrieved February 5, 2016 (www.brooklynbridgepark.org/press/2014-season-wrap-up-bbp-welcomes-visitors-from-greater-range-of-ny-public-programs-attract-160-000-attendees).
Brooklyn Bridge Park. 2016a. "About Us: Financial Information." Retrieved February 5, 2016 (www.brooklynbridgepark.org/pages/financial-information).
Brooklyn Bridge Park. 2016b. "Sustainability." Retrieved February 5, 2016 (www.brooklynbridgepark.org/pages/sustainability).
Carlson, Jen. 2016. "Did Beyoncé & Jay Z Buy a Controversial Pierhouse Condo?" *Gothamist,* January 11. Retrieved February 1, 2016 (http://gothamist.com/2016/01/11/beyonce_jay_z_pierhouse.php).

The City of New York. 2007. *PlaNYC: A Greener Greater New York*. The City of New York. Mayor Michael R. Bloomberg. New York: NYC Government.

The City of New York. 2011. *PlaNYC: Update April 2011*. The City Of New York. Mayor Michael R. Bloomberg. Retrieved February 5, 2016 (www.nyc.gov/html/planyc/downloads/pdf/publications/planyc_2011_planyc_full_report.pdf.).

Clarke, Katherine. 2015. "Brooklyn's Most Expensive Home: Brooklyn Heights Brownstone Listed for record $40M." *New York Daily News*, February 4.

Foderaro, Lisa W. 2014. "De Blasio Is Urged to Alter Housing Plans at Brooklyn Park." *The New York Times*, April 9.

Glen, Alicia. 2015. *Housing New York: A Five-Borough, Ten Year Plan*. The City of New York. Mayor Bill de Blasio. New York: NYC Government. Retrieved February 5, 2016 (www.nyc.gov/html/housing/assets/downloads/pdf/housing_plan.pdf).

Green NYC. 2016. "Mike Bloomberg's Record of Progress." Retrieved January 20, 2016 (http://progress.mikebloomberg.com/green-nyc/parks).

Gregor, Alison. 2013. "Condos That Fund a Brooklyn Park." *The New York Times*, November 22.

Hand, Scott M. and Otis Pratt Pearsall. 2014. "The Origins of Brooklyn Bridge Park, 1986–1988." Brooklyn Historical Society Catalogue (http://brooklynhistory.org/docs/OriginsBrooklynBridgePark.pdf).

Hurowitz, Noah. 2015. "Last Night: Heated Debate Over Towers at Brooklyn Bridge Park." *Brooklyn Paper*, July 31.

Kaysen, Ronda. 2015. "Where Shiny Meets Gritty." *The New York Times*, January 16.

Lees, Loretta. 2003. "Super-gentrification: The Case of Brooklyn Heights, New York City." *Urban Studies* 40(12): 2487–2509.

Levine, Mark. 2014. "New York Needs a Parks System Which Is Both Fair and Fabulous." *Huffington Post*, March 20. Retrieved February 5, 2016 (www.huffingtonpost.com/mark-d-levine/new-york-city-parks-system_b_5002092.html).

Lewis, Tammy L. 2000. "Transnational Conservation Movement Organizations: Shaping the Protected Area Systems of Less Developed Countries." *Mobilization* 5(1): 105–123.

Lyons, Richard D. 1985. "In Brooklyn Heights, A Spotlight on 87 Neglected Acres." *The New York Times*, October 27.

Moss, Jeremiah. 2012. "Disney World on the Hudson." *The New York Times*, August 21.

Nevius, James. 2015. "How Brooklyn Heights Became the City's First Historic District." *Curbed NY*, May 18. Retrieved February 5, 2016 (http://ny.curbed.com/archives/2015/03/18/how_brooklyn_heights_became_the_citys_first_historic_district.php).

New York City Department of Parks and Recreation. 2014. "NYC Parks: Framework for an Equitable Future." Retrieved February 5, 2016 (www.nycgovparks.org/about/framework-for-an-equitable-future).

NYC EDC. 2009. "Port Authority, New York City Sign Lease Extensions for Maritime Terminals in Staten Island, Brooklyn." Retrieved February 5, 2016 (www.nycedc.com/press-release/port-authority-new-york-city-sign-lease-extensions-maritime-terminals-staten-island).

New York State Urban Development Corporation, DBA The Empire State Development Corporation, and Brooklyn Bridge Park Development Corporation. 2006. *Brooklyn Bridge Park Civic and Land Use Improvement Project: Modified General Project Plan*. Modified Plan Adopted December 18, 2006.

OneNYC. 2015. "Mayor de Blasio and Parks Commissioner Silver Announce $15 Million in Conservancy Commitments to Community Parks." Retrieved February 5, 2016 (www1.nyc.gov/office-of-the-mayor/news/838-15/mayor-de-blasio-parks-commissioner-silver-15-million-conservancy-commitments-to).

Park Awards. 2016. Retrieved January 29 (www.brooklynbridgepark.org/pages/parkdesign#about-park-awards).

Perlman, Matthew. 2015. "Siggy's Owner On Closure: Brooklyn Heights Is Now Pricier Than Manhattan." *Brooklyn Paper*, February 20.

Pierhouse at Brooklyn Bridge Park. 2016. "Amenities." Retrieved January 25. 2016 (www.pierhouseny.com/amenities).

Robbins, Liz. 2014. "The Battle of Brooklyn Bridge Park." *The New York Times*, August 1.

Shakarian, Katrina. 2014. "For Richer & For Poorer: Tying the Park Equity Knot." *Gotham Gazette*, May 26. Retrieved February 5, 2016 (www.gothamgazette.com/index.php/government/5052-richer-poorer-park-equity-new-york-city).

Taylor, Dorceta. 2009. *The Environment and the People in American Cities, 1600s–1900s: Disorder, Inequality, and Social Change*. Durham, NC: Duke University Press.

Wen, Ming, Xingyou Zhang, Carmen D. Harris, James B. Holt and Janet B. Croft. 2013. "Spatial Disparities in the Distribution of Parks and Green Spaces in the USA." *Annals of Behavioral Medicine* 45(1): S18–S27.

Wisloski, Jess. 2005. "Heights Group: Lose the condos." *Brooklyn Paper*, 21 May.

Zimmer, Amy and Nigel Chiwaya. 2015. "Map: What are your chances of winning an affordable housing lottery?" Retrieved February 5, 2016 (www.dnainfo.com/new-york/20151027/midtown/map-what-are-your-chances-at-spot-affordable-housing).

5 The Gowanus Canal

From open sewer to the Venice of Brooklyn[1]

It is a bit unnerving to watch luxury condos going up on the banks of what is arguably the most toxic, stinking, and feared body of water in New York City, especially after its virus-infected contents flooded the neighborhood during Superstorm Sandy. The case presented here, that of the Gowanus Canal, has a relatively long history as a green gentrification site, with significant remediation intervention beginning in 1987. While the original canal was completed in the same era as Prospect Park, it was not conceptualized as a potential environmental amenity until the twenty-first century. It is an example of a brownfield site that is being cleaned up, in part through Superfund and in part by the green growth coalition, to become an environmental attraction. We provide an extended discussion of its history to illustrate the relationship among elites' economic choices, the quality of the water, and neighborhood demographics.

Cleaning up the Gowanus Canal has been on New York City's "to-do list" for decades. Why would 2010 be the year that the canal would gain Superfund status? We argue that the process of green gentrification explains the recent developments around the canal. We provide an historical analysis of the canal that demonstrates how economic decisions regarding the use of the canal altered its water quality, which, in turn, affected the quality of the residential areas around the canal and the constituency of the Gowanus neighborhood. The latest economic decision: to declare the canal a Superfund site and begin cleanup in earnest – greening the canal – is altering the constituency of the neighborhood yet again. The cleanup ultimately provides greater opportunities for real estate developers to invest in the area and increase housing values. An analysis of Superfund site cleanups found that housing values within one kilometer of sites increased 18 percent (Gamper-Rabindran, Mastromonaco and Timmins 2011). When sites are removed from the Superfund list, nearby demographics change: mean household income increases as does the percentage of college graduates (Gamper-Rabindran and Timmins 2011). In Gowanus, current low-income residents have been and will continue to be replaced by higher-income residents drawn to the revitalized ("greened") environmental resource. Light-industrial working-class jobs have been and will continue to be replaced by residences and services for new inhabitants. These processes lead to green gentrification.

History: from open sewer to the Venice of Brooklyn

The Gowanus Canal is one of America's most famously polluted urban waterways. Popularly conceived of as a stinking open cesspool, industrial sewer, and disposal site for mob hits, it has been found to host typhus, cholera, and live gonorrhea virus. It is also the site for Brooklyn's next round of luxury waterfront condominium developments. The Gowanus Canal's historic transformation from tidal marshland, to toxic dump, to urban environmental amenity illustrates the dynamic relationship between environment, economy, and social distribution. The nature of the socio-environmental dynamics that emerge from specific economic system-based transformations of the Gowanus ecosystem can be broadly analyzed as five distinct eras: colonization, industrial boom, industrial decline, early green gentrification, and, lastly, the era of Superfund designation and Superstorm Sandy. We draw upon published histories and news accounts to construct these eras, and to illustrate the recurring process of economic decisions leading to changes in water quality, which ultimately affect neighborhood constituency.

Starting with extractive development (oyster exports), through milling, to industrialization, and now residential real estate development, the primary engine of ecological and neighborhood change has been the interests of the growth coalition of each era, and each era has required or produced a different neighborhood composition. Despite Superstorm Sandy's momentary disruption of the redevelopment process in 2012, elites push on with development plans. The brief history that follows provides some context for the various ways that the site has been contaminated. In light of this long history as a dumping ground, it is all the more remarkable that the green growth machine is pressing forward with a cleanup for luxury real estate development.

Colonization

Ostensibly named for the leader of the Canarsee band of the Lenni-Lenape Indians who inhabited the site, Gowanus (Gowane's [*sic?*]) Bay became the site of the initial Dutch settlement of Brooklyn in 1636. The local ecosystem was a tidal inlet of saltwater marshland with many navigable creeks, the largest of which was eventually dubbed "Gowanus Creek." The large oysters hosted by this rich edge ecosystem became Brooklyn's first export, as barrels of oysters were shipped off to Europe in the seventeenth and eighteenth centuries. During the same period, tobacco plantations were established on former Canarsee maize fields, and parts of the marshland were drained (Burrows and Wallace 1999). The first tidewater gristmills of

New Netherland were also established in the Gowanus ecosystem in the mid-1600s, and millponds and canals were dug, using slave labor, to facilitate their operation (Alexiou 2015). The socioeconomically driven transformation of the ecosystem and its use, from an intact tidal marshland supporting renewable resource extraction (oystering), to one increasingly modified to support eotechnic (wood, water and wind-based) industry (milling) (Mumford 1934), would continue into the nineteenth century.

By the mid-1800s, Brooklyn was the fastest-growing city in the United States. The opening of the Erie Canal in 1825, and its expansion between 1834 and 1862, dramatically increased the importance of the Brooklyn waterfront. Erie Canal-based transshipment, combined with the arrival of the Industrial Revolution in Brooklyn, led to calls for the expansion of Brooklyn's docking and navigation facilities. Local elites argued for the construction of a canal to drain marshlands and raise property values, and to serve local industry (Alexiou 2015). The New York State legislature authorized the dredging of Gowanus Creek to create the Gowanus Canal in 1849. They authorized more extensive dredging in 1867 following a United States Army Corps of Engineers design. The canal was completed in 1869. The final design of the canal was chosen from a number of alternatives based primarily on its lower cost. The decision to create a 1.8-mile inland waterway with no outlet would have dramatic consequences for water quality, public health, and the area's long-term development. It was argued at the time that the ecosystem's 6-foot tides would effectively circulate water in and out of the canal. That premise would prove stunningly mistaken in short time. The draining of the millponds signaled the shift of the local economy from eotechnic (water and wind-powered milling) to paleotechnic (coal-powered, Industrial Revolution) production (Mumford 1934), as well as the increasing centrality of shipping. Over this long era, the population shifted from Lenni-Lenape to European settlers.

Industrial boom

The state-directed construction of the Gowanus Canal made the area one of the nation's first planned industrial development districts and succeeded in making it a central hub for local, regional, and national industrial growth. Industries quickly arose and expanded in response to the canal's construction including tanneries, soap makers, coal gas manufacturing plants, flour mills, plaster mills, cement works, paper mills, breweries, rope factories, sulfur producers, and paint, ink, and chemical plants. As a major shipment point, warehouses, and stone and coal yards proliferated nearby. Grain from the Erie Canal entered the city through the Gowanus. Stone from quarries in New Jersey came in through the Gowanus Canal and was used to build the now famous housing stock of brownstone Brooklyn. The expanding reliance on coal as a heating and power source, and the expanding demand for gas lighting in a rapidly growing Brooklyn made the

Gowanus Canal a major point of coal imports, coal gas manufacturing, and distribution. By 1880, the Gowanus Canal had helped make Brooklyn the fourth largest industrial city in the U.S. (Snyder-Grenier 1996).

The Gowanus industrial boom drew a large working-class immigrant population to the area to work in industry and shipping. Initially composed largely of people of Irish, Scandinavian, and German decent, they occupied the frame houses of the area which pre-dated the construction of brownstones in surrounding Park Slope, Cobble Hill, and Carroll Gardens. Brick row houses and small apartment buildings were added to existing housing stock to accommodate the expanding worker population, which would grow to include a sizable Italian component (Snyder-Grenier 1996). Brownstone construction in upland sections of the basin met the housing needs of the owner-and-manager class (Burrows and Wallace 1999). The pattern of workers housed downhill, downwind, and downstream from industrial effluent sources, and owners and managers housed uphill, upwind, and upstream of such facilities is well documented (Hurley 1995). The neighborhood of Gowanus quickly gained a reputation for rowdiness as working-class immigrants frequented the dozens of pubs that proliferated on Smith Street, with the neighborhood commonly referred to as the "Gashouse District" (Benardo and Weiss 2006). The working-class residents of industrial Gowanus were, of course, subjected to the toxic mélange of airborne industrial effluent at work and at home amid this concentration of nascent industrialization. Additionally, the neighborhood – built upon the remains of a tidal marsh in a flood basin – was subjected to the routine flooding of an area robbed of its natural water retention and drainage features, with particularly dramatic flood events in 1882 and 1890. The flooding increased exposure to the waterborne industrial effluent that was routinely discharged into the Gowanus Canal.

The rapid growth of South Brooklyn[2] in the mid-to-late nineteenth century, while being a source of demand and economic vibrancy for Gowanus, also imposed particularly noxious additional environmental burdens on its residents. With growth of the surrounding neighborhoods occurring at a rate of nearly 700 new buildings a year, population growth quickly outstripped sanitation planning. The raw sewage of surrounding neighborhoods naturally drained downhill to the Gowanus. When Brooklyn constructed the first municipal sewer system in the United States during the period of canal expansion (Melosi 1999), it expanded the range of sewage catchment and drained all of the human waste directly into the canal. The result of this municipal sanitation infrastructure project was to collect the waste from more affluent uphill brownstone neighborhoods, and concentrate it in the open sewer of working-class Gowanus (Miller 2014). The overwhelming stench of raw sewage and industrial effluent led some to call for the canal's elimination, although its centrality to the economy made that untenable (Gould 1991). By 1906, the canal was supporting 26,000 passages a year.

The contradiction between the noxious stench of the canal, and the rising property values resulting from the industrial boom and population growth around it, led to calls for some form of remediation that would preserve the commercial interests of both private industrialists and private real estate owners. The solution was found in publicly funded infrastructure. In an effort to correct the initial design flaw of the canal, the city sought to create water flow by constructing a 12-foot diameter, 6,280-foot long underground tunnel connecting the head of the canal to Buttermilk Channel in New York Harbor. Driven by a pumping station equipped with an enormous ship's propeller, the Gowanus "Flushing Tunnel" became operational on June 22, 1911 with great public fanfare (Alexiou 2015). Although not a panacea, the routine flushing of the canal with 200 million gallons of seawater a day substantially reduced the stench and the accumulation of both raw sewage and industrial effluent. However, even at that time, some noted that solving the problem of the Gowanus by dispersing its foul contents into the bay was not an adequate way to address contamination.

The peak of the Gowanus industrial boom occurred around the end of World War I. By this time, the Gowanus Canal was the nation's busiest and most polluted commercial and industrial canal, with roughly six million tons of cargo being moved annually (Miner et al. 2008). The Gowanus coal yards were handling as much coal as the rest of New York City combined. Despite the action of the flushing tunnel, the deposition of human waste into the canal necessitated routine dredging in order to keep the channel open. The Gowanus neighborhood would remain an ecologically toxic neighborhood to the present day but due to shifts in regional infrastructure, global shipping, and energy demand, its industrial and commercial centrality would wane rapidly at mid-century.

Industrial decline and ecological re-stagnation

The commercial and industrial decline of the Gowanus Canal foreshadowed the industrial decline of the nation as a whole and led the industrial decline of Brooklyn. A number of factors: local, regional, national and global, converged to spell the end of the Gowanus Canal as a focal point for urban industrial development. In the years following World War II, President Eisenhower's interstate highway project generated the infrastructure that would shift national commercial transportation from rail and barge to trucks. In New York City, this converged with Robert Moses's redesign of urban infrastructure to emphasize highways and auto transport at the expense of all other forms of urban transport. In 1951, Moses's raised Gowanus Expressway opened, connecting the Gowanus to the interstate highway system, and trucks became relatively cheaper and more convenient than using barges to transport goods. The Gowanus Expressway was devastating to the Gowanus neighborhood in other ways as well. The expressway bored through the community and helped inspire an exodus of the Irish,

Scandinavian, and German population, whose homes, commercial districts, community cohesion, and employment were all damaged by Moses's project (Caro 1975). Additionally, the expressway would become an ongoing source of air pollution that would rain down on the community and the canal as over 150,000 cars and trucks passed overhead daily.

Also following World War II, the scale and methods of commercial shipping began to shift, as containerization required larger ships, deeper harbors, more expansive yards, and an increasing reliance on trucking to and from ports. As containerization took hold, shipping shifted from Brooklyn to the expanding port facilities of New Jersey (Jackson 1998). Containerization also meant a dramatic reduction in longshoreman jobs, which had been the basis upon which nearby neighborhoods such as Carroll Gardens had attracted and retained its working-class, unionized, immigrant (Italian) population. The decline of Brooklyn's commercial waterfront would hit Gowanus early, and culminate with the closing of the Brooklyn Navy Yard in 1966. With the exception of Brooklyn's last small active commercial shipping port on Columbia Street, its waterfronts would go underused and into decay for the next half-century. The scale of national and global shipping had exceeded the capacity of a Gowanus Canal built for a rapidly passing era. In 1955, the Army Corps of Engineers suspended regular dredging of the canal, signaling its commercial insignificance.

While upscaled infrastructure had undermined the canal's role as a transshipment facility, changes in demand for one of the canal's primary industries fueled its decline as an industrial locale. When Brooklyn's natural gas infrastructure was connected to a transcontinental pipeline in 1950, the demand for coal gas and coal for home heating rapidly waned. Since coal had been a major source of barge traffic on the canal, the decline of this local industry rippled through the neighborhood's employment prospects, leading the decline of barge and tugboat work (Alexiou 2015). The coal gas industry was also the basis of the chemical and dye industries along the Gowanus, and an entire industrial sector left the landscape, although the consequences remain. The contamination left behind by a century of coal gas production has been a primary obstacle to the redevelopment of vast tracts along the Gowanus.

The final death blows to Gowanus's commercial and industrial vibrancy came with the breakdown of the flushing tunnel in the early 1960s. With the canal no longer vital to the city's economy and its formerly European (white) population exiting to be replaced by largely Hispanic (non-white) new immigrant groups, the city proved both financially and politically uninterested in repairing the canal's cleansing mechanism. Raw sewage, which was still routinely dumped untreated into the canal, would now remain in the stagnant water to mix with a legacy of industrial toxins and the spillage from the diminished oil industries that remained active along the canal. The stench from the canal, now returned to its pre-1911 potency, would be joined by the ongoing air contamination from Robert Moses's overhead expressways (Alexiou 2015). At the same time, in 1964, the Verrazano-Narrows Bridge linking Brooklyn with Staten Island (and thus New Jersey and the U.S. mainland) would finalize the interstate truck linkage making the canal obsolete (Pearsall 2013). As Brooklyn's manufacturing faded, poverty increased, and the Verrazano-Narrows Bridge facilitated white flight out of Brooklyn into Staten Island, leading Brooklyn's and Gowanus's population decline.

The city's abandonment of the canal cannot be separated from the change in the neighborhood's demographics, as both cause and consequence. In 1948, Robert Moses's Slum Clearance Authority under Title 1 initiated the construction of the Gowanus Houses project (see Figure 5.1),

Figure 5.1 Public housing projects in Gowanus

at the northern end of the canal. In 1966, another housing project, Wyckoff Gardens, was also established in the Gowanus neighborhood. The pattern of siting public housing in proximity to urban environmental hazards is well documented (Bullard 1990; Pellow 2002). The decline of the Gowanus economy generated an ideal spot for locally unwanted land uses to be hidden. As well-paid unionized jobs declined, white flight progressed, Puerto Rican in-migrants filled much of the pre-existing housing stock, and African-Americans came to occupy much of the public housing now located in this toxic hot spot. If Brooklyn was traditionally a low priority for a Manhattan-centric city government, the industrially decayed and economically obsolete Gowanus was near the bottom of city priorities as the municipality headed into the fiscal crisis of the 1970s. Gowanus became a model of "inner-city" disinvestment (McManus, et al. 1995). One hundred years after its construction, the Gowanus Canal was left to die and the population of its community would continue to change, and decrease, for decades to come.

But some long-term residents refused to walk away. The Gowanus Canal Community Development Corporation (GCCDC) was founded in 1978 as a nonprofit organization focused on the revitalization of Gowanus (McManus et al. 1995). It was inspired by a local business person, Salvatore "Buddy" Scotto, who would champion the cleanup of the canal for decades (Alexiou 2015). Here we find an early vision of this industrial and municipal "end pipe" as an environmental amenity. Although this vision of the festering Gowanus as "the Venice of Brooklyn" seemed remarkably quixotic, some developments in the 1970s lent hope. The Federal Water Pollution Control Amendments of 1972 and the Clean Water Act of 1977 provided a legal basis for local demands to clean up the canal (see Table 5.1). In 1974, the city took control of a 66-acre brownfield along the Gowanus that is arguably one of the most polluted sites in New York City, the site of a former gas plant with soil contaminated down to 150 feet

Table 5.1 Selected federal, state, and local policies affecting the Gowanus cleanup

Federal	Clean Water Act, 1977
	The Comprehensive Environmental Response, Compensation, and Liability Act (CERCLA aka Superfund) 1980
	President Clinton's Executive Order 12898 addressing environmental justice, 1994
	Environmental Protection Agency's Brownfield Program, 1995
State	New York Brownfield Cleanup Act, 2003
City	PlaNYC 2030; 2007
	Brownfield and Community Rehabilitation Act, establishing Office of Environmental Remediation and NYC Brownfield Cleanup Program, 2008

(McManus et al. 1995). The city designated the land to be used as a "Public Place" (see Figure 5.2), and a debate about its cleanup and use would begin (and last to the present day). In 1975, some dredging of the canal was initiated after a twenty-year hiatus. However, ongoing oil spills and fires from the remaining oil industry, and continuous sewer discharge, combined with the city's budget crisis, led to little in the way of water quality improvement or redevelopment.

Under federal pressure, the city constructed the $230 million Red Hook Water Pollution Control Plant in 1987 to treat the raw sewage headed for the canal. This first infrastructure to ever treat Gowanus-destined sewage had mixed success. While the routine dumping of raw sewage into the canal was finally terminated, the fourteen combined sewage overflow outlets (CSOs) linked to the canal continued to dump untreated human waste at every major rain event. To the present, the CSOs remain a major source of Gowanus Canal contamination and an obstacle to any repurposing of the Canal as an environmental amenity (see Figure 5.3). The 1990 census shows the opening of the Red Hook Treatment Plant to coincide with the neighborhood's population low point of 24,000 residents, roughly two-thirds of its historic peak.

Figure 5.2 Public Place

Figure 5.3 Combined sewer overflow into the Gowanus Canal

Early gentrification via artist colonization

By the 1990s, the gentrification of brownstone Brooklyn had picked up steam, and rising housing costs up-slope in surrounding Park Slope, Cobble Hill, Boerum Hill, and Carroll Gardens led would-be gentrifying in-migrants to seek out the cheaper housing stock in Gowanus. Out of its fiscal crisis now, the city started to look at the potential redevelopment of Gowanus that the GCCDC and other groups had been promoting. In 1994, reconstruction of the flushing tunnel was started, and completed in 1998. By this point in the canal's economic history, only ten primary industrial concerns were operating along the canal, including Bayside Oil. Early on, the abandoned warehouses and industrial infrastructure had begun to attract artists looking for affordable studio space in what would increas-ingly be defined as an "edgy" post-industrial landscape (see Figure 5.4) (Alexiou 2015). As early as 1983, an abandoned soap factory had been converted to arts space (Citizens for NYC 1998). Property values in the neighborhood rose roughly 40 percent between 1994 and 1998 (Nyman, Schwartz and Scanlon 2010). Rising property values in surrounding neigh-borhoods, and the in-migration of white, educated flag bearers of the so-called "creative class" captured the interests of city officials and developers. In 1998, Mayor Giuliani came out in support of the Brooklyn Commons development, a 500,000-square foot sports complex and multiplex theater on 9.4 acres of brownfield canal frontage formerly occupied by the U.S. Post Office. Although that development never materialized, local politicians began channeling substantial funds to the GCCDC to produce studies, redevelopment plans, and public open space for the Gowanus (see Table 5.2).

The return of white people to Gowanus was accompanied by the return of marine life to the canal. The renewed flushing tunnel was now pumping 215 million gallons of seawater through the canal daily, and killifish, crabs, and ducks were appearing in the canal. The New York City Department of Environmental Protection (DEP) dredged the canal in 1998, and in 2002 the U.S. Army Corps of Engineers entered into a cost-sharing agreement with DEP on a $5 million Ecosystem Restoration Feasibility Study of the Gowanus Canal area. Clearly, the rising property values of South Brooklyn and the potential to draw a steady influx of white, educated gentrifiers had made the ecological restoration of the Gowanus Canal feasible. In 1999, the Gowanus Dredgers Canoe Club began serving as a local environmental monitoring crew while sponsoring canoe rides along the canal. Other local groups also focused on the Gowanus environment and redevelopment, including Friends and Residents of the Gowanus Canal (FROGG), Urban Divers, and the Gowanus Canal Conservancy. By 2000, Ikea and Lowe's had both expressed interest in locating stores in the area (Table 5.3). Lowe's would ultimately build on the Gowanus and be required to include a small

Table 5.2 Selected public funding for Gowanus Canal and brownfields in NYC

1999	Assemblywoman Joan Millman provided the GCCDC with $100,000 for a bulkhead study and public access document
2000	The New York City Department of Parks and Recreation gave the GCCDC $270,000 to create three street-end open space parks as part of the Green Streets program
2001	Governor Pataki funded a $270,000 revitalization plan
2002	U.S. Army Corp of Engineers and NY Department of Environmental Protection allocated $5 million for Ecosystem Restoration Feasibility Study
2002	Congresswoman Nydia Velazquez allocated $225,000 for a comprehensive community development plan for Gowanus
2002	Borough President Marty Markowitz received $100,000 in state funds to identify areas for habitat restoration
1996, 2003, 2004, 2005, 2006, 2007	The City of New York has received six grants from the federal government for brownfields assessments, ranging from $200k to $800k (USEPA, Brownfields and Land Revitalization)

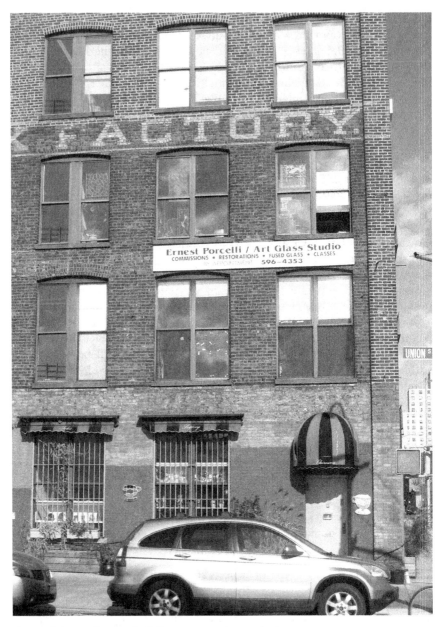

Figure 5.4 Box factory building converted to artists' space

canal-side public access park. The Lowe's park, across from the active scrap metal yard and Bayside Oil, remains largely unused. Between 2003 and 2007, the market price for industrial property in Gowanus rose from $108 to $270 per square foot (Nyman et al. 2010).

Table 5.3 Selected private proposals for development around the Gowanus Canal

1998	Brooklyn Commons: 500,000-square feet sports complex and theater (not developed)
2000	Ikea (developed elsewhere)
2000	Lowe's (developed and opened in 2004)
2003	Gowanus Green, mixed-use residential (status unclear, as of 2008 had entered a partnership with the city; ground breaking now slated for 2018)
2003	Whole Foods (received support from Community Board in 2011; opened in December 2013)
2006	Toll Brothers (zoning change granted to allow for residential project in 2009; pulled out after Superfund designation in 2010; Lightstone Group took over in 2012)
2015	Lightstone Group's 700-unit condominium project under construction

This state and private interest in the Gowanus facilitated expanding populations of crabs and artists. In 2003, Red Dive, an artist group, performed "Peripheral City: Rediscovering the Gowanus Canal." In the same year, the Gowanus Artists Open Studio Tour featured over seventy resident artists. A series of artist events and celebrations of the Gowanus environment became regular features of neighborhood culture. The possibility of a Gowanus Canal with crabs in its waters and artists along its banks became fodder for developers. Plans for a "Gowanus Green" housing development on a former coal gasification plant site, a canal-side Whole Foods supermarket, and numerous other residential and retail developments geared toward meeting the needs of new or future Gowanus residents proliferated (Table 5.3). Gowanus Green is noteworthy because it is proposed on land owned by the city, and the planning board for the development includes a local social justice organization, Fifth Avenue Committee. The plans call for 70 percent affordable housing. The developer, Hudson, Inc., was hired in 2008, but as of early 2016 had not broken ground on the site. The earliest estimates are for construction to begin in 2018. The city has been quite generous to potential developers in granting zoning changes to facilitate private development plans, and further zoning changes are a central piece of current redevelopment planning, as developers and the city seek to transition as much of the area from industrial to residential and commercial as local interests will allow. Twenty-five blocks of Gowanus were rezoned for non-industrial uses (Alexiou 2015). Such conversions have clear implications for the future class composition of the Gowanus neighborhood, as light-industrial employers are replaced with relatively expensive housing and retail space, and working-class jobs are lost to residents and low-wage service jobs.

Superfund designation and Superstorm Sandy

Two events in the early 2010s could have slowed, derailed or caused a major reconsideration of the green growth machine's plans for Gowanus. Both the necessity of major remediation of a highly toxic site, and the palpable threat of increased frequency of major flooding due to climate change might have inspired an urban sustainability plan for Gowanus with greater emphasis on the ecological and equity pillars of sustainability. The neighborhood flooded extensively during Superstorm Sandy, and new condo developments sit directly on the banks of the canal. However, the economic logic of real estate development trumped the eco-logic of a balanced approach to urban greening, with negative implications for environmental justice.

"Superfun Superfund?" [artist graffiti in Gowanus]

The rush to redevelop Gowanus hit a bump when, in 2010, the U.S. Environmental Protection Agency (EPA) designated the Gowanus Canal as a federal Superfund cleanup site. The cleanup is estimated to cost $300 to $500 million and to take up to twelve years to complete. Mayor Bloomberg and the real estate developers (the growth coalition) opposed Superfund designation, and countered with a city-controlled plan that was promoted as being much quicker to complete (Alexiou 2015). Both local government and private capital interests would be better served by a quick route to an official declaration that the canal was clean. Given the extent of contamination, and the quick short-run profits to be made in developing the contaminated sites, many area residents questioned the depth of the mayor's cleanup plan (Farrell 2012; Pearsall 2013). After much public debate, the 2010 Superfund designation had one immediate result. The Toll Brothers, a large developer firm, withdrew its residential development proposal, as it had threatened to do if the federal government became involved in the cleanup. Another developer quickly took their place. Artist colonization remains undeterred by Superfund status, and perhaps the status adds to the hip, edgy cachet of the locale (see Figure 5.5). In December 2010, the *Wall Street Journal* ran a story about the area titled, "Superfund Site Morphs into Cultural Hotspot" (Dollar 2010).

Regardless of the time that remediation takes to complete, or the fate of specific developers' plans, the forces driving the ecological restoration of the Gowanus Canal and its transformation from environmental hazard to urban environmental amenity are likely to remain powerful. The success of that ecological restoration lies at the heart of the future of the Gowanus neighborhood. A successful cleanup of the canal will ultimately raise property values (Hurd 2002), attracting in-migrants who can afford higher housing costs.

Figure 5.5 "Brooklyn's Coolest Superfund Site"

Superstorm Sandy

On October 29, 2012, despite bringing relatively little rain, and lower-than-hurricane-speed winds, Superstorm Sandy pushed a 13-foot storm surge into New York Harbor; flooded low lying coastal neighborhoods of New York City; knocked out electrical power in lower Manhattan; flooded a good portion of the subway system; destroyed housing on Staten Island, in the Rockaways, and elsewhere; set an entire neighborhood ablaze; and left thousands of New Yorkers without shelter, heat, power, and functional transportation infrastructure for months, and more (Youngman 2015). In Brooklyn, the storm surge pushed the sea up into and over the low lying neighborhood of Red Hook, and up the Gowanus Canal, sending sewage-laden waters over the banks, up the streets, and into the basements and ground floor residential, industrial, and commercial spaces of the Gowanus neighborhood. The Third Street and Carroll Street bridges were completely submerged. Floodwater spread out more than a block on either side of the canal, submerging the proposed sites for luxury condo developments. The area between Bond and Nevins Streets was turned into a 5-foot deep lake, inundating homes. Floodwater crashed through art spaces, upending large metal sculptural works, and mixed paint and chemicals with untreated sewage. Despite being in Flood Zone A (now Evacuation Zone 1), designated for mandatory evacuation, many Gowanus residents remained in their homes in an effort to protect their property and their pets. Having been warned to evacuate for Hurricane Irene, which did not produce Gowanus flooding, residents were understandably skeptical of weather hyperbole.

Flooding and power outages took the Gowanus Canal pumping station offline for thirty-three hours, causing 13 million gallons of untreated sewage to discharge into the floodwaters that still covered the neighborhood. As the flood receded the following day, the stench of polluted water and the sound of generators powering pumps to clear flooded basements filled the neighborhood. City officials sent emails warning residents to avoid skin contact with contaminated water, but the flood had left most affected residents without Internet access. The EPA (USEPA 2012) issued the following instructions to residents and volunteers who came to help:

- Remove or pump out standing water;
- Use bleach to kill germs;
- Wear rubber boots, rubber gloves and goggles;
- Clean hard things with soap and water. Then clean with a mix of 1 cup of household liquid bleach in 5 gallons of water ... Scrub rough surfaces with a stiff brush and air dry;
- Wash clothes worn during cleanups in hot water and detergent. These clothes should be washed separately than uncontaminated clothes.

Later test results would indicate that the Gowanus floodwaters contained very high levels of bacteria such as enterococcus due to raw sewage discharges. Enterococcus can cause diverticulitis, urinary tract infections, and meningitis. Levels of semi-volatile organic compounds of the type known to be a major component of Gowanus Canal sludge (such as PAHs – polycyclic aromatic hydrocarbons) were found in low levels in some on-land samples and were undetected in others.

Neither enterococcus nor storm surge flooding proved much of a deterrent to the green gentrification process. Little more than a year after Sandy, a sustainability-themed Whole Foods celebrated its grand opening on the banks of the Gowanus, and The Lightstone Group had broken ground on a 700-unit apartment complex, including 20 percent affordable housing, on the previously flooded development site abandoned by the Toll Brothers after Superfund designation (see Figure 5.6) (Alexiou 2015). The Gowanus area still commands its trendy image and has become a "real estate hot spot" (Krisel 2015). Global warming floods and Superfund stigma have proven less powerful than the green growth machine. What remains to be seen is how much of the working-class employment and population will survive this experiment in urban greening.

Figure 5.6 Lightstone Group condo development on the banks of the Gowanus

Neighborhood demographics

As noted earlier, in the Brooklyn real estate world, the boundaries of neighborhoods shift according to their desirability. The boundaries of gentrifying neighborhoods stretch to encompass more territory so that properties on the periphery can command higher rents and sales prices. Neighborhood boundaries are fluid and the real estate industry is a leader in shifting these boundaries to meet their marketing needs, often despite the disagreement of long-term residents. Other times, residents join together to name their neighborhoods. For instance, Carroll Gardens was chosen as a name by its residents and designated such in the 1960s. Historic preservation groups, such as those that created the Boerum Hill Historic District, also do this.

In this context, it can be tricky to define the borders of the Gowanus neighborhood. There are a few ways we do this: 1) using real estate borders, 2) using geographic boundaries, 3) using census tracts, and 4) considering residents' self-identification.

Of the four ways in which we consider what constitutes the "Gowanus neighborhood," the real estate borders contain the least area (see Figure 5.7). This makes sense given its bordering neighborhoods. These neighborhoods – Carroll Gardens to the west, Boerum Hill to the north, and Park Slope to the east – have well-established names and have already been gentrified. At this stage in its development, it is more likely to see properties close to the Gowanus Canal being marketed as "Park Slope" or "Boerum Hill" than the inverse. There is more real estate money to be made by absorbing Gowanus into other neighborhoods with high-priced names and well-established identities when possible. As such, it is not surprising that only one of the large real estate brokers' offices (Corcoran) in Brooklyn have "Gowanus" listed as a neighborhood. The *New York Times* recently added it to its searchable neighborhoods in its real estate section. In 2011, in their "Neighborhood Guides," Corcoran Real Estate brokers describe the neighborhood:

> Gowanus, often referred to as "G-Slope" (because it is just west of Park Slope) is a neighborhood with an industrial, edgy feel, yet Gowanus offers a nice sense of community and a number of homes to buy ... The most anticipated real estate development in Gowanus is the area bordering the Canal. New planned developments along the Gowanus Canal include a large mixed use building with lots of new apartments to buy and a spacious, green park ... Lowe's Home improvement opened a few years ago and Whole Foods is coming too. Plus the trendy boutiques of Park Slope and Carroll Gardens are just a stone's throw away ... On summer nights, a diverse group of neighborhood dwellers share grilled food and drinks at the outdoor Gowanus Yacht Club. Gowanus also boasts an annual Artists Studio Tour where over 120 artists open up their studies to the public.
>
> (Corcoran Group 2011)

Corcoran is trying to create a hip new name ("G-Slope") for this area that does not conjure existing negative connotations associated with the canal while also capitalizing on Park Slope's appeal. No one else uses "G-Slope" to refer to this area, not even five years later. Also, the "G-Slope" is being sold as a soon-to-be gentrified area with existing and promising new amenities, such as Whole Foods. As reported in Anguelovski (2015: 185):

> Activists talk about the Whole Food Effect: When chains like Whole Foods open a store, residents claim that the company knows that the neighborhood is ripe for socio-economic changes. After store opening, policy reports have shown that real estate prices tend to increase. For example, in Portland, price premiums for homes located close to specialty grocery stores are estimated to range from 5.8 percent to 29.3 percent.
>
> (Anguelovski 2015)

Corcoran's own boundaries don't actually work for the sales pitch it is giving. The Gowanus Yacht Club (a clever name for a dive bar) is located three blocks west of the canal in an area that Corcoran does not actually consider part of the "G-Slope." The *New York Times* map of the neighborhood does include the Yacht Club (and the west side of the canal).

The Gowanus neighborhood looks bigger than the "G-Slope" if you look at census tracts, geographic boundaries, and community groups' ideas about what constitutes Gowanus. For analytic and data collection purposes, census tracts make sense for understanding the area around the canal. The census tracts surrounding the canal (see Figure 5.7) overlap significantly with the geography of the area and with Gowanus community groups' definitions of the area. The canal is in the lowlands. The west side of the canal (Carroll Gardens, census tracts 75 and 77) slopes gently down to the canal, flattening out over the bridge, into the east side of the neighborhood (Corcoran's "G-Slope," census tracts 125, 123, 121, and 117; note that these were the tract numbers prior to 2010: in 2010, tract 123 was changed to tract 119). It remains flat to the eastern most end of these tracts where a very clear upward slope begins into Park Slope. North of the canal (Boerum Hill, census tracts 71 and 127) is also flat. For the most part, the flat lowland geography defines the area around the canal as "Gowanus."

The west, north, and east sides of the canal are very different. To give a sense of the differences among these sides, we analyzed data from the U.S. Census Bureau (1990, 2000, and the 2010–2014 American Community Survey). Carroll Gardens is most residential, and has already gentrified. Its residents are predominantly white and educated, with high incomes and high housing values. At least three community groups focused on the canal are located in this area (FROGG, the Gowanus Conservancy, and the GCCDC). Also on this side of the canal is Public Place, a 6-acre site owned by the city, for which numerous housing developments have been proposed

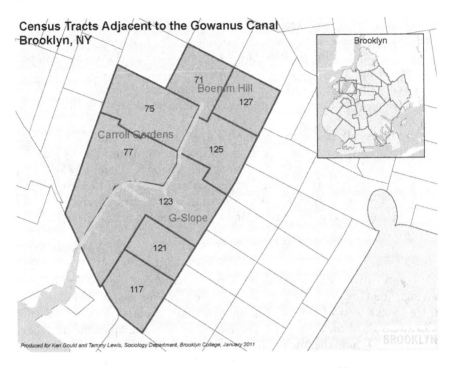

Figure 5.7 Census tracts adjacent to the Gowanus Canal, Brooklyn

over the years, including Gowanus Green most recently. Boerum Hill to the north, is mixed with light industry and residences, with almost all residences one block beyond the canal. Boerum Hill Historic District, established in 1983, abuts the Gowanus Houses, a large housing project. One block to the east are Wyckoff Gardens, another housing project. Boerum Hill has very high housing prices, but lower than Carroll Gardens; the incomes and education levels are also significantly lower. The percentage of black residents is higher than the percentage of white. The east side, the "G-Slope," presently has the lowest density of housing and the fewest residents of the three neighborhoods due to its partially industrial character. Its median housing prices are the lowest of the three sides, and its incomes are in the middle. The area is more white than black. Numerous developments have been proposed for this area, which hosts the new Whole Foods.

These areas have seen significant demographic shifts over time (Table 5.4). In 1990, the area was much more like Brooklyn overall (compare to Table 3.2), though a bit whiter, poorer, with lower home values, and comparable rents. Over time, however, from 1990 to 2014, Gowanus diverged from Brooklyn. It whitened, richened, became more educated, and home values and rents increased at a faster rate than Brooklyn. For instance,

Table 5.4 Demographic changes in neighborhoods surrounding Gowanus Canal, 1990–2014

		1990	*2000*	*2014*	*Change over time, 2000–2014*	*Change over time, 1990–2014*
	Population change	20,961	22,512	24,409	8%	16%
Race	White (%)	55.6%	52.6%	57.6%	5%	2%
	Black (%)	24.5%	20.0%	14.7%	–5%	–10%
Class	Median household income 2013 ($)	$45,893	$52,930	$74,297	40%	62%
	Families below poverty line (%)	25.1%	21.7%	13.7%	–8%	–11%
Social power	Bachelors degree or higher (%)	23.4%	33.6%	54.7%	21%	31%
Housing	Owner occupied housing units (%)	20.0%	21.3%	26.5%	5%	7%
	Median single family owner occupied home value 2013 ($)	$283,411	$442,812	$909,221	105%	221%
	Median rent 2013 ($)	$859	$1,005	$1,571	56%	83%

Sources: 1990 U.S. Census Bureau, Social Explorer
2000 U.S. Census Bureau, Social Explorer
2014 American Community Survey, Social Explorer, 5-year estimates

during that period Brooklyn's percentage of whites decreased by 3 percent to 44 percent of the total population in 2014. Gowanus's increased by 2 percent to contain 58 percent whites in 2014. In the same period, median household income in Brooklyn declined by 1 percent to end at just about $46,000 in 2014. Gowanus's income increased by 62 percent to end just over $74,000. The percent of individuals with bachelor's degrees rose in Brooklyn by 15 percent, ending at 32 percent with degrees. In Gowanus, that percentage increased by 31 percent, ending at 55 percent. Finally, housing values in Brooklyn increased 66 percent, ending at a median value of over $557,000; for Gowanus, the comparable increases are 221 percent with a median value of $909,221. For rents, the story is the same. Brooklyn increased by 44 percent, with a median of $1,189; in Gowanus, the increase was 83 percent and a median of $1,571. Trends in the Gowanus neighborhood departed from Brooklyn's. Gowanus gentrified in part due to the promise of "the Venice of Brooklyn."

Nearly 400 years after colonization of the Gowanus tidal basin, nearly 150 years after completion of the canal, and after more than a half-century of industrial decline, the Gowanus Canal is being "greened" and consequently gentrified in the second decade of the twenty-first century. What forces, processes, and interests converged after a century and a half to attempt to transform this open sewer and industrial tailpipe into an environmental amenity?

The green growth machine

No single group or historic event marked a turning point for the Gowanus. Instead, a confluence of historical conditions and social actors created this environmental redevelopment possibility. Long-term de-industrialization decreased the canal's economic significance. A shorter-term economic boom in Brooklyn, especially after the terror attacks on Manhattan on September 11, 2001, created a demand for housing in the borough. The neighborhoods around the canal had already gentrified significantly, leaving Gowanus an outlier in its near-surroundings. Its neighboring attractions and *in situ* potential drew attention from private real estate developers.

Government mandates, initiatives, and rhetoric reinforced these economic trends. For instance, federal water quality legislation (Clean Water Act) required that the Gowanus meet certain environmental standards. New York State's Brownfield Cleanup Program and The New York State Brownfield Opportunity Area Program (BOA) – both established in 2003 – made funds available to address the contamination of the canal and the lands around it. Two of the ten priorities in Mayor Bloomberg's PlaNYC: A Greener, Greater New York, his major sustainability initiative, directly affect canal redevelopment. The plan promises to "Create more homes for almost a million more New Yorkers, while making housing more affordable and sustainable" and to "Clean up all contaminated land in New York" (PlaNYC 2007). And in 2009, the Obama administration called for a jump-start toward a national "green economy," drawing heavily on the advocacy of the Apollo Alliance, a coalition of organized labor, environmental and business organizations, whose goal is to transition the U.S. to clean, renewable energy.[3] Since 2014, Mayor de Blasio's affordable housing initiative, which promises to add 80,000 units in ten years, also looks to the Gowanus and the city-owned land at Public Place as a promising space on which to build.

This political-economic context dovetailed with social trends. Upper-middle-class urban residents were supporting "sustainability" movements, such as urban food movements, and seeking "green housing." These Brooklynites represent Brooklyn's growing "sustainability class," akin to Florida's (2002) "creative class" with overt sustainability-oriented values and the wealth to express their environmental concerns through high-end consumption. Older community groups, such as the GCCDC who had long sought to clean up the Gowanus, found allies in these groups, and in the artists who had started to colonize the Gowanus neighborhood. The emerging political opportunity structure coupled with the interest of private developers, the local government, long-term residents, new residents (the artists), and a large potential group of sustainability-class in-migrants converged to make 2010 the moment that the Gowanus Canal's clean-up would begin in earnest and the stinking canal would begin to turn in everyone's imagination into the basis for an urban environmental amenity. This vision was undeterred by the flooding caused by Superstorm Sandy in 2012.

Gowanus as the Venice of Brooklyn?

If the Gowanus Canal is successfully remediated through Superfund over the course of the next decade, what are the long-term implications for neighborhood change? What are the redistributional impacts of Gowanus remediation and redevelopment? Who will inhabit "the Venice of Brooklyn?" The green growth machine's plans for the Gowanus economy includes a reduction in the number of working-class light-industrial jobs not requiring formal education. While "light-industrial jobs" are included in the vision of the new Gowanus, these new jobs are largely based on artist production by the formally educated "creative class." The new arts-industry employers threaten to displace the existing iron, marble, machine, lumber, casket, concrete and scrap metal works still providing neighborhood employment (see Figure 5.8).

A redeveloped Gowanus also promises more higher-end retail and service economy jobs (restaurants, clubs, galleries, boutiques, etc.) aimed at serving the gentrifiers (of Gowanus and surrounding brownstone neighborhoods). It seems reasonable to project that those employed in the greened Gowanus will be whiter and better educated than those in the current valley of brownfields (Bryson 2012). As the fields go from brown to green, those employed will go from brown to white.

More speculatively, "edgy" industrial facilities may ultimately be redefined as local health, environmental, and aesthetic nuisances by second-wave gentrifiers. As real estate prices increase, pressure to convert structures still in use for light industry to residential and service use may pick up, generating a green coalition for a second round of Gowanus rezoning. Gowanus's light-industrial employers are already feeling the pinch of the conversion of properties from industrial to residential use (Bowles

Figure 5.8 South Brooklyn Casket Company

2002). This process would be the urban equivalent of the rural phenomenon, associated with "rurbanization;" urbanites attracted to rural farming communities only later to agitate against the noises, smells, and effluents of agricultural production, and seeking to restrict agricultural uses of the ecosystem.

The trends in residential demographics are already clear. Whites with higher educational attainment continue to move in to Gowanus. As housing costs in the neighborhood continue to increase while local employment for non-college educated residents decreases, the poorer and less educated population will be pushed out. These processes are likely to have a disproportionate impact on the Latino population of the community, though community groups, such as the Fifth Avenue Committee – a group that works on social justice, including "displacement caused by gentrification" – are actively opposing this (Fifth Avenue Committee 2016). The Fifth Avenue Committee sits on the board of Gowanus Green, which promises affordable housing, but this construction is at the bottom of Hudson, Inc.'s project list. According to Hudson, Inc.'s website, "Seventy percent of the units will be affordable to households with incomes between 30 percent and 130 percent of area median income" (Hudson, Inc. 2016). By the time that these are available, low-income residents will already be displaced. According to a news account, the median home price in 2009 was $630,500 and in June 2015 had jumped to $1,474,000. Median rents in the same period went from $1,900 to 2,750 (Albrecht 2015).

The public housing projects (Gowanus Houses and Wyckoff Gardens) will somewhat stabilize the black population, but as increasingly isolated and anomalous pockets of poverty with low average educational attainment. Low-wage service employment opportunities for this constituency may increase as large businesses like Lowe's and Whole Foods continue to occupy former industrial properties. Such a trend is clear in neighboring Red Hook, where both Ikea and Fairway Market draw black employees from the Red Hook Houses, the largest public housing project in Brooklyn. As with the possibility of future rezoning demands, it is not unreasonable to speculate that gentrification of the Gowanus neighborhood will lead to increased local and developer pressure to tear down housing projects to be replace with "integrated mixed income public housing," aimed at decreasing and decentralizing this population.

We expect that a cleaner and greener Gowanus Canal will be primarily accessed by, and enhance the quality of life of, more white, well-educated neighborhood in-migrants, and longer-term residents of nearby brownstone neighborhoods. In contrast to the population who lived adjacent to the open sewer version of the Gowanus Canal, those who live adjacent to the Green Gowanus will be whiter, wealthier, and better educated.

Green gentrification: stronger than the storm

The increasing density of Gowanus gentrifiers on the banks of the canal will require structural mitigation-infrastructure to keep their condos above floodwaters. Such mitigation will be provided by private developers and will be included in the price of canal-front condos, in a neoliberal model of urban sustainability and climate change adaptation. The wealthy will utilize their private capital to float above the storms, in contrast to the working class that was left to pump them out of their basements after Sandy. Some of the broader infrastructure costs will also be borne by governments, which will be pressed to provide services to areas with high real estate values.

Superstorm Sandy could have been a wake-up call for Gowanus, and for New York City as a whole. However, despite years of talk and largely superficial nods to urban sustainability and resiliency under the leadership of Mayor Michael Bloomberg, the dominance of real estate interests in New York City's growth machine militated against meaningful reconsideration or redirection of its development paradigm. The new administration of Mayor Bill de Blasio, who was elected in 2013, may require a higher percentage of "affordable" housing in new developments, but is unlikely to reverse larger trends in housing markets. The premium placed on waterfront property simply overwhelms concern for the increased frequency of coastal flooding in the Anthropocene. Likewise, major new waterfront developments at Hudson Yards on Manhattan's west side, the Domino Sugar site in Brooklyn, and Coney Island proceed with only minor nods to increased flooding risk. While the logic of adaptation to ecological conditions argues for a staged retreat from coastal flood zones, the logic of capital argues for increased investment in real estate with water views, even if that water is primarily a sewage outfall.

In Gowanus, Sandy-related flooding was arguably less of a hit to the gentrification process than was Superfund designation. After Sandy, The Lightstone Group moved ahead with its 700-unit condominium complex on the banks of the canal, despite objections from Gowanus's city councilman. Arguing that its initial plans took full account of federal flood prevention standards, the development corporation stated that, "The project was designed to exceed federal 100-year storm standards by significantly elevating the development above the 100-year flood plain" (WNYC News 2010). That appears to be the primary response of developers bent on capitalizing on waterfront real estate by increasing coastal population density – build but elevate, so as to be able to have enterococcus-infested waters wash under and around luxury residential development. Whole Foods opened on a brownfield on the banks of Gowanus in December of 2013 with an overt sustainability theme (see Figure 5.9). Shopping for organic kale chips on an urban brownfield in a coastal flood zone next to a combined sewer overflow while parking your car in a solar-lit lot is certainly a "light" version of environmental consciousness. The paradox from an environmental justice standpoint is that the next time the Gowanus floods its banks in a major storm event, it will flood a much wealthier, and better-educated community, because the economic logic of the urban redevelopment treadmill is stronger than the storm.

Green chickens or green eggs?

Did early gentrifiers instigate the greening of the Gowanus, or is it a larger green growth machine that has instigated greening (betting on future gentrification)? We argue that the early artist-gentrifiers are only one small segment of a much larger green growth coalition that converged to generate the green growth machine in Gowanus. The gentrification of brownstone and "bridge and tunnel" Brooklyn drew developer interest in identifying new prospects for profit in less obvious locations. The existence of a small artist colonization of the Gowanus neighborhood served as a marker for just such a potentially profitable real estate locale.[4] But full-on gentrification of the neighborhood – and thus maximization of the profitability of real estate investment for urban green growth machine elites ("treadmill elites") (Schnaiberg and Gould 2000) – would require state intervention for both urban rezoning to convert industrial tracts into

Figure 5.9 Solar-powered Whole Foods parking lot

residential developments, and brownfield and canal remediation to trans-form environmental hazards into environmental amenities. As McManus et al. observed more than twenty years ago, "Restoring the Gowanus could lead to an economic renewal of the entire Gowanus region because it would make the area attractive to developers" (1995: 61).

It is the green growth machine – the convergence of state and private capital interests in transforming both the social and ecological landscapes – that makes Gowanus greening possible. The support of community groups (both early gentrifiers and long-term residents) makes such greening politi-cally viable (Hamilton and Curran 2013; Pearsall 2013). The existence of first-wave gentrifying artists makes such greening marketable. And a pool of potential upper-middle-class gentrifiers (both from within Brooklyn, and from the Manhattan diaspora) makes greening the Gowanus profitable. Housing prices in Gowanus rose 52 percent from 2004 to 2012 when Sandy hit and have shown no sign of stopping since then. The median asking price for a home in Gowanus in 2015 was $1.4 million, up from $0.6 million in 2009 (Albrecht 2015). In the meantime, the affordable housing units prom-ised for inclusion in the Gowanus Green development slated for Public Place await the brownfield remediation required before ground breaking can begin. More than 56,000 people applied for the eighty-six affordable housing units in The Lightstone Group's 430-unit luxury condo develop-ment (Katz 2016). Such figures offer little hope for the effective mitigation of displacement pressures on Gowanus residents.

The green growth machine, operating as an urban greening treadmill, will move the green redevelopment of the Gowanus forward while creating greater housing segregation and inequality. In other words, it will create economic growth in the short term, with the long-term consequences of social dislocations and displacement of ecologically damaging production to other, less well-regulated locales as Brooklyn and the U.S. continue to deindustrialize (Schnaiberg and Gould 2000; Gould, Schnaiberg and Pellow 2008). The Gowanus Canal is being greened now, after serving a century and a half as an industrial and municipal sewer, because city government and private real estate capital both understand urban greening to be an engine of gentrification. The green growth machine serves the interest of what we call the "sustainability class," which will displace the working-class neighbors of the Gowanus Canal. In this way, "sustainable" consumption replaces working-class jobs and residents.

Notes

1   Excepts from the following chapter are republished with permission of Rutgers University Press, from Gould, Kenneth A. and Lewis, Tammy L. 2016. "Green Gentrification and Superstorm Sandy: The Resilience of the Urban Redevelopment Treadmill in Brooklyn's Gowanus Canal." In *Taking Chances: The Coast After Hurricane Sandy*, Karen M. O'Neill and Daniel J. Van Abs (eds). New Brunswick, NJ: Rutgers University Press, 145–63.
2   South Brooklyn is the northeast area of the borough, south of Brooklyn Heights, including the neighborhoods of Cobble Hill, Red Hook, Gowanus, Carroll Gardens, and the Columbia Street Waterfront District.
3   The reference to the Apollo space missions indicates its support of a government commitment to scientific breakthroughs in the clean energy sector (www.bluegreenalliance.org/apollo).
4   Jessica Miller (2014) notes that this early gentrification was partially led by the idea that the area would be environmentally remediated in the future.

Bibliography

Albrecht, Leslie. 2015. "Gowanus Affordable Development Still Years Away as Home Prices Soar." Retrieved January 4, 2016 (www.dnainfo.com/new-york/20150624/gowanus/gowanus-affordable-housing-development-still-years-away-as-home-prices-soar).
Alexiou, Joseph. 2015. *Gowanus: Brooklyn's Curious Canal.* New York: NYU Press.
Anguelovski, Isabelle. 2015. "Alternative Food Provision Conflicts in Cities: Contesting Food Privilege, Injustice, and Whiteness in Jamaica Plain, Boston." *Geoforum* 58: 184–194.
Benardo, Leonard and Jennifer Weiss. 2006. *Brooklyn by Name: How the Neighborhoods, Streets, Parks, Bridges, and More Got Their Names.* New York: NYU Press.
Blue Green Alliance. Retrieved February 1, 2016 (www.bluegreenalliance.org/apollo).
Bowles, Jonathan. 2002. "Red Hook and Gowanus Reborn." Retrieved June 6,

2011 (www.nycfuture.org/content/articles/article_view.cfm?article_id=1055&article_type=0).

Bryson, Jerome. 2012. "Brownfields Gentrification: Redevelopment Planning and Environmental Justice in Spokane, Washington." *Environmental Justice* 5(1): 26–31.

Bullard, Robert D. 1990. *Dumping in Dixie: Race, Class and Environmental Quality*. San Francisco, CA: Westview Press.

Burrows, Edwin G. and Mike Wallace. 1999. *Gotham: A History of New York City to 1898*. New York: Oxford University Press.

Caro, Robert A. 1975. *The Power Broker: Robert Moses and the Fall of New York*. New York: Vintage Books.

Citizens for NYC. 1998. *The Neighborhoods of Brooklyn*. New Haven, CT: Yale University Press.

The City of New York. *PlaNYC: A Greener Greater New York*. 2007. Mayor Michael R. Bloomberg.

Corcoran Group. 2011. "Gowanus." Retrieved January 12, 2011 (www.corcoran.com/nyc/Neighborhoods/Display/43).

Dollar, Steve. 2010. "Superfund Site Morphs into Cultural Hotspot." *The Wall Street Journal*, December 15.

Farrell, Shanna. 2012. "The Gowanus Canal: Local Politics of 'Superfund' Status." In *The World in Brooklyn: Gentrification, Immigration, and Ethnic Politics in a Global City*. Judith N. DeSena and Tomothy Shortell. eds. New York: Lexington Books, 185–210.

Fifth Avenue Committee. 2016. "FAC's Mission." Retrieved January 27, 2016 (http://fifthave.org/index.cfm?fuseaction=Page.ViewPage&pageId=556).

Florida, Richard. 2002. *The Rise of the Creative Class*. New York: Basic Books.

Gamper-Rabindran, Shanti and Christopher Timmins. 2011. "Hazardous Waste Cleanup, Neighborhood Gentrification, and Environmental Justice: Evidence from Restricted Access Census Block Data." *American Economic Review* 101(3): 620–624.

Gamper-Rabindran, Shanti, Ralph Mastromonaco and Christopher Timmins. 2011. "Valuing the Benefits of Superfund Site Remediation: Three Approaches to Measuring Localized Externalities." Working Paper No. 16655, National Bureau of Economic Research.

Gould, Kenneth A. 1991. "The Sweet Smell of Money: Economic Dependency and Local Environmental Political Mobilization." *Society and Natural Resources: An International Journal* 4(2): 133–150.

Gould, Kenneth A. and Tammy L. Lewis. 2016. "Green Gentrification and Superstorm Sandy: The Resilience of the Urban Redevelopment Treadmill in Brooklyn's Gowanus Canal." In *Taking Chances: The Coast After Hurricane Sandy*. Karen M. O'Neill and Daniel J. Van Abs. eds. New Brunswick, NJ: Rutgers University Press, 145–163.

Gould, Kenneth A., David Naguib Pellow and Allan Schnaiberg. 2008. *The Treadmill of Production: Injustice and Unsustainability in a Global Economy*. Boulder, CO: Paradigm Publishers.

Hamilton, Trina and Winifred Curran. 2013. "From 'Five Angry Women' to 'Kick-ass Community': Gentrification and Environmental Activism in Brooklyn and Beyond." *Urban Studies* 50 (8): 1557–1574.

Hudson, Inc. 2016. "Gowanus Green." Retrieved January 27, 2016 (http://hudson-inc.com/gowanus-green/).

Hurd, Brian H. 2002. "Valuing Superfund Site Cleanup: Evidence of Recovering Stigmatized Property Values." *Appraisal Journal* 70: 426–437.

Hurley, Andrew. 1995. *Environmental Inequalities: Race, Class, and Industrial Pollution in Gary, Indiana, 1945–1980.* Chapel Hill, NC: University of North Carolina Press.

Jackson, Kenneth T. 1998. *The Neighborhoods of Brooklyn, 2nd Edition.* New Haven, CT: Yale University Press.

Katz, Miranda. 2016. "Over 50,000 People Apply for Affordable Housing On the Banks of the Gowanus." *Gothamist*, January 11.

Krisel, Rebecca Salima. 2015. "Gentrifying a Superfund Site: Why Gowanus, Brooklyn is Becoming a Real Estate Hot Spot." *Consilience: The Journal of Sustainable Development* 14(2): 214–224.

McManus, Maureen, Keith W. Jones, Nicholas L. Clesceri and Ivor L. Preiss. 1995. "Renewal of Brooklyn's Gowanus Canal Area." *Journal of Urban Technology* 2(2): 51–64.

Melosi, Martin V. 1999. *The Sanitary City: Urban Infrastructure in America from Colonial Times to the Present.* Baltimore, MD: Johns Hopkins University Press.

Miller, Jessica. 2014. *Super Fun Superfund: Urban Waterfront Redevelopment. Gentrification, and Displacement on the Gowanus Canal of Brooklyn, New York.* Unpublished doctoral dissertation. Department of Earth and Environmental Sciences, City University of New York.

Miner, Dorothy, Julie Foster, Kristina Nugent, Tara Rasheed, Caroline Stephenson and Rosalind Streeter. 2008. *Gowanus Canal Corridor.* Columbia University. Retrieved January 27, 2016 (http://issuu.com/proteusgowanus/docs/2008_gowanus_corridor_historic_buildings_-_columbi).

Mumford, Lewis. 1934. *Technics and Civilization.* New York: Harcourt Brace Jovanovich.

Nyman, J.S., Schwartz, H. and Scanlon, R. 2010. *Reconsidering Gowanus: Opportunities for the Sustainable Transformation of an Industrial Neighborhood.* The Steven L. Newman Real Estate Institute of Baruch College-CUNY.

Pearsall, Hamil. 2013. "Superfund Me: A Study of Resistance to Gentrification in New York City." *Urban Studies* 50(11): 2293–2310.

Pellow, David Naguib. 2002. *Garbage Wars: The Struggle for Environmental Justice in Chicago.* Cambridge, MA: The MIT Press.

Schnaiberg, Allan and Kenneth A. Gould. 2000. *Environment and Society: The Enduring Conflict.* Caldwell, NJ: Blackburn Press.

Snyder-Grenier, Ellen. M. 1996. *Brooklyn! An Illustrated History.* Philadelphia, PA: Temple University Press.

United States Environmental Protection Agency. 2012. "Cleaning Up After Hurricane Sandy: Gowanus Canal Area." (www.riverkeeper.org/wp-content/uploads/2012/11/gowanus-canal-cleaning-after-sandy.pdf).

WNYC News. 2012. "Development Near Gowanus Canal Moves Forward After Sandy" Retrieved March 6, 2014 (www.wnyc.org/story/252523-builder_moves_forward_after_sandy/).

Youngman, Nicole. 2015. "Understanding Disaster Vulnerability: Floods and Hurricanes." In *Twenty Lessons in Environmental Sociology* (2nd Edition). Kenneth A. Gould and Tammy L. Lewis. eds. Oxford University Press, 231–245.

6 Contested spaces
Bush Terminal Park and Bushwick Inlet Park

Putting the social equity pillar back in

The concept of sustainable development rests on three pillars: ecological integrity, economic security, and social equity. In urban sustainability policy, ecological integrity has largely been operationalized as greater energy efficiency, increased access to green space, decreased automobile congestion, and climate change resilience (Fitzgerald 2010). The economic component has been commonly operationalized as economic growth rather than economic security, with rhetorical emphasis on green jobs, green entrepreneurship, and neoliberal public-private partnerships to support parks and urban bike programs (Alkon 2012). The social equity pillar has, for the most part, been ignored or at least de-emphasized in urban sustainability policy. The result of this configuration of the three pillars of sustainability has been urban greening that promotes what we might call "light green growth." At its best, this approach creates jobs in the retrofitting of older buildings to meet new energy efficiency standards, better bike lanes and alternative transportation access, more opportunities for composting, and adds green public space (Fitzgerald 2010). At its worst, this one-and-a-half pillar sustainability model – with economic growth at the forefront, ecological integrity included where it proves profitable, and social equity largely absent – promotes development that uses a thin veneer of environmental consideration to keep the ecologically unsustainable game of limitless economic growth alive, while generating deepening social inequality (Redclift 2006). Green gentrification is both a vehicle for such distorted urban sustainability policies, and a predictable outcome of market-driven urban development schemes in the Anthropocene. On some level, recent efforts at urban greening demonstrate little more socio-ecological consciousness than that which inspired the construction of Prospect Park 150 years ago. Build an attractive environmental amenity and it will raise property values, allow developers to profitably flip real estate, expand the tax base and allow the wealthier among us access to the transcendental powers of nature (Taylor 2009).

Within the "treadmill of production" (TOP) (Schnaiberg 1980; Schnaiberg and Gould 2000), the constituency to support an urban economic (growth) pillar will always be present and powerful. In a city like New York, that constituency will always be rooted in real estate. In the Anthropocene, urban environmental awareness has reached a point at which a constituency for at least some consideration of ecological integrity is increasingly a given. That constituency may accept the merely profitable green initiatives,[1] or push to constrain the economy within ecological limits.[2] However, neither the treadmill nor the Anthropocene naturally generate or ensure a mobilized constituency to support urban social equity. Although the treadmill routinely generates disenfranchised groups receiving disproportionate environmental burdens, and few socio-environmental benefits, it does not routinely generate a consciousness that results in calls for slowing growth or redistributing costs and benefits. The social justice component therefore often serves as the most volatile variable in the three-pillar equation, and the one most likely to be ignored unless organized citizen-workers actively engage the urban political economy, demanding that their voices are heard and that policies reflect their interests (Gould, Schnaiberg and Weinberg 1996). Without social justice activists pushing for social equity concerns to be built into urban greening initiatives, green gentrification, displacement, expanding inequality and environmental injustice are likely social outcomes of urban sustainability plans in a capitalist political economy.

Prospect Park restoration proceeded without strong voices for social equity outcomes, and without public policy intervention to mitigate displacement pressures. Real-estate market forces were left alone to respond to environmental amenity improvements, and access was redistributed to those with more wealth and away from those with less. Brooklyn Bridge Park (BBP) construction moves toward completion in a neighborhood that already serves the needs of the wealthiest population in Brooklyn. The BBP brings hyper-gentrification to the 1 percent, who are poorly positioned to argue their equity case against the 0.1 percent. Gowanus Canal remediation proceeds without strong, unified and coordinated community opposition to the displacement pressures that a cleaner and greener Gowanus will bring. However, there are contested spaces in Brooklyn where the threat of green gentrification was anticipated, where communities are organized, and where resistance against green displacement is strong. These communities have seen the negative social equity impacts of urban greening and gentrification in other neighborhoods, and are demanding that the social pillar be built back into urban sustainability plans. These communities are further emboldened by the transition from Mayor Bloomberg, arguably the architect of social equity-blind urban greening in New York City, to Mayor de Blasio, who ran for office on a social equity platform.

Mayor Bloomberg's PlaNYC for a "Greener, Greater New York" did not fully ignore social equity concerns (Rosan 2012). Within each of its ten areas of topical foci, some note of equity issues is made. For example, the section on housing includes the need to create affordable housing while expanding total housing stock and making it more sustainable. The section on open space notes the need to "expand access to parks and open space in communities where they have been scarce" (The City of New York 2007). However, Mayor de Blasio's OneNYC plan elevates social equity from one of many considerations to a primary organizing principle for his administration's vision of the city's development future. OneNYC begins by noting the four "lenses" through which the plan looks at the future: growth, equity, sustainability, and resilience. The vision articulated in the plan aims for a "growing, thriving city," a "just and equitable city," a "sustainable city," and a "resilient city" (OneNYC 2015). This is much closer to the three pillars of sustainability approach in which equity concerns are equally weighted with economy and environment. The political opportunity structure became more conducive for New York City's urban greening initiatives in 2007 with the transition from Republican to Democrat in the Governor's office, and again in 2009 with the transition from Bush to Obama in the White House (Hamilton and Curran 2013). The political opportunity structure improved – in terms of resistance to the gentrification associated with urban greening – in 2014 with the transition from Bloomberg to de Blasio in City Hall.

Two cases that illustrate this resistance to green gentrification in Brooklyn are the conflicts surrounding Bush Terminal Park (BTP) in the Sunset Park neighborhood, and Bushwick Inlet Park (BIP) on the Greenpoint-Williamsburg waterfront. In these cases, strong community organizations responded early to redevelopment plans, defended their environmental interests and their rights to access environmental amenities, and demanded public policy intervention to prevent displacement. As Tarry Hum notes:

> Greenways, waterfront parks, and access are the material victories of environmental justice struggles and will greatly improve the living environment of poor communities of color. However, the overarching goals of self-determination, engaged citizenry in public policy and city planning decisions, and creating sustainable communities are tested again in the revalorization of waterfront industrial neighborhoods as potential sites for creative entrepreneurs and workers, recreation, and tourism. The right to stay in a neighborhood is central to community empowerment and control. Exerting that right as a strategy to counter "environmental gentrification" will require new resources and alliances.
>
> (Hum 2014: 209)

With a city government overtly committed to social justice, there may be no better time for such public policy demands. The outcomes at these contested spaces will tell us much about the extent to which urban sustainability initiatives can be designed and implemented in ways that are consistent with environmental justice in a hot real-estate market like Brooklyn's.

A brief history of the Greenpoint and Williamsburg neighborhoods

The Greenpoint-Williamsburg waterfront has been a focal point of urban greening efforts to convert dilapidated waterfront brownfield sites into a series of waterfront parks, greenways and high-density luxury condominium developments. The two neighborhoods have distinct histories, but are unified through inclusion in Community Board 1, and through a waterfront redevelopment vision promoted by the green growth machine (see Figure 6.1).

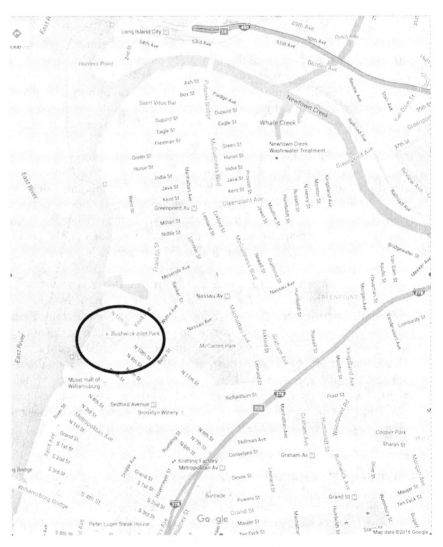

Figure 6.1 Map of Greenpoint-Williamsburg, highlighting Bushwick Inlet Park

Williamsburg

Williamsburg is now an iconic gentrification hot spot. The "bridge and tunnel" gentrification of Brooklyn in the late twentieth and early twenty-first century is most notable for the hipster enclave that transformed Williamsburg into an artsy indie music cliché. Rural Williamsburg began to industrialize along its East River waterfront in the 1820s, when a ferry service to Manhattan was established. Distilleries, foundries, shipyards, and sugar refineries were built, along with the suburban homes of the wealthy. By 1870, the Domino Sugar refinery was producing more than half of the sugar consumed in the U.S. Around the same time, Cornelius Vanderbilt, Charles Pratt, and Jim Fisk all built mansions in Williamsburg. This wealthy enclave changed dramatically in 1903 when the Williamsburg Bridge linked the neighborhood to Manhattan's lower east side, and Williamsburg became densely populated with eastern European immigrants. In the 1940s, the south side became a center for Hasidic Jewish communities, joined later by Puerto Rican and Dominican immigration. Robert Moses's Brooklyn-Queens Expressway cut the western, waterfront section of Williamsburg off from the rest of the neighborhood in 1957. The deindustrialized spaces of Williamsburg became the vortex for the hipster Brooklyn gentrification that made the possibility of greening the waterfront attractive to developers and the city. That waterfront greening with upscale housing could potentially draw in new residents with greater wealth but less flair.

Greenpoint

Greenpoint has been later to gentrify than Williamsburg due to both its greater distance from the bridge and its famously polluted active industrial sites along Newtown Creek. A long-time Polish enclave, Greenpoint is nonetheless feeling the pressures generated, in part, by a gentrification-saturated Williamsburg and the 2005 waterfront rezoning from industrial to residential. In the 1840s, Greenpoint transitioned from farming to shipbuilding, attracting Irish immigrants in the 1850s and Italian immigrants in the 1870s (DeSena 2009). As shipyards declined, other industries emerged, making Greenpoint an industrial center not unlike Gowanus. Printing, petroleum refining, glass-making, and pottery attracted a new immigrant workforce with a dominant Polish contingent. Industrial effluent contaminated Newtown Creek, which, like the Gowanus Canal, would receive Superfund designation in 2010. Shipbuilding and much of the heavy industry departed following World War II. Contamination attracts other "locally unwanted land use" (LULUs) (Gould 2006), and so Greenpoint became home to an incinerator (now closed), a sewage treatment plant, and one of the largest oil spills in U.S. history (Prud'homme 2010). Immigration from Puerto Rico contributed to the Greenpoint population in the 1950s, but did not generate the white flight experienced in other Brooklyn neighborhoods

(DeSena 2009). In the early 1990s, gentrification was welcomed by many long-term residents as a sign that racial transition was reversing, but the scale of continued gentrification threatened community cohesion (DeSena 2005, 2009). Rents for two-bedroom apartments increased by 50 percent between 1997 and 2002 as more young, educated, creative-class gentrifiers "discovered" the neighborhood (DeSena 2009).

Bushwick Inlet Park: "Centerpiece of the Greenpoint-Williamsburg Waterfront"

The New York City Department of Parks and Recreation describes Bushwick Inlet Park as follows:

Bushwick Inlet Park is the centerpiece of the Greenpoint-Williamsburg Waterfront. This park incorporates natural and urban structures, bringing Greenpoint's waterfront and natural areas into the community around it. Visitors can admire the views or use the park's facilities for active recreation. The park includes a multipurpose field for soccer, football, lacrosse, field hockey, rugby, and ultimate Frisbee, a green building with a green roof, a viewing platform, playground and public access to the waterfront. The green building, which is the park's headquarters, is designed to achieve high environmental performance standards with a highly efficient heating-cooling system that uses geothermal wells, heat pumps and radiant floors. It has a green roof with a shade structure composed of photovoltaic cells that provides solar energy power to the building, and a rainwater collection system to provide irrigation water to the green roof (New York City Department of Parks and Recreation 2016).

On its website, the Friends of Bushwick Inlet Park, tell a somewhat different story:

In 2005, after months of negotiations and overriding the vote against it by Community Board 1, the City rezoned almost the entire Greenpoint and Williamsburg waterfront, paving the way for the development of residential towers where there had once been low-profile industrial buildings and radically increasing the potential population (and consequent impact on local infrastructure) in the neighborhood. In the 2005 Waterfront Rezoning Agreement the City explicitly provides the community with some remediation for this impact in the form of affordable housing units and park space. Ten years later, with massive development underway and tens of thousands of new residents, neither promise has been delivered (Friends of Bushwick Inlet Park 2016).

The small park referred to by the New York City Department of Parks and Recreation is just a piece of the 28-acre park promised to the community. Plans for the small first phase of the park described above were unveiled in 2008. Thus far, the first phase is all that has materialized. A key piece of the waterfront property included in the larger park plan is the 11-acre CitiStorage site, a privately owned parcel that has continued to be in dispute while the value of that waterfront land has soared (Figure 6.2). A generous eminent domain ruling has encouraged the property owner to ask $500 million for the parcel, which community activists call a "ransom" demand (Lanham 2015b). As land values increased, the pressure from the growth machine to designate all or part of the property for luxury tower development also increased. Without this parcel for the park, and the remediation of the adjacent Bayside Oil site, the rapidly gentrifying and gentrified neighborhoods of Greenpoint and Williamsburg could be essentially walled off from the water by luxury towers from the Williamsburg Bridge to Newtown Creek.[3] That development trajectory would privatize the waterfront and associated green space for luxury condo-owning newcomers.

On December 31, 2015 Mayor de Blasio announced that, "the administration would never accept a rezoning here [the proposed park site] that did not have the support of the councilman and community" (Hogan 2015). This announcement followed months of community activism by Friends of Bushwick Inlet Park and others responding to news that the private owner of the CitiStorage site was actively seeking to sell to developers rather than

Figure 6.2 Bushwick Inlet Park with CitiStorage Building

to the city, which would incorporate it into the park. That organized community intervention has been a key feature of the fight for affordable housing and access to environmental amenities since Mayor Bloomberg promised that the site would be part of Bushwick Inlet Park when the waterfront was rezoned in 2005. Here we see a community organized to fight for public urban greening rather than privatized access. Will that promised greening materialize in what is now a gentrification hot spot, and will community efforts to get the city to include significant affordable housing in development plans be enough to mitigate displacement?

Revision of the waterfront

As with much of the rest of New York City's extensive shoreline, the increasingly deindustrialized Greenpoint-Williamsburg waterfront came to be defined as a dilapidated wasteland. In the 1980s, debates about the waterfront's future focused on the wisdom of protecting remaining industry, attracting industrial redevelopment, or repurposing the area for residential development. As the fact of deindustrialization as a long-term national trend in a global economic context began to sink in, urban waterfront spaces came to be reimagined as environmental amenities. Greenpoint-Williamsburg's dilapidated wasteland slowly came to be seen by developers and city officials as waterfront property with sweeping Manhattan views (NYC Department of Planning 2011). Waterfront that was once useful to capital for production and transportation came to be useful to capital for consumption as quality-of-life enhancements for urban residents. This trend swept through the deindustrialized Great Lakes and down the deindustrialized east coast. In New York City, where real-estate capital is a dominant player in the local growth coalition, this notion of abandoned waterfront as future green space and condo towers proved wildly popular. As early as 1992, the administration of Mayor Dinkins released a 256-page comprehensive waterfront plan that projected the conversion of much of the formerly industrial shoreline to green space and residential development (Department of City Planning 1992). Vision 2020, the New York City Comprehensive Waterfront Plan, further specified where working waterfronts would be preserved and where they would become green residential growth centers (NYC Department of Planning 2011). As seen in previous chapters, Brooklyn Bridge Park emerged from piers abandoned for half a century, and the putrid Gowanus Canal became redefined as waterfront property. The Greenpoint-Williamsburg waterfront followed this same path.

As early as 1987, a developer sought zoning changes from the city to build a public promenade and condos on the Greenpoint-Williamsburg waterfront. One commenter noted that, "The waterfront will be a key factor … it could trigger the rest of the area." (Foderaro 1987). This is before the artist colonization of Williamsburg had transformed the neighborhood. We see here an early vision of greening the waterfront as a lynchpin for generating gentrification. However, such waterfront visions were slow to materialize, and inland Williamsburg gentrified for other reasons while the waterfront continued to decay.

In the 1990s, the demographics of the Greenpoint-Williamsburg waterfront began to shift. The area nearest to the East River became a little whiter, and a little wealthier. The percentage of white dwellers increased from 49.1 percent to 56.9 percent, while the percentage of black dwellers declined from 10.1 percent to 4.7 percent. The percentage of families below the poverty line decreased from 34.1 to 22.4, and median household income grew from $31,429 to $46,391. The most dramatic shift was a near-tripling of the percentage with bachelor's degrees from 11.6 percent to 33.4 percent, indicating the arrival of the "creative class. Demographic shifts in the twenty-first century would be much more dramatic (see Table 6.1).[4]

As late as 2000–2003, conflicting visions of the waterfront continued to do battle, as a proposal to reindustrialize the waterfront with a power plant mobilized community activists (Hays 2000, 2001; Newman 2003). It is worth noting that community groups argued that the power plant would add to their already disproportionate burden of exposure to environmental bads (see Figure 6.3) (Bahrampour 2000; Newman 2003). The Bloomberg administration was sympathetic to a residential development vision, as it had committed to adding 60,000 residential units to the city, and the waterfronts offered the last remaining urban space for such large-scale housing expansion (DeSena 2009). Once the growth coalition determined that the waterfront would indeed transition from an industrial to a service economy function, community activists mobilized for environmental goods to replace environmental bads.

Community intervention in the planning process

By 2002, another developer was proposing "a public esplanade along the river to rival the promenade in Brooklyn Heights," drawing the connection to the wealthiest residential neighborhood in Brooklyn where Brooklyn Bridge Park was built (McGeveran 2002). At the same time, neighborhood activists were pushing local elected officials to create a park at Bushwick Inlet. In 2003, Mayor Bloomberg announced a rezoning plan that would put to rest the idea of reindustrialization, and pave the way for a combination of green spaces and major housing developments along the waterfront. Bloomberg's vision included a green waterfront path similar to that included in plans for Brooklyn Bridge Park. Almost immediately, a coalition of community leaders began calling for more affordable housing to be included in redevelopment plans (Hays 2003) as a bulwark against displacement. Greenpoint in particular has a long history of organized community engagement with City Hall regarding municipal services and development (DeSena 2009). As the rezoning plan was being negotiated through a Waterfront Rezoning Task Force, the organized community fought back

Table 6.1 Demographic changes in Greenpoint and Williamsburg, 1990–2014

		1990	2000	2014	Change over time, 2000–2014	Change over time, 1990–2014
	Population change	6,399	6,522	12,335	89%	93%
Race	White (%)	49.1%	56.9%	74.6%	18%	26%
	Black (%)	10.1%	4.7%	5.5%	1%	–5%
Class	Median household income 2013 ($)	$31,429	$46,391	$75,232	62%	139%
	Families below poverty line (%)	34.1%	22.4%	8.5%	–14%	–26%
Social power	Bachelor's degree or higher (%)	11.6%	33.4%	62.9%	30%	51%
Housing	Owner occupied housing units (%)	11.8%	10.6%	19.6%	9%	8%
	Median single family owner occupied home value 2013 ($)	$368,132	$284,833	$823,872	189%	124%
	Median rent 2013 ($)	$624	$879	$1,582	80%	154%

Sources: 1990 U.S. Census Bureau, Social Explorer
NB For 1990, for home value, a weighted mean for two of the tracts was used because there were zeros for two tracts
2000 U.S. Census Bureau, Social Explorer
2014 American Community Survey, Social Explorer, 5-year estimates

against initial proposals that included only 25 percent affordable housing units, demanding instead a "40 percent guarantee" (DeSena 2009). They enlisted local officials who vowed to block the project if more affordable housing was not included. Having already faced a wave of artist- and hipster-led gentrification, long-term residents were well aware of the displacement threat posed by such a major housing and green space proposal. Creative-class activists rallied for additional green space in the plan (DeSena 2009).

Figure 6.3 Bayside Oil site on Bushwick Inlet

In the case of the Greenpoint-Williamsburg waterfront, rather than green-led gentrification, we have a plan for *greened gentrification*, which is a packaging of urban greening with luxury condo development.[5] What the green growth coalition proposed for this site was an array of public green space amenities (parks, ball fields, esplanades, and bike paths) coupled with massive housing developments. The growth coalition was seizing the greening moment, and using increased demand for urban environmental amenities to enhance housing values for developments. In this way, public investments in greening would subsidize the enhanced values of private investments in housing (a different take on public-private partnerships).

While some greening was included in the growth proposal, the neighborhood organized to alter development plans to enhance sustainability. Activists demanded both more green space (the ecological pillar of sustainability), and more affordable housing (the social equity pillar of sustainability). The *New York Sun* (Gardiner 2005) reported "Community groups have been fighting the plan aggressively for about two years, saying that the Mayor's proposal does not include enough 'affordable housing' or 'park space'." The success of organized community intervention in the planning process is reflected in the fact that the final rezoning plan increased the extent of green space from forty-nine to fifty-four acres, and the percentage of affordable housing units from twenty-five to thirty-three (Son 2005). On the other hand, activists had demanded seventy acres of park space and 40 percent affordable housing. The fifty-four green acres that were included in the plan included the 28-acre Bushwick Inlet Park, of which only six acres had been built by 2016. The rezoning plan represents the most extensive use of inclusionary zoning to create affordable housing in New York City to date (DeSena 2009). The plan also included a small Industrial Business Zone to preserve manufacturing jobs.[6] DeSena (2009) argues that the Bloomberg Administrations' strategic commitment to "A Greener New York City" and "Affordable Housing" originated from his experience with the Greenpoint-Williamsburg rezoning process.

The 2005 rezoning of the Greenpoint-Williamsburg waterfront allowed for the construction of 30- to 40-story residential towers. One major development following that green growth coalition initiative was the Greenpoint Landing development that will include ten high-rise luxury towers, but also public green space, and three 6-story below-market residential buildings. Of the 5,500 residential units included in the entire project, 1,400 are slated for families making between 40 and 60 percent of the area median income (which is $77,700 for a family of three in New York City) (Furfaro 2015). While such a massive development project will undoubtedly change the neighborhood, the inclusion of a substantial percentage of below-market units is intended to lessen displacement pressures as the waterfront is cleaned and greened. Some working-class families will gain access to water views and new parks, reducing environmental injustice impacts. Those results represent over a decade of organized community activism, and significant public policy response.

The Greenpoint Landing site sits to the north of Bushwick Inlet Park, in the Greenpoint neighborhood. The other mega-development slated for the Greenpoint-Williamsburg waterfront is the redevelopment of the Domino Sugar factory site, to the south of Bushwick Inlet Park, in the Williamsburg neighborhood. The 11-acre waterfront site, home to Domino Sugar production from 1856 to 2004, was initially slated to remain industrial and commercial. However, the 2005 rezoning allowed for residential development of the site. The property was sold in 2012 for $180 million to a developer planning massive luxury housing towers. Community residents forcefully opposed the initial development plans. A revised plan was approved in 2014. Now, under Mayor de Blasio, the number of "affordable," below-market rate residential units was increased from 660 to 700 out of 2,300 new living spaces. The new plan also includes 60 percent more publicly-accessible open space, including a public park along the waterfront and a public square at the 1882 sugar refinery building. Here again, persistent and aggressive organized community activism was able to push elected officials to require public policy interventions that would expand environmental amenities and reduce environmental inequality.

Delivering the goods, late or never?

As the condo towers rose, much of the promised green space failed to materialize. A project that was sold to the community as urban greening delivered very little green, aside from the money generated by luxury housing for developers. Although the city had promised the green space, it failed to secure the land on which to construct it. In the meantime, as rezoned developments went up, so did land values. Proposals for a power plant at the Bushwick Inlet site were revived, likely used as a ploy by the landowner to delay sale while property values escalated. It took until 2008 to finally put that idea to rest, but much of the 10,000 units of new luxury housing were already up or in process. Another lot included in the park plan was still being used by the Metropolitan Transit Authority (MTA) as a parking lot in 2009 (Belenkaya 2009). On the city's annual It's My Park Day, community activists led a protest march from the Bushwick Inlet Park site to the MTA parking lot site, asking Where's My Park? (Durkin 2009b). The MTA finally vacated the property in 2011. An "occupy the inlet" event marked the tenth anniversary of the city's unfulfilled 28-acre park promise (Lanham 2015a). The social equity pillar fared no better than the environmental pillar. By May of 2009, none of the 1,345 affordable housing units that the City had promised to date had been built (Durkin 2009a).

Figure 6.4 Condo tower at Bushwick Inlet Park

By 2012, seven years after the rezoning agreement, one FieldTurf soccer field at Bushwick Inlet and a signature green park building was all the community had to show for urban greening. The Bloomberg administration indicated that they were still committed to creating the green space some-day, but cleanup costs and land acquisition had led to major cost overruns. With much fanfare surrounding Bloomberg's successful creation of the High Line and Brooklyn Bridge Park, perhaps the legacy value of yet another signature urban green space was less compelling. His successor, Mayor de Blasio, while more committed to the social equity pillar, is far less commit-ted to the environmental pillar (if for no other reason than that will always be associated with his predecessor). Private financing of some of the green space is now being proposed. What currently stands as Bushwick Inlet Park features a park maintenance building that was named one of the top ten U.S. green buildings in 2014. It includes ground source heat pump wells, rainwater harvest and storage, and drip irrigation (Cockram 2014). Although this feature may help sell condos as an associated amenity, it does little to green the neighborhood and improve the quality of life for long-term residents. Neighborhood rents continue to rise, as do land acquisition costs to complete the greening. The rezoning and subsequent development, as well as inflated eminent domain judgments, drove up the cost to the City of delivering on its urban sustainability promises (Gonzalez 2015, Kimmelman 2015).

Mayor de Blasio wants to cut park funding in order to shift scarce resources toward his own, equity-focused initiatives. A critic for the *New York Times* noted that this is "a big disappointment and a missed opportu-nity to spread social equity and environmental justice." (Kimmelman 2015). Concerns that the mayor would rezone some of the waterfront parcels for development to pay for a more attenuated green space were relieved when he declared he would not rezone Bushwick Inlet Park land without the support of the community (Hobbs 2015). But the parks remain unbuilt (see Figure 6.5), as does most of the affordable housing. Com-munity leaders charge that the city lied about green space and affordable housing in order to get rezoning approval in 2005. Neighborhood protests have become a regular feature of life around the waterfront. Activist claim that "thousands of poorer residents have been priced out," and that "this community has lost 10,000 Latino residents in the past 10 years" (Furfaro 2013).

As indicated in Table 6.1, in the first fourteen years of the twenty-first century, the population of the Greenpoint-Williamsburg waterfront nearly doubled. At the same time, the population of Brooklyn as a whole increased only 4 percent, indicating a densification along the flood-prone waterfront during the era of climate change resilience planning. The in-migrants to the waterfront were largely white, wealthy, and educated, and they were paying premium prices for home purchases and rentals. Between 2000 and 2014, the percentage of the Greenpoint-Williamsburg waterfront population that

Figure 6.5 "Behold Bushwick Inlet! Stop! The Towers! Where's Our Park?"

was white increased from 56.9 to 74.6, whitening at a rate five times faster than the rest of the borough over that period. Families below the poverty level shrunk from 22.4 percent of the population to 8.5 percent, a 14 percent decrease that far exceeded the 2 percent decrease for Brooklyn as a whole. The percentage with bachelor's degrees along the Greenpoint-Williamsburg waterfront nearly doubled to 62.9 percent, increasing at twice the Brooklyn rate. Median monthly rent also nearly doubled from $879 to $1,582, while the median single-family owner-occupied home value nearly tripled from $284,833 to $823,872. Rents on the Greenpoint-Williamsburg waterfront increased 80 percent compared to 31 percent for Brooklyn overall, and home values were up 189 percent compared to 80 percent for Brooklyn. It is in the context of this dramatic, site-specific demographic shift that the Greenpoint-Williamsburg waterfront rezoning was negotiated. Obviously, any affordable housing being built in 2016 was arriving too late to mitigate displacement, and the promise of green space, if fulfilled, would accrue to gentrifiers.

Although the Greenpoint-Williamsburg waterfront community was successful at pushing the equity pillar into the green growth machine's plans, it has been less successful at getting the machine to deliver on its environmental and social equity promises. In 2016, a number of affordable housing units were under construction, but as DeSena (2009) predicted, those may be arriving too late to mitigate displacement (see Figure 6.6).

Figure 6.6 Affordable housing construction

An important question that remains at both major Greenpoint-Williamsburg waterfront brownfield redevelopment sites is how the new below-market rate housing units, once they are completed, will be distributed. If they are distributed by open lottery, as affordable housing commonly is in New York City, the inclusion of below-market rate housing in the Greenpoint-Williamsburg waterfront developments could provide social equity *and* displacement. That is, environmental justice would be achieved by building in class (and likely racial) diversity in access to water-front living and other environmental amenities. However, if those units are not first made available to long-term neighborhood residents, that popula-tion could still be displaced as local housing costs rise and affordable units are distributed to working-class applicants from other neighborhoods. Only local distribution of affordable units can insure that hard-won environ-mental equity structures in urban greening plans also mitigate local displacement pressures.

Growth is the word

What is revealed in the case of Greenpoint-Williamsburg is that the primary object of the green growth machine is growth. Green is often pursued only to the extent that it enhances growth. If green sells, as it does in Brooklyn today, then green growth is good. In the Greenpoint-Williamsburg water-front, green needed only go as far as the initial planning stages in order to gain the acquiescence of the local population. Rather than greening as an engine of growth, here we see the promise of greening as greasing the wheels of the growth machine. It is also clear that the equity component of urban sustainability would have been much more limited under the Bloomberg administration had the community not organized to demand greater mitigation of displacement through inclusionary zoning (DeSena 2009; Maantay 2002). Growth coalitions, green or not, will reliably promote growth but less reliably promote greening (when greening raises real-estate values), and will promote equity to the extent forced to by citizen-workers and municipalities.

A brief history of the Sunset Park neighborhood

In a city known for its heterogeneity, and a borough known for its ethnic neighborhoods, Sunset Park is notable for its ethnic diversity. It is named for a 25-acre park constructed in the 1890s, and has been home to waves of immigrant ethnic enclaves since Dutch colonization. The neighborhood was settled by refugees of the Irish potato famine in the 1840s. Poles, Norwegians, and Finns arrived in the 1880s and 90s; Italians at the turn of the century; Puerto Ricans in the 1950s and 60s; and, beginning in the 1980s and 90s, other Latin Americans and Asians. While once famous for its "Little Norway" and "Finntown," it is now famous for its "Chinatown."

The industrialization of the Sunset Park waterfront can largely be attributed to Irving T. Bush, who in the 1890s purchased the waterfront property of Ambrose Park for the location of a risky 250-acre shipping terminal scheme. Defying skeptics, Bush Terminal proved a huge success, expanding along the shore for twenty blocks and employing thousands directly, and thousands more in secondary concerns. The Sunset Park neighborhood economy and community became synonymous with the shipping terminals and warehouses of Bush Terminal. Waves of immigrant labor were employed on the Sunset Park waterfront which, in addition to shipping, included the Bethlehem Steel Shipyard, the American Machine and Foundry Company (makers of bowling alley equipment and vending machines), Topps Chewing Gum, Colgate Palmolive-Peet, and the American Can Company (Hum 2014) (see Figure 6.7).

Economic decline came in waves. The Third Avenue elevated subway line was suspended during the Great Depression, and eventually replaced in the 1950s with Robert Moses's Gowanus Expressway, which cut off the piers from the community, and covered the once thriving commercial strip. Following World War II, containerization moved commercial shipping to the deeper ports of New Jersey, the large industrial facilities closed, and many older residents moved to the growing suburbs. Housing deteriorated in the neighborhood, and many homes were abandoned. Bush Terminal was renamed Industry City in 1960 and in 1965 it was purchased by an

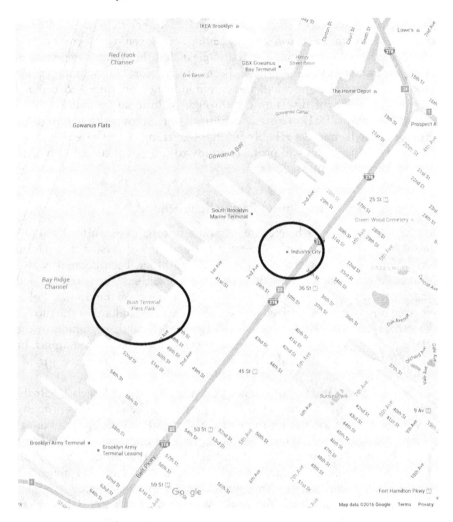

Figure 6.7 Map of Sunset Park, highlighting Bush Terminal Park and Industry City

investment group led by Harry Helmsley. The Economic Opportunity Act of 1964 designated Sunset Park a federal poverty area. The opening of the Verrazano-Narrows Bridge in that same year facilitated white flight out of the area. The Immigration and Nationality Act of 1965 facilitated the repopulation of the neighborhood. In the decades that followed, low housing costs attracted waves of new immigrants to Sunset Park including large Mexican, Dominican, Ecuadorian, Indian, and Chinese populations (Hum 2014). These ethnic communities rehabilitated housing and restored neighborhood vitality, with many employed in the garment sweatshops that occupied waterfront warehouses in the 1980s and 90s. The non-Hispanic

white population of Sunset Park declined from 91 percent in 1960 to 14
percent in 2000 (Hum 2014). In 2010, Sunset Park was 44 percent Latino
and 38 percent Asian (Hum 2014).

Unlike the Greenpoint-Williamsburg waterfront, the economic profile of
Sunset Park does not diverge substantially from that of Brooklyn as a
whole. Between 2000 and 2014, Sunset Park median household incomes
remained unchanged, while Brooklyn's rose only 3 percent (Table 6.2).[7] The
percentage of families below the poverty level declined 2 percent in Sunset
Park, the same percentage as Brooklyn as a whole. While only 16.2 percent

Table 6.2 Demographic changes in Sunset Park, 1990–2014

		1990	2000	2014	Change over time, 2000–2014	Change over time, 1990–2014
	Population change	5,948	8,559	9,862	15%	66%
Race	White (%)	48.5%	38.3%	35.5%	−3%	−13%
	Black (%)	9.8%	10.8%	12.2%	1%	2%
Class	Median household income 2013 ($)	$40,359	$39,427	$39,236	0%	−3%
	Families below poverty line (%)	32.3%	24.7%	22.5%	−2%	−10%
Social power	Bachelor's degree or higher (%)	9.9%	11.1%	16.2%	5%	6%
Housing	Owner occupied housing units (%)	23.8%	23.5%	26.5%	3%	3%
	Median single family owner occupied home value 2013 ($)	$364,787	$236,842	$465,490	97%	28%
	Median rent 2013 ($)	$840	$902	$1,187	32%	41%

Sources: 1990 U.S. Census Bureau, Social Explorer
2000 U.S. Census Bureau, Social Explorer
2014 American Community Survey, Social Explorer, 5 year estimates

of Sunset Park residents had bachelor's degrees in 2014 compared to about a third of all Brooklynites, the rate of increase at 46 percent was about the same, even though the total increase (5 percent) was lower. The value of single-family owner-occupied homes increased 97 percent in Sunset Park, more than the 80 percent average for Brooklyn, but the median price of those homes was still below the Brooklyn median at $465,490. Median rent in Sunset Park was nearly identical to that of Brooklyn as a whole, as was the rate of increase. Between 2000 and 2014, when Greenpoint-Williamsburg waterfront was undergoing a major demographic transformation, Sunset Park was stable. Of course, census data misses a lot of the undocumented population in Sunset Park. Nevertheless, the overall picture of relative stability is accurate.

Sunset Park is a densely populated Asian-Latino, working-poor neighborhood with Mexican being the dominant Latino group and Chinese being the dominant Asian group. It is also one of the last surviving industrial centers in New York City, with a largely informal labor force reaping relatively low wages (Hum 2014). It is this diverse working-poor, and working-class Hispanic and Asian community that faces the threat of green gentrification now, as developers and gentrifiers "discover" waterfront access, loft spaces, more affordable housing, and the new Bush Terminal Park green space.

Figure 6.8 Adjacent Chinese and Ecuadorian neighborhood restaurants

Bush Terminal Park: working-class green space or gentrification trojan horse?

The New York City Department of Parks and Recreation describes Bush Terminal Park as follows:

> A quiet natural space in the industrial section of Sunset Park, Bush Terminal Piers Park is a lovely waterfront park with spectacular views of the area's tidal pools and the Bay Ridge Channel. This site, once a port complex, was cleaned up and opened as a public park in 2014. Visitors to the park can enter at 43rd Street, and walk along the waterfront esplanade past the tide ponds and restored wetlands. Visitors will find two multipurpose soccer and baseball fields as well as a nature preserve that allows a fun glimpse into Brooklyn's wild side.
>
> (The New York City Department of Parks and Recreation 2016)

The park was constructed on a remediated brownfield site: four abandoned piers on the industrial waterfront of the Sunset Park neighborhood of Brooklyn. The park owes its existence to tireless community advocacy, the support of local elected officials, and federal, state and city funding from numerous agencies and programs.

UPROSE, a Puerto Rican-originated, Latino-based, multi-ethnic community organization in Sunset Park, now in its fiftieth year, describes its role in the neighborhood mobilization behind the park's establishment as follows:

> UPROSE was instrumental in the initial planning stages for Bush Terminal Piers Park. Our role consisted of advocating for a post-brownfield waterfront park in a community suffering from a severe lack of open space, a disproportionate amount of environmental burdens, and an utter absence of waterfront access. Over the years, we have pushed for the park to reflect the needs and visions of the Sunset Park community and maintained pressure on public entities to prioritize its completion.
>
> (UPROSE 2016)

Bush Terminal Park's construction relied heavily on the largest grant ever awarded by the State for the remediation of a brownfield site (Fried 2006). The site had been contaminated by illegal dumping in the 1970s, and fenced off since the early 1980s. In the 1990s, the community, led by UPROSE, agitated for a waterfront park when the city was working on port redevelopment plans. As an UPROSE spokesperson noted, "the lack of open space and environmental amenities is an exacerbating factor in our working-class community of color that already faces significant environmental burdens" (Oder 2014). Funding for brownfield remediation was secured in 2006, and the park was included in the New York City Economic Development

Corporation plan in 2009. However, remediation costs quickly exceeded projections, and the green space was delayed and scaled back. When the park was finally opened in 2014, only eleven acres of the promised twenty-two acres were included. Neither the children's playground, nor the environmental center was constructed. Only one of the two entrances was created, the lighting was not installed, and a picnic and concessions area was fenced off. Critics noted that "Bush Terminal Park is decidedly lacking in amenities and imaginative design elements" (Kensinger 2015) in contrast to the stunning Brooklyn Bridge Park built for the borough's richest community. As at Bushwick Inlet Park on the Greenpoint-Williamsburg waterfront, activists continue to organize to have their park completed. In Sunset Park, such mobilization led to the creation of a second park entrance and a community-led design for the children's playground (NYC EDC 2015). In January of 2016, neither lighting, playground, nor the environmental center were in place (see Figure 6.9).

At the park's opening, congresswoman Nydia Velázquez noted that "The opening of Bush Terminal Piers Park is a long-awaited step in making Sunset Park's waterfront accessible to Brooklyn's working families," framing the park as an urban greening project aimed at serving existing community residents, who had long mobilized for public waterfront access (New York City Department of Parks and Recreation 2014). However, at that same opening, New York Secretary of State Cesar A. Perales stated,

Figure 6.9 Bush Terminal Park

"Bush Terminal Park serves as a reminder that neighborhood revitalization anchored in strong community planning can bring about tremendous change" (New York City Department of Parks and Recreation 2014). Planning rooted in community participation is a central element of process justice (Agyeman 2005). What is potentially ominous in Mr. Perales's statement is how "neighborhood revitalization" and "tremendous change" is interpreted. Is revitalization and change ultimately going to serve the needs of Sunset Park's largely working-class and working-poor Latino and Asian community, or is Bush Terminal Park going to anchor efforts to attract the "sustainability class" to gentrify the waterfront? The *Wall Street Journal* went so far as to frame Bush Terminal Park as the lynchpin of an overtly green gentrification scheme: "No real-estate project in New York seems complete these days without a lavish amenity space. On Brooklyn's waterfront, even an industrial district now boasts its own park" (Paletta 2015). Calling this environmental justice community victory a "real-estate project" is to use fighting words, and clearly indicates how the growth machine understands urban environmental amenities. Just as the park opened, a property one block from the park sold for nearly 20 percent above asking price (Barbarino 2014). The *Wall Street Journal* went on to note the neighborhood transition that the green growth machine seeks to generate: "Bush Terminal Park ... attracts not merely neighborhood residents long-isolated from their waterfront, but also a growing population of employees in creative industries that fill the surrounding warehouses." (Paletta 2015). Is Bush Terminal Park an urban environmental amenity for a working-class and poor-people-of-color community, or the catalyst for the green growth machine's real-estate schemes?

Re-visioning the waterfront

As was the case with the Greenpoint-Williamsburg waterfront, there are clearly competing visions of the Sunset Park waterfront. Sunset Park's waterfront is not nearly as fully deindustrialized as that of Greenpoint-Williamsburg, so it still supports many working-class and working-poor jobs. Waterfront employment increased 10 percent between 2000 and 2008 – although waterfront employment is still lower than it was in the early 1990s (NYC Department of Planning 2011). The Sunset Park waterfront also remains potentially viable as a working port facility, as the water is deep enough to support modern shipping. Community activists, anchored by the leadership of UPROSE, have promoted an overtly environmental justice-oriented vision of the space's future. They seek to repel additional environmental health burdens (like power plants), reduce ongoing environmental exposures (from the Gowanus Expressway, for example) preserve working-class jobs, promote "green" port facilities, establish a waterfront greenway and additional park space, increase safe public access links to the waterfront, and retain and expand affordable housing (Hum 2014; Sze

2007; UPROSE 2013, 2016). This comprehensive, three-pillared approach to urban sustainability planning is contrasted with the green growth machine's vision of a greened and gentrified Sunset Park waterfront, anchored by Industry City.

Industry City is a transformation of Irving T. Bush's century-old waterfront industrial site into a commercial, creative class-oriented gentrification magnet. The site is a 30-acre swath of waterfront including sixteen buildings. From the 1990s forward, artists priced-out of other gentrifying neighborhoods began to relocate into many of the formerly industrial spaces on the Sunset Park waterfront, including the Industry City complex. Many of the buildings were badly damaged by Superstorm Sandy, and are now being renovated and rented as upscaled light-industrial and commercial space, displacing many of the artists (Satow 2014). The developers describe the first phase of this extra-local vision of the waterfront, "transforming ground floor and lower levels into a pedestrian-friendly series of shops, showrooms, event spaces and courtyards, loosely organized around themes such as food and food production, children and family, and home goods" (Industry City 2016). The developers, who include a lead developer of the Brooklyn Navy Yards, seek to attract the artisanal production that forms the center of millennial Brooklyn kitsch. The growth machine's vision is that artists will be followed by foodies, artisanal producers, creative-class entrepreneurs, and alternative consumers (Hum 2014). A Chelsea Market-style food court was added, and a public walkway was designated as "Innovation Alley" (deMause 2015) (see Figure 6.10). The space includes artisanal shops, including a gluten-free bakery, butcher, coffee shop, candy maker, and an open area where artists and "makers" who work on upper floors and other buildings on the "campus" can eat in a Wi-Fi friendly environment. In 2016 the space also included a gallery exhibit on "Social Ecologies."

The threat is manyfold. First, although the revived Industry City remains industrial and commercial, the new "maker economy" prized by developers has substantially lower employment capacity than the garment manufacturers, construction suppliers, auto shops, furniture makers, moving companies and other businesses that currently occupy the waterfront (Hum 2014, 2016). And it remains unclear if these new industries will employ long-term Sunset Park residents or attract new employees (as indicated by *The Wall Street Journal*) who will then seek residential relocation to the neighborhood. The combination of a new waterfront park, new artisanal producers, and an overt effort to market the area as "Williamsburg South" (deMause 2015), DUGO (Down Under the Gowanus Overpass) (Hum 2014), and "the SoHo of Sunset Park" (Satow 2014) constitutes a serious displacement threat.

There is concern that eventually waterfront condos with sweeping views of the harbor will replace industrial spaces, and the inland affordable housing of the working-poor and working-class immigrant community will

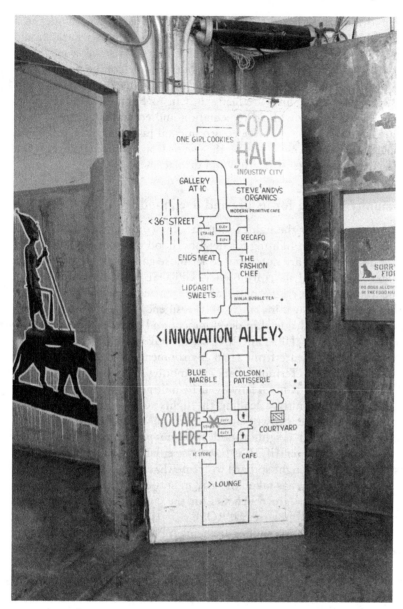

Figure 6.10 Guide to the food hall at Industry City

be flipped to gentrifiers. Real-estate brokers already report increased interest and prices in the neighborhood (Cullen 2015), and tenants already report harassment in rent-stabilized units (deMause 2015). The Brooklyn Nets professional basketball team took a large amount of square footage in Industry City for their new front office and practice facilities, adding to the appeal of the neighborhood to outsiders. The Industry City model is a distinctly white, wealthy, and non-local vision of what Sunset Park should be. It is not a vision that originates with, or is geared to serve, a neighborhood population that is 66 percent Latino, one-third below the poverty line, with 63 percent having high school as their highest educational attainment (Hum 2016). And battle lines are being drawn. As Hum (2014: 169) notes "While demands for brownfield remediation and equitable access to open spaces are central to Sunset Park's environmental justice agenda and goals, the challenge remains how to ensure that waterfront improvements do not lead to transformative gentrification and displacement."

A community fighting for its life and livelihood

Sunset Park is ready for the fight. Long-standing community organizations like UPROSE have been fighting for neighborhood quality-of-life improvements for decades, and are not about to let those gains become the catalyst for the displacement of its constituency. UPROSE describes itself as "an intergenerational, multi-racial, nationally recognized community organization that promotes sustainability and resiliency through community organizing, education, leadership development and cultural/artistic expression in Brooklyn, NY" (UPROSE 2016). UPROSE played a central role in the re-visioning of the waterfront as an environmental amenity, fighting for and co-designing Bush Terminal Park, promoting and co-designing plans for the Brooklyn Waterfront Greenway (a 14-mile green bike route connecting waterfront communities), leading the fights to prevent LULU sitings, and helping to secure brownfield remediation funding. Of course, a polluted, contaminated neighborhood with no public waterfront access would be less prone to gentrify. It is just those environmental resources that groups like UPROSE fought so hard to create that outsiders seek to appropriate. And so UPROSE has taken the lead in anti-gentrification organizing, determined to retain the green benefits for the community that demanded them. As Elizabeth Yeampierre, UPROSE's dynamic and effective leader, has stated, "What our communities are being told is that unless we live next to a waste transfer station or a power plant, we don't deserve to live there" (Hum 2014: 191).

UPROSE is a founding organization in the Protect Our Working Waterfront Alliance (POWWA). POWWA sponsored a Columbus Day rally in 2015 with the theme, "There is nothing innovative about displacement" and unfurled a banner with Columbus landing on the Americas with an Industry City flag. The rally drew attention to what the activists say is a wave of tenant harassment and local business closings as rents increase and owners seek to profit from the interest in Sunset Park from outsiders. Elizabeth Yeampierre asked those at the rally, "What did Columbus say? We made "fine servants." I think Industry City thinks we make fine servants too – to their economy, and to the people that they're bringing into Sunset

Park." The POWWA Facebook Page describes the group's goals, principles and vision as follows:

> The Sunset Park industrial waterfront is being threatened by land speculation, potential rezonings, and high-end commercialization inconsistent with blue-collar manufacturing. The preservation and expansion of a blue-collar manufacturing base is crucial to the economic viability of a working-class community like Sunset Park.
>
> The loss of blue-collar jobs and the displacement of working-class businesses and residents is a devastating narrative that has unfolded in other neighborhoods; it must not be allowed to occur in Sunset Park. The following principles seek to ensure local economic development, equity, and resilience in Sunset Park:
>
> 1 Ensure community control over infrastructure and planning projects in Sunset Park.
> 2 Protect the economic needs of long-time residents, workers and businesses. Local residents and businesses are increasingly facing flat wages, heavy rent burdens, and the threat of displacement. Ensure that economic development on the waterfront directly benefits the local community.
> 3 Expand blue-collar union, career-track jobs. Manufacturing jobs pay twice the annual salary of service sector jobs in much of the city. Promote businesses and career opportunities at all skill levels, career advancement, and income mobility. Commercialization of the waterfront threatens to replace blue-collar manufacturing with service jobs.
> 4 Promote the development of maritime-dependent industrial uses. Maritime-dependent uses reduce truck traffic and emissions.
> 5 Protect land zoned for manufacturing. Restrict any rezonings or zoning variance applications that reduce land zoned for manufacturing to accommodate commercial or residential uses. Rezonings and variances lead to land speculation, which result in rising rents and displacement of existing jobs.
> 6 Incorporate climate adaptation and resiliency into waterfront development.
>
> (POWWA 2016)

What is clear in these principles, in addition to a comprehensive vision of environmental, economic, and social sustainability, is the centrality of rezoning to the future of the community. Sparked by a 2007 proposal for an "acontextual" 100-foot tower in a residential neighborhood, the community effectively fought for a rezoning plan for part of Sunset Park. The rezoning plan was approved in 2009 to mixed reviews from the Latino-Chinese community coalition that had participated in the rezoning process.

The rezoning imposed height limits on new construction, and preserved retail corridors, but still allowed for some densification through inclusionary zoning in specific corridors, which threatened to bring in gentrifiers (Hum 2014). This early action did help to preclude widespread high-rise, high-density construction and rapid neighborhood displacement. In 2015, another proposal to "upzone" (increasing building heights to facilitate densification) parts of Sunset Park, ostensibly to generate more affordable housing, was defeated. Critics charged that the new zoning would encourage developers to replace existing affordable housing with high-density projects with both affordable and more expensive units. As one Community Board member noted, "We don't build affordable housing in Sunset Park, we preserve it. It's already existing, our pressure is that we're losing it" (Lynch 2015). In 2016, Industry City developers are looking for waterfront rezoning to establish retail and a large hotel on its property. Thus far, Mayor de Blasio has not approved the creation of a "special innovation zoning district" on the Sunset Park waterfront to allow for what some have dubbed a "$1B Brooklyn hipster mega-project" (Hawkins 2015). With such rezoning comes the risk of retail-creep, where retail pushes out manufacturing, and residential-creep, where the large hotel becomes the starting point for long-term residential development on the waterfront. In his 2016 State of the City address, Mayor de Blasio proposed an ambitious streetcar-based infrastructure plan that would link waterfront neighborhoods from Sunset Park to Williamsburg. This project, if it goes through, will lay the groundwork for further green gentrification.[8]

Last best hope

Sunset Park represents perhaps the last best hope for achieving truly sustainable urban greening in Brooklyn. As Tarry Hum (2014: 4) has stated, "urban policy and planning initiatives for sustainability and resilience must foreground racial equity and justice in Sunset Park's revalorized local landscape of postindustrial economic growth and post-Hurricane Sandy rebuilding." The community is well organized and deeply engaged in the planning process, with a community-based organization, UPROSE, that understands the importance of process justice. UPROSE operates on environmental justice principles in its quest to improve the quality of life in the neighborhood. And the potential of community disintegration through green gentrification has been anticipated and is well understood (Hum 2014). Steadily increasing levels of Asian-American homeownership may reduce displacement pressures (Treskon 2012). Community leaders are well connected to, and well respected by, local elected officials. Despite some early gentrification, the neighborhood still retains its race, class, and ethnic character. The de Blasio administration ran on a social equity platform whose centerpiece was affordable housing, and is overtly committed to racial justice. If it is possible to achieve "just sustainability" (Agyeman

2005) in Brooklyn, if urban sustainability that includes all three pillars is possible in a global city, if it is possible to attain environmental justice in the context of a capitalist political economy, it should happen in Sunset Park in this decade.

Comparative resistance

In both Greenpoint-Williamsburg and Sunset Park we see communities demanding more green space and greater public waterfront access. In Greenpoint-Williamsburg, the community demanded green space and waterfront access as compensation for a waterfront rezoning from industrial to residential that threatened to wall off the East River with a line of high-rise luxury condos. In contrast, the Sunset Park community mobilized for green space and waterfront access largely independent of rezoning plans, employing an environmental justice frame. That is, where Greenpoint-Williamsburg was largely reactive to externally generated waterfront redevelopment initiatives, Sunset Park was proactive in promoting a locally generated vision of a revitalized waterfront that included green space.

Despite these differences, both communities demanded a future waterfront neighborhood that included more green space, greater public waterfront access, and affordable housing to defend against displacement. In these cases, we see grassroots urban greening initiatives rather than top-down greening plans. Growth coalitions were receptive to these community demands since they were consistent with larger citywide visions of a renewed waterfront as the site of urban environmental amenities (NYC Department of Planning 2011). Citizen groups formed a key element of the local green growth coalition in these two cases. On the Greenpoint-Williamsburg waterfront, activists sought to add greening to growth. In Sunset Park, activists sought green waterfront amenities and green waterfront job growth. Both communities, however, understood that urban greening generates gentrification pressures, although their strategies for both greening and defending against green gentrification differed. Interestingly, in both cases, the promised waterfront parks have been very slow to appear and have been greatly attenuated in their size and scope to date. Bushwick Inlet Park remains just six recreational acres of a 28-acre plan, and the promised waterfront esplanades remain incomplete.[9] Bush Terminal Park is smaller and has fewer facilities than originally planned, and the waterfront greenway has yet to fully develop.

Both communities also chose to amplify demands for a more environmentally clean, publically accessible waterfront while mobilizing against proposals to locate polluting power plant facilities on their respective waterfronts (Sze 2007). Activists in Greenpoint-Williamsburg and Sunset Park argued that their communities were already disproportionately burdened with exposures to multiple sources of environmental contamination. In this sense they each used an environmental equity frame in arguing that their communities should be the location of fewer environmental bads, and more environmental goods. Both neighborhoods fought the market tendency to distribute environmental bads to locations already hosting LULUs and made an environmental justice argument for public policy intervention in markets to distribute green space where markets would otherwise distribute polluting facilities. In the end, both communities were victorious in their fights against power plant sitings, and both were victorious in negotiating for urban environmental amenities in their place. In these cases, process justice resulted in greater distributive justice outcomes (Agyeman 2005).

The Greenpoint-Williamsburg community demanded affordable housing construction through inclusionary zoning in the 2005 redevelopment plan as a bulwark against the displacement impact of proposed high-rise, high-rent, high-cost towers. Sunset Park, engaging at a stage prior to the major gentrification pressures faced by Williamsburg in particular, seeks to retain existing affordable housing, and rejects most "upzoning" even with new affordable housing guarantees. Sunset Park does not lack affordable housing; Williamsburg does.[10]

Whereas Greenpoint-Williamsburg largely accepted the transition of its waterfront from industrial to residential, demanding new affordable units and greening as compensation, Sunset Park has fought to retain the working-class employment capacity of its industrial waterfront. UPROSE and POWAA oppose rezoning that transitions industrial waterfront to residential development, understanding that it is those working-class jobs that allow Sunset Park residents to sustain a walk-to-work, working-class community. The city supports retention of much of the working waterfront in Sunset Park, although it promotes transition to a greater share of creative-class jobs touted in the "maker economy" (NYC Department of Planning 2011). Sunset Park residents largely reject the creative-class industries that Williamsburg has built its identity around in recent decades, seeing such enterprises as part of a larger gentrification threat. Creative-class enterprises had already displaced many traditional working-class waterfront jobs in Greenpoint-Williamsburg when the 2005 rezoning conflicts were resolved. Whereas Greenpoint-Williamsburg retains a small Industrial Business Zone, much of the Sunset Park waterfront is included in the Southwest Brooklyn Industrial Business Zone. Again, Sunset Park activists have understood the environment as "where we live, work, and play" and have sought to integrate more environmentally friendly employment, green amenities, and affordable housing into an integrative community vision (Hum 2014). This is different than leveraging new luxury condo tower approvals against demands for more greening and inclusionary zoning.

At both the Sunset Park and Greenpoint-Williamsburg waterfronts, community mobilization and participation in planning processes is evident and impactful. However, by being pre-mobilized and early to engage in the visioning process, the Sunset Park community has been able to set the terms and parameters of redevelopment plans more effectively. One lesson to draw from this is that communities need to be organized before green gentrification threats emerge, articulate a vision for their community, and demand process justice in redevelopment planning from the outset. History is unkind to those who mobilize late.

Finally, another lesson to be drawn from these two cases of community intervention in the green gentrification process is that sequencing matters. Not only do communities need to be organized early, but they also need to get the ordering of new developments right to maximize greening and minimize displacement. In Greenpoint-Williamsburg, luxury towers started going up before green space property was purchased (see Figure 6.11). This

Figure 6.11 Waterfront luxury condo towers in Williamsburg

raised the cost of greening and both delayed park construction and reduced city enthusiasm for following through on its green promises. Similarly, affordable housing construction started too late to prevent substantial displacement. While affordable housing will eventually generate a more mixed income community, it will not do so with the long-term residents who have already been forced away from the waterfront. Greenpoint-Williamsburg was somewhat successful in attaining procedural justice, but much less successful at achieving substantive justice (Agyeman 2005).

Ideally, the affordable housing must go in and be filled (or effectively retained) first, cementing long-term working-class residents in place. Then green space should follow (with affordable housing units potentially reducing land values for city purchase). Only after neighborhoods have been stabilized and greened should the new, less affordable, high-density structures be permitted to go up as the city seeks to accommodate developers and an increasing urban population.

The alternative is to sell such plans as a full neoliberal package, with developers committed to paying for public green space and affordable housing in exchange for the right to profit from urban greening through new luxury construction. Even in that neoliberal model, sequencing would matter: first equity, then environment, and then economy. In Sunset Park, the affordable housing is there, and the community is fighting any zoning changes and waterfront developments (Industry City) that might threaten it. The greening has been started, originating with community demands rooted in an environmental justice frame. Working-class jobs retention and expansion is sought, with development plans measured against the extent to which they provide climate-adaptive local employment for long-term residents (Hum 2014). Some upzoning has been allowed, but limited. It remains to be seen if Sunset Park can green without substantially gentrifying. Greenpoint-Williamsburg has largely lost that fight. Not only must all three pillars of sustainability have equal policy salience, but in a global city where real-estate markets tend to dominate other interests, the sequence in which each pillar is implemented is likely to be of critical importance to the distributive outcome of urban greening plans.

Notes

1   Schnaiberg's (1980) economic synthesis.
2   Schnaiberg's (1980) managed scarcity or ecological syntheses.
3   With the exception of pocket parks at Grand Ferry Park, the attenuated Bushwick Inlet Park, and the WNYC Transmitter Park.
4   For 1990 and 2000, we analyzed census tracts 551, 555, 557 and 577. These were reconfigured in 2010 and for later analysis we use 551, 555, and 557.
5   This is much like the park-condos package that emerged at Brooklyn Bridge Park, except that in that case, the community accepted condos as the price of the park, whereas in the Greenpoint-Williamsburg waterfront case, the commu-

nity demanded more parks in exchange for the condos. To both communities, the greening was desirable but the condos were not.

6   Industrial Business Zone designations are flexible, and do not fully prohibit all non-industrial land uses (Hum 2014).
7   For all years, we analyzed census tracts 2, 18, 20 and 22.
8   In his proposal, Mayor de Blasio presents this streetcar plan as providing public transit linkages for the numerous public housing projects built near the Brooklyn waterfront in its industrial (environmental bads) era. However, he proposes to pay for the project through the taxes generated by new residential developments that such waterfront infrastructure will inevitably inspire in the urban greening era.
9   The waterfront esplanades were to be constructed by private tower developers and turned over to the City Parks and Recreation Department once completed (DeSena 2009).
10 Greenpoint retains more affordable housing because it has had fewer gentrification pressures until recently. A relatively stable Polish community has actively fought displacement over the years (DeSena 2005), and proximity to active industrial sites and pollution has reduced desirability.

Bibliography

Alkon, Alison Hope. 2012. *Black, White, and Green: Farmers Markets, Race, and the Green Economy.* Athens, GA: University of Georgia Press.
Bahrampour, Tara. 2000. "Neighborhood Report: New York Up Close; Residents See Health Risks in New Generating Plants." *The New York Times*, December 24.
Barbarino, Al. 2014. "Sunset Park Development Sells for Nearly $20 M." *Commercial Observer*, April 4. Retrieved January 19, 2016 (https://commercialobserver.com/2014/04/sunset-park-development-sells-for-nearly-20m/).
Belenkaya, Veronika. 2009. "Waterside Park is Still a Dream." *New York Daily News*, March 9.
The City of New York. 2007. *PlaNYC: A Greener Greater New York.* The City of New York. Mayor Michael R. Bloomberg. New York: NYC Government. Retrieved February 5, 2016 (www.nyc.gov/html/planyc/downloads/pdf/publications/full_report_2007.pdf).
Cockram, Michael. 2014. "Going with the Flow." *Architectural Record.* 202(6).
Cullen, Terrence. 2015. "Brooklyn's Sunset Park Is About Much More Than Just Industry City." *Commercial Observer*, September 24. Retrieved January 18, 2016 (https://commercialobserver.com/2015/09/brooklyns-sunset-park-is-about-much-more-than-just-industry-city/).
deMause, Neil. 2015. "As Industry City Promises a New Sunset Park, Some Residents Fight to Maintain the Old One." *City Limits*, October 27, Retrieved January 18, 2016 (http://citylimits.org/author/neil-demause/).
Department of City Planning. 1992. *Comprehensive Waterfront Plan: Reclaiming the City's Edge.* The City of New York.
DeSena, Judith. 2005. *Protecting One's Turf.* New York: University Press of America.
DeSena, Judith. 2009. *Gentrification and Inequality in Brooklyn: The New Kids on the Block.* New York: Lexington Books.

Durkin, Erin. 2009a. "Affordable Apts. On Waterfront Still Far On Horizon." *New York Daily News*, May 20, p. 51.

Durkin, Erin. 2009b. "Williamsburg, Greenpoint Residents Say City Hasn't Delivered on Park Spaces Key to Rezoning Set-Up." *New York Daily News*, May 14.

Fitzgerald, Joan. 2010. *Emerald Cities: Urban Sustainability and Economic Development*. New York: Oxford University Press.

Foderaro, Lisa W. 1987. "A Metamorphosis for Old Williamsburg." *The New York Times*, July 19.

Fried, Joseph P. 2006. "In the Works, Another Park for a Bit of the Waterfront." *The New York Times*, May 30.

Friends of Bushwick Inlet Park. 2016. Retrieved January 7, 2016 (www.bushwickinletpark.org).

Furfaro, Danielle. 2013. "Greenpointers: City Lied About Parks, 'Affordable Housing'." *The Brooklyn Paper*, May 24.

Furfaro, Danielle. 2015. "Greenpoint Mega-Development's Below-Market Buildings Will Segregate the Poor, Say Neighbors." *The Brooklyn Paper*, June 29.

Gardiner, Jill. 2005. "Mayor's Brooklyn Rezoning Proposal Is in the Sites of Community Groups." *New York Sun*, April 4.

Gonzalez, Juan. 2015. "Ambitious Brooklyn Park Plan Remains Benched After Nearly a Decade." *New York Daily News*, April 4.

Gould, Kenneth A. 2006. "Promoting Sustainability." In *Public Sociologies Reader*. Judith Blau and Keri Iyall Smith. eds. Lanham, MD: Rowman and Littlefield, 213–229

Gould, Kenneth A., Allan Schnaiberg and Adam S. Weinberg. 1996. *Local Environmental Struggles: Citizen Activism in the Treadmill of Production*. Cambridge, MA: Cambridge University Press.

Hamilton, Trina and Winifred Curran. 2013. "From 'Five Angry Women' to 'Kick-ass Community': Gentrification and Environmental Activism in Brooklyn and Beyond." *Urban Studies* 50(8): 1557–1574.

Hawkins, Andrew. 2015. "Developers Unveil $1B Brooklyn Hipster Mega-Project." *Crain's New York Business*, March 9. Retrieved January 18, 2016 (www.crainsnewyork.com/article/20150309/BLOGS04/150309863/developers-unveil-1b-brooklyn-hipster-mega-project).

Hays, Elizabeth. 2000. "Power Barge Hearing Set State Agency Bows to Demand for Added Public Input." *New York Daily News*, December 11.

Hays, Elizabeth. 2001. "Power Plant Plan Jeered Greenpoint, Williamsburg Activists Berate Developer." *New York Daily News*, June 25.

Hays, Elizabeth. 2003. "Plea for Affordable Homes Activists Worry Waterfront Rehab Will Shut Out Poor." *New York Daily News*, June 27.

Hobbs, Allegra. 2015. "De Blasio: I Won't Rezone Promised Bushwick Inlet Park Land for Apartments." *The Brooklyn Paper*, December 31.

Hogan, Gwynne. 2015. "City Reverses Stance on CitiStorage Site After Community Pressure." *DNAinfo*, December 31. Retrieved January 7, 2016 (www.dnainfo.com/new-york/20151231/greenpoint/city-reverses-stance-on-citistorage-site-after-community-pressure).

Hum, Tarry. 2014. *Brooklyn's Sunset Park: Making a Global Immigrant Neighborhood*. Philadelphia, PA: Temple University Press.

Hum, Tarry. 2016. "Sunset Park Redevelopment Proposal Misses the Mark." Gotham Gazette. Retrieved January 6, 2016 (www. gothamgazette.com/

index.php/opinion/5666-sunset-park-redevelopment-proposal-misses-the-mark-tarry-hum).

Industry City. 2016 "History." Retrieved February 6, 2016 (http://industry city.com/history/).

Katinas, Paula. 2015. "Menchaca's Goal: 'I Want to be Part of a Movement'." *Brooklyn Daily Eagle*, September 17.

Kensinger, Nathan. 2015. "Finally, a Park Grows in Brooklyn's Last Industrial Pocket." *Curbed NY*, March 5. Retrieved February 4, 2016 (http://ny.curbed. com/archives/2015/03/05/finally_a_park_grows_in_brooklyns_last_industrial_ pocket.php).

Kimmelman, Michael. 2015. "Price Tag on a Brooklyn Park Reaches $225 Million, and That's Only the Beginning." *The New York Times*, June 2.

Lanham, Robert. 2015a. "There's an Occupy the Inlet Event this Weekend at Bushwick Inlet Park." *Free Williamsburg*, August 5. Retrieved February 6, 2016 (http://freewilliamsburg.com/theres-an-occupy-the-inlet-event-this-weekend-at-bushwick-inlet-park/).

Lanham, Robert. 2015b. "Times Says Bushwick Inlet Park Could Cost Another Half Billion in 'Ransom' Money." *Free Williamsburg*, June 1. Retrieved February 6, 2016 (http://freewilliamsburg.com/times-says-bushwick-inlet-park-could-cost-another-half-billion-in-ransom-money/).

Lynch, Dennis. 2015. "Upzone Backfire! Bared 7: Rezone for 'Affordable' Housing Would Have Opposite Effect." *The Brooklyn Paper*, November 20.

Maantay, Juliana A. 2002. "Industrial Zoning Changes in New York City and Environmental Justice: A Case Study in 'Expulsive' Zoning." *Projections: The Planning Journal of Massachusetts Institute of Technology* 3: 63–108.

McGeveran, Tom. 2002. "Developer Klein Makes a Big Bet on Waterfront." *New York Observer*, May 13.

New York City Department of Parks and Recreation. 2014. "NYC Parks Joins NYC Economic Development Corporation and The Sunset Park Community to Cut the Ribbon on New Bush Terminal Piers Park." Retrieved January 7, 2016 (www.nycgovparks.org/parks/bush-terminal-park/pressrelease/21263).

New York City Department of Parks and Recreation. 2016. "Bushwick Inlet Park." Retrieved January 7, 2016 (www.nycgovparks.org/parks/bushwick-inlet-park).

New York City Department of Planning. 2011. "Vision 2020: New York City Comprehensive Waterfront Development Plan." Retrieved February 6, 2016 (www.nyc.gov/waterfront).

Newman, Andy. 2003. "For a Stretch of Brooklyn Waterfront, Many Dreams Are Contenders." *The New York Times*, February 6.

NYC EDC. 2015. "Sunset Park Vision Plan." Retrieved February 6, 2016 (www.ny cedc.com/project/sunset-park-vision-plan).

Oder, Norman. 2014. "Impatience Grows Over Promised Brooklyn Waterfront Park." *City Limits*, May 20. Retrieved February 4, 2016 (http://citylimits.org/ 2014/05/20/impatience-grows-over-promised-brooklyn-waterfront-park/).

OneNYC. 2015. "Mayor de Blasio and Parks Commissioner Silver Announce $15 Million in Conservancy Commitments to Community Parks." Retrieved February 5, 2016 (www1.nyc.gov/office-of-the-mayor/news/838-15/mayor-de-blasio-parks-commissioner-silver-15-million-conservancy-commitments-to).

Paletta, Anthony. 2015. "A Park Revives Some of Brooklyn's Waterfront." *The Wall Street Journal*, July 15.

POWWA. 2016. Protect Our Working Waterfront Alliance Facebook Page. Retrieved January 19 (www.facebook.com/POWWA-1517168355247981/).

Prud'homme, Alex. 2010. "An Oil Spill Grows in Brooklyn." *The New York Times,* May 15.

Redclift, Michael. 2006. "Sustainable Development (1987–2005) – An Oxymoron Comes of Age." *Horizontes Antropológicos* 12(25): 65–84.

Rosan, Christina D. 2012. "Can PlaNYC make New York City 'greener and greater' for Everyone? Sustainability Planning and the Promise of Environmental Justice." *Local Environment,* 17(9): 959–976.

Satow, Julie. 2014. "Industry City, the SoHo of Sunset Park." *The New York Times,* January 17.

Schnaiberg, Allan. 1980. *The Environment: From Surplus to Scarcity.* New York: Oxford University Press.

Schnaiberg, Allan and Kenneth A. Gould. 2000. *Environment and Society: The Enduring Conflict.* Caldwell, NJ: Blackburn Press.

Son, Hugh. 2005. "Mike Makes Housing Deal." *New York Daily News,* May 3, p. 37.

Taylor, Dorceta E. 2009. *The Environment and the People in American Cities, 1600s–1900s: Disorder, Inequality, and Social Change.* Durham, NC: Duke University Press.

Treskon, Mark. 2012. "Constructing an oppositional community: Sunset Park and the politics of organizing across difference." In *The World in Brooklyn: Gentrification, Immigration, and Ethnic Politics in a Global City.* Judith DeSena and Timothy Shortell. eds. 2012. New York: Lexington Books.

UPROSE. 2013. "Sunset Park Brownfield Opportunity Area Nomination Study Report." New York State Department of State. Retrieved February 6, 2016 (http://uprose.org/wp-content/uploads/2015/04/UPROSE-Sunset-Park-BOA-Nomination-Study.pdf).

UPROSE. 2016. "Uprose." Retrieved February 6, 2016 (http://uprose.org/).

7 Making urban greening sustainable

Green gentrification is the enemy of sustainability

Urban greening is a global phenomenon evident in cities around the world from New York to Cape Town to Shanghai. Cities compete to attract attention to their new parks, waterfront esplanades, river walks, bike paths, greenways, and pedestrian malls. They routinely tout their new LEED certified buildings, clean energy initiatives, and public transit improvements. Urban greening, however, does not necessarily contribute to sustainable development. Urban greening that increases inequality undermines the social conditions necessary to attain sustainability at higher scales, and reduces the quality of life locally for those near the bottom of the stratification system.

The treadmill of production, the political and economic arrangement of institutions and interests that promote economic growth as the dominant social goal, produces increasing environmental degradation and increasing inequality. What makes these arrangements an ever-quickening treadmill is that the institutional commitments to growth are so entrenched that the primary solution – to the dual problems of ecological decay and social inequality promoted by this political economy – is accelerated growth. Calls for steady-state economics or de-growth do not even make it to the level of debate (Kallis et al. 2012).[1] Alternatives such as these are absent from policy discussions. In the treadmill model, growth is viewed as generating the financial resources necessary to address environmental problems (primarily through structural mitigation and technological innovation), and the economic opportunities to lift those at the bottom of the stratification system out of poverty (through job creation and/or social welfare revenues). (Schnaiberg 1980; Schnaiberg and Gould 2000; Gould et al. 1996; Gould et al. 2008).

In the urban context, treadmill of production interests are manifest in local growth coalitions (Molotch 1976; Logan and Molotch 1987), where municipal governments, developers, and citizen-workers' interests coalesce around schemes to increase municipal revenues, profits, and job opportunities. In the twenty-first century, the environmental disruption impacts of treadmill-fueled growth have begun to produce a broad consensus in global cities (and elsewhere) that urban greening must be integrated into municipal planning (Evans 2002). Because the treadmill prescribes growth as the only possible solution to the environmental problems caused by growth, urban growth coalitions have greened. Green growth machines have developed to address urban environmental problems, and to capitalize on widespread environmental concerns, interests, and tastes. Green growth coalitions seek to promote urban development that promotes growth around the production and restoration of urban environmental amenities (Gould and Lewis 2012), structural mitigation of environmental risks (like sea level rise and increased coastal flooding) (O'Neill and Van Abs 2016), and technological innovation (green buildings and "cleantech" industries) (Goldstein 2013). The push for urban greening is a global phenomenon, with urban greening proponents contributing to a worldwide exchange of urban greening ideas, technologies, and initiatives (Sze 2015; Cohen forthcoming; Montero 2015). There is now a global urban green growth machine, which profits from urban environmental problems and their solutions. Since most of those solutions are predicated on economic growth, to a large extent they promise to contribute to the global production of the very problems they ostensibly seek to address.

Urban green growth coalitions have vested interests in two pillars of the sustainable development paradigm: economic (growth), and environmental. This two-pillar approach that omits the crucial social equity pillar, inevitably leads to the maldistribution of environmental goods and environmental bads in the urban context. That is, green growth is aimed at addressing the urban environmental problems generated by the treadmill, through growth schemes that are ostensibly ecologically more sustainable. Because growth generates *both* environmental problems *and* social inequality, green growth aimed at mitigating environmental problems not only fails to address the social inequality impacts of growth, but may actually utilize those inequality impacts to create the impression of greening. That is, green growth tends to shift environmental bads to less socially visible locations. On a global scale this can be seen in countries that claim great improvements in environmental quality (greened growth) by offshoring their polluting industry and their waste (Pellow and Smith 2006; Pellow 2007). Some places, inhabited by whiter and wealthier populations, are greened while environmental inequality is increased. Similarly, urban elites promote a green growth that increases urban inequality.

In global cities, the green growth machine increases urban inequality by distributing environmental amenities upward in the stratification system and environmental bads downward in the stratification system. A primary mechanism through which this negative redistribution is achieved is green gentrification. As we have seen, the construction or restoration of urban environmental amenities intersects with real estate markets and institutional racism in ways that tend to push the working poor, working class, and people of color away from environmental amenities, and redistributes access to such amenities to wealthy, white populations. Green gentrification exacerbates the amenity gap between environmental refugees and the environmentally privileged, in a neocolonial process of resource appropriation. Urban environmental improvement therefore increases inequality in general, and environmental inequality in particular. This is just as true when urban environmental amenities are the result of grassroots, bottom-up initiatives as when they are part of a green growth coalition development scheme. The inattention to the social equity pillar of sustainability – an inattention which is structurally generated by the political economy – results in urban greening that increases environmental racism and classism in terms of access to environmental amenities and exposure to environmental risks. As the urban sustainability plans of the green growth coalition redistribute environmental goods from poor to rich and from people of color to whites, they do so in a political-economic context in which goods attract goods and bads attract bads. Greened locales are more likely to attract other amenities (like public bicycles, and private organic food stores). Locales without such green amenities, to which poorer residents and citizens of color are pushed by market forces and racial discrimination as other locales are greened, are more likely to attract environmental hazards (like bus depots and power plants). Urban sustainability produces environmental injustice unless citizen-workers force public officials to intervene in markets and undo patterns of institutional racism to place the social equity pillar centrally in urban-greening plans.

The inequality produced by green gentrification has implications for environmental policy and the social capacity to address environmental problems on a global scale, far beyond the boundaries of any particular urban complex. Environmental inequality severs the feedback loop between social systems and ecosystems that is necessary to achieve sustainability on a planetary scale (Gould 2006). If urban elites are separated from the environmental consequences of their decisions, and are instead surrounded by environmental amenities while being insulated from environmental hazards, their capacity to comprehend the severity of environmental threats is attenuated, and their sense of environmental well-being is enhanced. Since sustainable development involves trade-offs between social benefits and environmental costs (Gould and Lewis 2015) an arrangement by which power-holding decision-makers receive both the majority of the social benefits of these trade-offs *and* the majority of environmental amenities, skews their perception in ways that makes them deaf, dumb, and blind to the actual costs of their actions. At the same time, green gentrification ensures that environmental costs in the form of hazards, and those who suffer from them, will be out of sight and out of mind, rendered socially invisible by the urban political economy. Green growth coalitions achieve just this type of ecological insularity through green gentrification in general, and especially through the neoliberal public-private partnership mechanism utilized in many urban sustainability initiatives (Greenberg 2009). Greening policies that produce urban environmental "citadels" (Friedmann and Wolff 1982; Smithsimon 2010) undermine the possibility of sustainable development.

The neoliberal city and the inverted quarantine

Public-private partnerships are a preferred approach to urban greening in the twenty-first century (Gotham and Greenberg 2014). This makes sense, as growth coalitions are by their very nature public-private partnerships, and neoliberal ideology increasingly legitimates the privatization of functions formerly performed by the public sector. Urban greening, climate adaptation, and resilience planning is taking place in an era of austerity (Shi et al. 2015). Austerity budgets imposed on municipalities empower private capital to direct urban trajectories by control and distribution of scarce resources for preferred projects. In terms of urban environmental amenities, such neoliberal arrangements allow elites to prioritize which amenities will be constructed or remediated: where, in what ways, when, and for whom. Public-private partnerships therefore allow public resources like parks, canals, and waterfronts to be utilized by urban elites as part of their inverted quarantine. The inverted quarantine is a private approach to environmental safety through the mechanism of purchasing insularity from generalized environmental harms (like paying for bottled water instead of publicly funding clean water supplies (see Flint, Michigan), or buying organic produce rather than mobilizing for regulation of pesticides) (Szasz 2007). The inverted quarantine distributes environmental safety by wealth, and fosters a retreat from public policy and political mobilization in response to growing environmental threats. The inverted quarantine thus enhances the severed feedback loop between social system actions and ecological impacts and, like green gentrification, is predicated on environmental inequality.

Public-private partnerships in urban greening encourages private funding for the parks and environmental amenities that are situated next to private donors. It allows the "gentry" to control the fate of amenities in their neighborhoods (or ones they choose to appropriate). By using private funds to improve and thus gentrify certain amenities (so-called public goods), they capture public goods for themselves, using real estate markets and institutional racism to distance others from these goods. The environmentally privileged (Park and Pellow 2011) can then withdraw support from public funding for parks without personal consequence. Why should elites pay for public parks budgets when the public parks they prefer are reconstructed to their liking? Rich communities get better parks (like Prospect Park and Brooklyn Bridge Park) and, in these times of austerity budgets, poor communities get budget cuts for their parks (like most NYC parks in poor and people-of-color communities). Public-private partnerships, rather than a form of public engagement, are more properly understood as a mechanism by which the rich withdraw from the public sector *and* get their public amenities improved. In doing so, the feedback loop between environmental conditions and those most empowered to make pro-environmental changes is further severed, as *their* public green spaces look great.

A green treadmill grows in Brooklyn

New York City, as the primary global city of the most powerful country on Earth, emerged as a leader in urban sustainability planning under the administration of Mayor Michael Bloomberg. The dual commitment to urban greening and urban growth manifest in PlaNYC is a model of the green growth machine in the context of the treadmill. New York City's green growth model is evident in the choice to use green space production to generate real estate development in neighborhoods around Prospect Park and Brooklyn Bridge Park. The green growth model is similarly evident in the choice to increase density in flood-prone areas like Gowanus and the Greenpoint-Williamsburg waterfront, using structural mitigation to rise above the tides. The green growth model is also evident in the construction of green buildings in Bushwick Inlet Park and Brooklyn Bridge Park, and in efforts to attract green "creative class" industries to the Sunset Park water-front. Green growth with scant attention to equity is the hallmark of the New York City model of urban sustainability, which the green growth machine seeks to replicate worldwide.

As the green growth machine intersects with real estate markets and insti-tutional racism in Brooklyn, we see the environmental inequality impacts manifest themselves through processes of green gentrification. The neigh-borhoods around Prospect Park richened and whitened as the green space was restored, distributing access away from, and displacing, the working class and people of color. The construction of Brooklyn Bridge Park hyper-super-gentrified Brooklyn Heights and the surrounding neighborhoods, drawing the mega-rich toward the amenity already constructed for the wealthiest Brooklynites. In Gowanus, a fetid canal that had been allowed to fester for half a century is now being greened as the green growth machine sees its profit potential. Whereas the working class and people of color were allowed to live near the canal when it was a waste dump, they are being green gentrified away from it as it is transformed into an environmental amenity. On the Greenpoint-Williamsburg waterfront, communities demanded green space, public access, and affordable housing in exchange for luxury densification. Ten years after reaching agreement, the public green space has proved too expensive to provide, the affordable housing is still not built, but many of the luxury towers are already up. Finally, in Sunset Park, the construction of Bush Terminal Park and the start of the waterfront greenway have helped attract the green growth machine, and working poor and working-class people of color are forced to fight to avoid being displaced from the waterfront they themselves greened.

In Brooklyn, as elsewhere, the environmental inequalities generated by green gentrification processes set in motion the accelerated polarization of environmental distribution, as goods attract goods, and bads attract bads. A restored Prospect Park attracted new bike lanes, public bicycles, a farmers market and other quality-of-life enhancements, concentrating environmental goods among the gentrifiers. Brooklyn Bridge Park similarly attracted new bike lanes, public bicycles, and free kayaking. A greener Gowanus now hosts a sustainability-themed Whole Foods with an organic greenhouse and solar power-lit parking lot. Even Bush Terminal Park helped draw in a gluten-free, organic bakery to Industry City that, like the Gowanus Whole Foods, is priced to attract gentrifiers rather than to serve long-term residents (see Figure 7.1). It is worth recalling that the Sunset Park waterfront was attracting power plants and waste transfer stations before it caught the eye of the green growth coalition.

Figure 7.1 Organic, gluten-free bakers, Brooklyn-made

The inverted quarantine of neoliberal public-private partnerships for urban greening has produced two enclaves of environmental splendor in Brooklyn. Prospect Park gets better and better, with meticulous ecological restoration, well-equipped playgrounds, two new ice skating rinks, and well-manicured ball fields. One can hardly imagine an environmental care in the world, using your public bike on the new bike lanes to access the farmers market to buy artisanal bread and organic produce, or taking your kids to the playground or for a winter skate. Surely the global environment is getting better, and is consistent with the growth that allows you to pay for living in such an expensive neighborhood. Brooklyn Bridge Park is even more impressive, with its sustainable rain catchment system, bike lanes, beach volleyball, kayaking and sweeping harbor views, all surrounded by multimillion-dollar homes. It would be hard to find any place in New York City, or any global city, where the environmental quality of life is higher. And while green gentrification fueled by public-private partnerships improve the quality of life for the richest Brooklynites, much of the rest of the city experiences austerity in the form of Parks and Recreation Department budget cuts. The parks near the environmental bads continue to degrade (despite Mayor de Blasio's commendable commitment to greater park equity), as the "hallmark," "signature," and "destination" parks flourish. Bushwick Inlet Park is less than 25 percent complete over the same period in which Brooklyn Bridge Park was constructed. Bush Terminal Park has been scaled back while new amenities are added to Prospect Park and Brooklyn Bridge Park. It is worth noting that the New York City public parks budget was *cut* under Mayor Bloomberg, resulting in reduced maintenance and reduced personnel. Inequality in access to urban parks is a nationally recognized environmental-justice issue (Wen et al. 2013) plaguing global cities as disparate as New York and Los Angeles (The City Project 2011, 2012). However, the problems of urban environmental amenity budget cuts are meaningless to the wealthiest Brooklyn neighborhoods. They live in a world where the environment is improving, without the rest of us in it.

Although Michael Bloomberg's New York City model of urban greening has received global attention, it is not a model of sustainable development. As David Harvey observed, "In New York City, the billionaire mayor, Michael Bloomberg, is reshaping the city along lines favorable to developers ... He is, in effect, turning Manhattan into one vast gated community for the rich" (Harvey 2008: 38). PlaNYC 2030 was the environmental amenity plan for that community. It is its inequality impacts that make Bloomberg's approach to urban greening the antithesis of sustainable development. The greening benefits and quality-of-life enhancements of the model are laudable, but their maldistribution makes them untenable. If we are to achieve sustainable development in the context of global cities, market mechanisms and neoliberal public-private partnership won't get us there – at least not left to their own devices. Organized communities

Figure 7.2 Bill de Blasio campaign rally at Brooklyn's Borough Hall

demanding environmental justice must force the state to intervene with public policies that promote a more just sustainability (Agyeman 2005).

Bottom-up urban sustainability: pushing back against markets and institutional racism

Communities must organize for anti-market, anti-racist public policy interventions

Left to their own devices, market forces and institutional racism will generate increasing environmental inequality from urban-greening initiatives through processes of green gentrification. However, as DeSena (2009: 87) notes regarding gentrification in Brooklyn, "global capitalism is not always entirely successful in realizing its objective. Local communities can mediate and mitigate structural and global forces on behalf of ordinary people." One lesson that is clear from our case studies of green gentrification is that working-class communities and communities of color must push back, demanding state intervention as public policy for the retention and/or production of affordable housing to mitigate displacement. That such housing is commonly referred to as "below-market rate" appropriately labels such citizen-worker movements as anti-market movements. That is, calls for urban greening without displacement are calls for non-market approaches to sustainability. Such calls are part of what Harvey (2008: 23) refers to as "the right to the city":

> it is far more than the individual liberty to access urban resources: it is a right to change ourselves by changing the city. It is, moreover, a common rather than an individual right since this transformation inevitably depends upon the exercise of a collective power to reshape the process of urbanization.
>
> (Harvey 2008: 23)

Communities have tried to shape their neighborhoods and use their power to transcend the market's calculus, with varying levels of success.

With green gentrification specifically, and gentrification generally, communities often engage at the early stages of development in debates over rezoning. This is especially so in cases of brownfields redevelopment, when cleanup is often predicated on rezoning; this is the time when the community has the opportunity to share its vision for what the brownfield can become. Inevitably, in this era of greening, community visions are often of open, green spaces. Some visions also include jobs. However, the green growth coalition does not see much "green" (money) in community green visions. Their profit-generating ideas compete with park visions, and the outcome in most of these cases is luxury condos with a green twist. Collectively visioning the future of a site engages communities in process justice; however, that level of participation and input rarely leads to outcome justice. Partial-outcome justice is sometimes achieved by way of concrete policy decisions. When brown sites are rezoned to include residences, as they have been in most of the cases in this book, a second policy debate takes place. While there are numerous housing policies that can be applied to prevent displacement (see Causa Justa :: Just Cause 2014), in Brooklyn the debate has largely centered on the creation of affordable housing.

The idea of "affordable housing" implies that most housing is unaffordable. When a community demands that a certain percentage of new construction fits within affordable housing guidelines, it is also a concession to adding a (typically much higher) percentage of unaffordable units. For this reason, residents of Sunset Park resisted the addition of new developments with affordable housing and instead are seeking to maintain the affordable housing that they already have. They want to avoid development that would increase rents in the area and displace current residents. Another policy that could have that effect would be some sort of rent control, but that is not currently politically viable (although some apartments are included in the city's 1969 rent stabilization program that restricts the rate of rent increases). In a similar move, activists in Lefferts Gardens resist the addition of new housing units, which would include affordable housing, in their neighborhood. This is ironic in that Mayor de Blasio's plan for affordable housing seeks to aid housing pressures for the working class and communities of color, such as those living in Sunset Park and Lefferts Gardens. These communities have flipped the script: they are resisting new developments that would contain 30 percent affordable housing and 70 percent market-rate (unaffordable) housing for gentrifiers. Not only is such housing problematic from an economic point of view, they also argue that it would decrease their quality of life by increasing the density of their neighborhoods. The quality-of-life argument is one that the wealthier, whiter residents of Brooklyn Heights also make.

The structural (climate change, ecological crisis), and cultural (green trendiness) imperatives for urban greening as flood protection, pollution reduction, health and fitness space, quality of life enhancements, etc. are only likely to increase, so greening will continue as an urban trend. There are multiple paths to, and outcomes for, urban greening. Thus far, urban-greening initiatives in global cities tend toward what we might call low-road, high-inequality scenarios. Such approaches to urban greening are consistent with both Hugh Stretton's (1976) "the rich rob the poor" scenario for elite-centered environmentalism, and with Allan Schnaiberg's (1980) "managed scarcity" scenario in which modest levels of environmental protection are achieved largely through socially regressive means. In New York City, widening economic and social divides became particularly acute under Mayor Bloomberg (Hum 2014), who is recognized as a global leader in promoting urban sustainability. At least in global cities, neoliberal urban greening predicated on increasing inequality is the leading model. However, high-inequality scenarios of urban greening are not sustainable in the long term because the equity pillar is a necessary condition of sustainable development. Urban greening that contributes to long-term socio-ecological sustainability must be a form of just sustainability because equity is necessary for the social system-ecosystem feedback loop to function effectively, and because the great majority of the population that is increasingly alienated from the benefits of urban sustainability will reject environmental protection if it is equated with impoverishment and scarcity for them and luxury for the few.[2]

Organized neighborhoods are more resilient in the face of green-gentrification pressures. Communities therefore need to organize now to take control of development within their own neighborhoods. The control of information is a powerful tool in development conflicts, and pre-organized communities are more likely to receive information about development plans early, and to be able to disseminate it widely (Weinberg and Gould 1993). Strong community organization facilitates early, proactive intervention in development planning, rather than late, reactive response to development plans originating from outside of the neighborhood. Organized communities are also more likely to build relationships and alliances with local elected officials, which improves information flows and increases political leverage. A neighborhood like Sunset Park, with a half-century-old community organization and long-term relationships with elected officials is far better positioned to exert its will on the local development trajectory than others. Neighborhoods with more political power (like Brooklyn Heights) have more control over development processes, and strong community organizations are an important component of neighborhood power, especially in communities with relatively few resources, like Sunset Park (Gould 1992). Additionally, to the extent made possible by local history and demographics, self-identification as an environmental-justice community provides an effective "master frame" with which to clarify interests, generate support, and make claims. An environmental-justice frame applied to urban-greening initiatives places the equity pillar of sustainability in the center of development conflicts.

Sequencing matters

In order to achieve integrated economic, environmental and equity-focused sustainable urban development, attention must be paid to sequencing. Land values respond to zoning changes and the creation or restoration of green amenities. If municipalities are to secure the land and remediation for green spaces, that land acquisition must precede rezoning for residential development. In order to prevent displacement, affordable housing units must be constructed and sold or rented prior to luxury housing units. Municipalities must buy land for green amenities when prices are lower. They can then make land available to developers through rezoning or other means after new green amenities raise property values. Only once the neighborhood has been secured against displacement pressures, and enhanced by quality of life-improving environmental amenities, should developers be allowed to break ground on luxury units aimed at urban densification. Displacement is only mitigated when affordable housing is secured or created first, and when access to affordable units is limited to those within the neighborhood. New York City's lottery system for the distribution of affordable housing units pits long-term neighborhood residents against all others seeking reasonable housing costs in the luxury city.

Table 7.1 summarizes the five cases in our analysis. Based on the discussion above, there are a few key analytic points we would like to highlight. First, when communities did not request affordable housing, the green growth coalition did not provide it voluntarily. Since the city did not have mandatory inclusionary affordable housing, which would require that all new development include a certain percentage of affordable housing, rezoning and new development was negotiated on a case-by-case basis. When communities don't demand it (as in Prospect Park and Brooklyn Bridge Park), it isn't added by private developers. In the case of Brooklyn Bridge Park (BBP), the community is resisting it, but the city may require it.

Second, there was community participation (process justice), in each case. The existence of this did not appear to affect the outcomes. However,

Table 7.1 Comparison of cases

Case	Prospect Park	Brooklyn Bridge Park	Gowanus Canal	Greenpoint-Williamsburg Waterfront	Sunset Park
Type	Restoration of existing environmental amenity (park)	Rezoned from industrial to park and residential	Rezoned from industrial to residential; Superfund cleanup and brownfield restoration	Rezoned from industrial to residential; new green spaces promised	Limited rezoning for higher density; working waterfront remains; new park
Status	Completed	Nearing completion	In process	In process	Nearing completion
Community response	Supported restoration; no discussion of affordable housing	Supported park, resisted affordable housing	Supported cleanup and affordable housing	Demanding green space and affordable housing	Demanding green space, housing stability, and job retention
Self-identified environmental justice community group	No	No	No	No	Yes
Greening initiators	Neighborhood elites prodding city	Neighborhood elites responding to city	Neighborhood elites, government officials and real estate developers	Community groups and government officials	Community group
Process justice	Limited	Yes	Yes	Late	Early
Outcome justice	No	Yes and no	No	No	Maybe
Affordable housing policy implemented	No	No, being resisted	Yes	Yes	Being debated
Extent of gentrification compared to Brooklyn	High	Medium; already super-gentrified	High	High	Similar to Brooklyn overall

the timing of participation did. Sunset Park's community organizations were organized before the threat of green gentrification. This level of organization at an early stage may be a key factor in the current housing stability in Sunset Park. At the other end of the spectrum, the Brooklyn Heights Association in BBP intervened early and was able to have their vision of the Harbor Park replace other city visions, though they had to concede to the city by providing condos in the park for maintenance. Even the white wealthy community had to give concessions to the green growth coalition. Finally, Sunset Park's relative success in resisting gentrification may be due in part to the existence of a strong community organization, their focus on working-class jobs, and the fact that a relatively large number of light-industrial and other employers remain active on their waterfront. Unlike areas closer to Manhattan, like the docks just south of Brooklyn Bridge Park, the economic benefits of the working waterfront may still outweigh real estate development. The question is, whose economic benefit is it? Once the docks to the north succumb to green gentrification, as we predict they will, it may only be a matter of time until Sunset Park can no longer bear the gentrification pressure. They might look to Prospect-Lefferts-Gardens residents for ideas about what a winning (or losing) strategy looks like for fighting off the creep of green gentrification.

An important motivation for this research is to make it useful to communities resisting green gentrification, because they are the key to making urban greening truly sustainable. Based on our findings, we recommend the following actions for communities that are vulnerable to green gentrification and/or are already resisting it:

1   Place environmental justice (EJ) at the center of your resistance. Draw upon other environmental-justice organizations for support and strategies. Build EJ-consciousness within the neighborhood.
2   Build alliances. Concentrate efforts on workers in the neighborhood. Workers fighting for their jobs can align with residents fighting for their neighborhood. Build relationships with local elected officials.
3   Do not equate participation in the process with success. It is often only one early piece of the puzzle.
4   Build solidarity within the community to resist zoning changes. The zoning battle is often the first stage of green gentrification. Without zoning changes from industrial to residential, displacement is less likely to occur. Enlist local elected officials as allies.
5   Generate alternative visions that include green space and jobs for neighborhood residents that are economically viable. Be proactive, not reactive.
6   If areas are rezoned to include residential zones, fight for high proportions of affordable housing and ensure that local residents have first priority for that housing (followed by other priority groups).

Figure 7.3 UPROSE leading the People's Climate March in New York City

7   When greening and affordable housing is promised, be sure that the sequencing follows the logic outlined above to ensure that residents actually get what they are promised and are not disappointed by the green growth coalition that defaults on promises due to economic logics.

The actions recommended above are consistent with calls for blue-green alliances (Obach, 2004; Gould, Lewis and Roberts 2004), an environmentalism rooted in livelihood struggles – much like environmental movements of the Global South (Taylor et al. 1995; Guha and Martinez-Alier 1997; Gedicks 2001) – and they aspire to a vision of *buen vivir* (Lewis 2016).

Greening the global city

As a global city, New York City has a "hot" real estate market, and in recent years Brooklyn's real estate has been hotter than Manhattan's. We believe that the "heat" of an urban real estate market matters in terms of the displacement and environmental inequality impacts of urban greening initiatives. Real estate markets in global cities tend to be hotter than others, since the demand for residential and commercial space is global rather than regional or local. Luxury condos in Brooklyn attract wealthy potential buyers from every continent in a way that luxury condos in Cleveland, Ohio or Guayaquil, Ecuador do not. As centers of global capital (Friedman 1986; Sassen 2001; Taylor 2004), demand for housing in global cities (no matter how many weeks per year they may actually be occupied) tends to remain high, and real estate values tend to climb. Growth coalitions constantly seek new neighborhoods from which to extract greater value, as global cities densify and/or expand. This means that gentrification pressures in global cities are high in general, and thus urban greening in such cities is going to generate green gentrification. New urban environmental amenities are exactly the kind of opportunity that global city growth coalitions look for to extract increased value from a locale. And global city growth coalitions understand that by producing an urban environmental amenity they can generate profit by appropriating environmental resources from one class for another. Primary motivations behind urban greening in global cities include attracting "knowledge workers" and the "creative class" (whom we loosely equate with the "sustainability class") – using green urbanism as a form of lifestyle-branding and gaining a competitive edge in global city rankings (Greenberg 2014; Hu 2015; Sze 2015). Global cities may therefore be the most difficult urban areas to green without increasing environmental inequality and thus undermining sustainability. Urban greening is a global phenomenon, and so is gentrification (Atkinson and Bridge 2005).

The global urban green growth machine

Greening cities is all the rage. There is no shortage of lists of green or green-est cities, with rankings varying widely depending upon the criteria used in assessment. Municipal governments compete globally to raise their green status and profile (Hu 2014; Sze 2015). There is a global urban-greening industry driven by just such competition and promoted by private foundations, international financial institutions, private firms and academics, which encourages acontextual replication of specific green amenities, infrastructures and policies (Montero 2015). The Brazilian city of Curitiba is perhaps the most common reference point for urban greening, in part because of its early leadership, and in part due to its apparent successes. However, what is often left out of the Curitiba narrative is how different the political-economic context in which those gains were achieved is from those faced by other cities today. There are things that are achievable in a military dictatorship, especially regarding urban infrastructure, that are more complex to attain in neoliberal regimes.

In her book *Fantasy Islands* (2015), Julie Sze problematizes what she calls eco-authoritarianism for impeding the emergence and engagement of civil society that is essential for sustainable development. Sze critiques China's urban greening, which is rooted in global city competition and top-down technocratic ecological modernization (Mol and Spaargaren 2000). She notes that it is bound to fail on social grounds, as it tends to exacerbate social injustice. China's urban greening, like New York's and that of other global cities, focuses on green buildings, energy efficiencies, and green spaces within the constraints of a green-growth ideology. In China, just as in Michael Bloomberg's New York, urban sustainability consists of two pillars: economic (growth), and environmental, with the third social equity pillar off the table (Sze 2015). Urban greening is pursued to the extent that it accelerates rather than impedes the Chinese treadmill of production (Schnaiberg 1980; Schnaiberg and Gould 1994; Gould, Pellow, and Schnaiberg 2008). The green-growth machine in Shanghai and its surroundings aims to remake the image of the city (and the country) as more ecologically sound through site-specific urban development projects and the creation of more urban green space (Sze 2015). However, the major site-specific (British engineered) urban-greening project, Dong'tan, has stalled (Pearce 2009; Sze 2015) and the creation of urban green space in Hangzhou is inflating nearby property values and thus generating green gentrification and associated environmental injustice (Wolch et al. 2014). This inattention to equity is a common theme throughout most global city urban greening schemes.

While Bogotá is lauded for its efficient public transit system, Copenhagen for its progress toward carbon neutrality, Mexico City for air quality improvements, Berlin for its central city Environmental Zone, Singapore for its zero-waste goals, and London for its energy efficiency, very few of the accolades make any reference to equity issues in urban greening (Grist 2007; Pantsios 2014; Schwartz 2013). In 2013, the city of Barcelona released its *Barcelona Green Infrastructure and Biodiversity Plan 2020*. It is an elaborate and ambitious plan for securing, expanding, and constructing green space throughout the city. Nowhere in the plan's summary documents are references to the issues of housing, equity, or gentrification. This is especially troubling in a city famous for its green space-implicated gentrification following the 1992 Olympics, and its current, enormous 22@ urban regeneration project aimed at gentrifying an underused industrial district (Lindmäe 2016). Urban greening is being pursued by global cities in a neoliberal era in which both sustainability and gentrification are viewed as urban regeneration and growth strategies. Upon the release of the *Barcelona Green Infrastructure and Biodiversity Plan 2020*, the International Union for the Conservation of Nature noted, "The city of Barcelona is leading the way in creating space for nature to protect biodiversity and achieve environmental objectives but also to improve the well-being of its citizens, create jobs and business opportunities" (IUCN 2013). Barcelona creates jobs and business opportunities, in part, through displacement (Dot et al. 2010).

Sydney, Australia's urban-greening plan, *Sustainable Sydney 2030*, was released in 2008, one year after New York's *PlaNYC 2030*. Unsurprisingly, there are many similarities. Sydney's plan takes a green-growth, neoliberal, two-pillar approach to urban sustainability, with some slight nods to urban equity issues. *Sustainable Sydney 2030* seeks to use the greening of a global

Figure 7.4 Public bicycles in Barcelona

city to facilitate growth and increase global competitiveness, with all of the green-gentrification issues one might expect. Inner-city densification has led to high-rise gentrification. Green redevelopment strategies have included "high-rise apartments for the creative class especially in the traditionally industrial waterfront zones," (Hu 2014: 4553) in addition to the construction of new green spaces and bike paths. Equity elements of the plan include a commitment to 7.5 percent affordable "social" housing, and for every resident to live within a three-minute walk of a "continuous green link" (bike path or pedestrian corridor) (City of Sydney 2013).

Cape Town, South Africa has also leapt onto the global urban sustainability stage. In 2014 the Ethisphere Institute identified it as one of the ten cities most likely to be a global sustainability center by 2020. In this case the city's green credentials are centered on energy initiatives including a commitment to having 10 percent of homes using solar power, and 10 percent of the city's total energy consumption coming from renewable sources by the year 2020 (d'Allant 2014). Cape Town was the first African city to develop an "Energy and Climate Change" strategy, and it purchases some electricity from South Africa's first commercial wind farm (Toffa 2014). In 2014, it marked the opening of the most modern photovoltaics factory on the African continent. Such leadership in renewable energy is, of course, commendable, but this environmental progress is made in an urban context in which vast swaths of the black population live in abject misery on flood plains without basic services. As d'Allant (2014) observes, it is essential to "avoid situations in which the 'green' discourse justifies further investment in the wealthiest areas at the expense of the poorest" in Cape Town.

Perhaps the most hopeful signs come from one of the world's largest and most unequal cities. In 2014, the Brazilian City of São Paulo unveiled a new strategic masterplan that included a number of urban sustainability principles. It is noteworthy that the plan was not sold internationally as a great urban-greening initiative, but rather as an attempt to solve a number of the city's longstanding problems, many of which have a strong environmental component. Much of the plan centered on transportation infrastructure and transit-oriented development. São Paulo's traffic congestion is famous, and the masterplan seeks to reduce automobile use through densification along public transit corridors, elimination of parking space requirements for new buildings, and adding dedicated bus lanes and bike lanes (see Figure 7.5) (Institute for Transportation and Development Policy 2014). It also proposes to locate new affordable housing developments (10 percent of new housing) in transit-oriented development zones (Cavalcanti 2014). These developments complement an earlier (2012) Sustainable Urban Development Plan focused on affordable housing and green space (SP-Urbanismo 2012). That plan gets the sequencing right by necessity, as its first phase is to construct affordable "social" housing to replace favelas along proposed greenway areas, and then use the freed space created by upzoning affordable housing to create green corridors. If done well, the plan should produce urban greening without displacement, as long as the social housing is not replaced through market mechanisms down the road. Nonetheless, the masterplan is heralded as promoting "sustainable growth" (Institute for Transportation and Development Policy 2014).

Figure 7.5 São Paulo bus rapid transit lanes

Clearly, most global cities – from London to Tokyo, Los Angeles to Stockholm – are greening. In many cases the effects of such urban greening is leading to green gentrification. In the United States, two powerful cities we are interested in analyzing with regard to green gentrification are San Francisco and Chicago (Florida 2015). Like New York City, both San Francisco and Chicago are global cities with industrial waterfronts and ambitious greening plans. San Francisco consistently ranks among the top green cities in the United States overall, and its clean air and water and abundant parks are noteworthy. Its greening programs are spread throughout many agencies. It has a Climate Action Plan and is mandated by law to have a Sustainable Communities Strategy (The Mayor's Office of Long-Term Planning and Sustainability 2013: 18). The mission of its Department of the Environment is to create "visionary policies and innovative programs that promote social equity, protect human health, and lead the way toward a sustainable future," and environmental justice is presented on their website as an explicit piece of the work that they do (SF Environment 2015). Nevertheless, San Francisco is one of the most expensive places to live in the United States and is especially interesting due to its already high degree of gentrification and gentrification-related political conflicts (Misra 2015). The role that greening plays in such gentrification in San Francisco and the greater Bay Area is not yet known.

Chicago also ranks among the top U.S. cities in green city rankings such as SustainLane (Karlenzig et al. 2007). Mayor Daley wanted to make the city the "greenest city in America," and he led by putting a green roof on City Hall (Karlenzig et al. 2007). Noteworthy from our green-gentrification perspective, the city flipped brownfields into its highly successful Millennium Park. The election of Mayor Rahm Emanuel did not stop Chicago in its green pursuits. In 2012, the city developed its Sustainable Chicago 2015 plan that includes seven interconnected themes, the first being economic development and job creation. Another one, "parks, open space and healthy food" echoes PlaNYC in its goal for Chicagoans to live within a ten-minute walk of parks. In the report of its 2012–2015 high-lights, the city notes, "Once-in-a-generation parks were opened: Northerly Island, 606, Rosehill, La Villita and Maggie Daley. Rebuilt or refurbished 225 playgrounds throughout the city through Chicago Plays!" (City of Chicago 2015). The distribution of these destination parks and playground upgrades, and their effects, are, we hypothesize, related to this work on green gentrification.

Just green enough in global cities?

The particular dynamics of global cites present a problem for those promoting an urban environmental strategy rooted in the concept of "just green enough" (Curran and Hamilton 2012). The just green enough approach to urban sustainability seeks to identify that tipping point in the urban environmental amenity production process where an area becomes attractive to growth coalitions. Rather than greening generated as real estate development schemes, just green enough looks to grassroots, bottom-up and/or publicly supported urban greening largely independent of private investment capital interests (Wolch, Byrne, and Newell 2014). We believe that such strategies have much merit but are unlikely to work as well in global cities as they are elsewhere. Just green enough depends on where that growth coalition attraction tipping point is, and that boundary is likely to be largely defined by how hot or cold a real estate market is. In shrinking rustbelt cities like Detroit, Michigan or Youngstown, Ohio, urban greening is unlikely to substantially increase the potential to appropriate environmental resources up the stratification scale, except perhaps when implemented in the very hottest urban locations in such cities. These are urban areas dealing with collapsing real estate markets in increasingly sparsely populated residential neighborhoods where greening might stabilize property values, not hyper-inflate them (Schilling and Logan 2008). Gary, Indiana, a deindustrialized city with declining population and a high poverty rate, has a Director of Environmental Affairs and Green Urbanism. The city is using the U.S. Department of Agriculture's Local Foods, Local Places initiative to convert vacant land into urban farms, and use food hubs to "revitalize downtown" (Pete 2016). Converting vacant land in Gary or Detroit into an urban farm, park or other green amenity, will increase or stabilize property values, but is not going to attract developers looking to a global market for luxury condominiums in urban centers.[3] A new water-front park in Sunset Park, Brooklyn would likely have a different trajectory. Between those extremes there is a wide range of neighborhoods with very different green-gentrification tipping points. In general, urban greening is likely to have less severe inequality impacts the colder the urban real estate market is. Greening environmental-justice communities in cold markets is going to have a better long-term environmental-justice trajectory than doing so in global cities. This implies that community-generated initiatives for urban environmental equity will require less forceful public policy intervention and protection than similar initiatives in global cities. In global cities, organized communities must seize the state sufficiently to defend against the appropriation interests of capital.

Urban greening is an important twenty-first century global phenomenon, and one that has particular dynamics in global cities. Greening in global cities is typified by efforts to remake urban spaces in ways that are more ecologically sound (in perception, if not always in effect) and that generate economic growth. Urban greening tends to appropriate environmental resources from one class to another through processes of green gentrification, and in doing so increases urban inequality in general and environmental injustice in particular. Because sustainable development requires social equity in both process and outcome, the current wave of urban greening in global cities does not enhance sustainability. By increasing

Figure 7.6 "End" sign at Domino Sugar redevelopment site in Williamsburg

the distance between power holders and the marginalized, and between those experiencing the costs of the current global development trajectory and those reaping the benefits from it, urban greening in global cities further disables the feedback mechanism between social system and ecosystem which is necessary if sustainable development is to be achieved. It is our hope that this volume will contribute in some small way to the empowerment of civil society and the emboldening of public policymakers to act on their behalf in the struggle for environmental justice and a just sustainability.

Notes

1 Bauhardt (2014: 60) outlines the degrowth critique of capitalism: "The concept challenges the assumption that economic growth leaves people better off and happy. The production of goods and services is supposed to improve living conditions: the ongoing growth of production and consumption is assumed to raise living standards and well-being. The ecological crisis tells us that this story of social progress through economic growth is highly questionable."
2 The equity pillar is also essential to attaining sustainability because high inequality will ultimately require increasing levels of repression, which is socially and ecologically costly.
3 It may, however, designate an area as purified, indicating that green has been added and brown people have been removed, signifying its readiness for reinvestment (Clement and Kanai 2015).

Bibliography

Agyeman, Julian. 2005. *Sustainable Communities and the Challenge of Environmental Justice.* New York: New York University Press.

Atkinson, Rowland and Gary Bridge. 2005. *Gentrification in a Global Context: The New Urban Colonialism.* New York: Routledge.

Bauhardt, Christine. 2014. "Solutions to the Crisis? The Green New Deal, Degrowth, and the Solidarity Economy: Alternatives to the Capitalist Growth Economy from an Ecofeminist Economics Perspective." *Ecological Economics* 102: 60–68.

Causa Justa::Just Cause. 2014. "Development without Displacement: Resisting Gentrification in the Bay Area." (www.acphd.org/media/343952/cjjc2014.pdf).

Cavalcanti, Maria Fernanda. 2014. "São Paulo's New Master Plan Prioritizes Sustainable Urban Development." *The City Fix.* August 7. Retrieved January 29, 2016 (http://thecityfix.com/blog/sao-paulo-brazil-master-plan-prioritizes-sustainable-urban-development-people-oriented-mobility-public-participation-maria-fernanda-cavalcanti/).

City of Chicago. 2015. "Sustainable Chicago 2015: Action Agenda 2012–2015 Highlights and Look Ahead." Retrieved January 28, 2016 (www.cityofchicago.org/content/dam/city/progs/env/Sustainable_Chicago_2012-2015_Highlights.pdf).

City of Sydney. 2013. *Sustainable Sydney 2030 Community Strategic Plan.* Council of the City of Sydney: Sydney, Australia.

Clement, Daniel and Miguel Kanai. 2015. "The Detroit Future City: How Pervasive Neoliberal Urbanism Exacerbates Racialized Spatial Injustice." *American Behavioral Scientist.* 59(3): 369–385.

Cohen, Daniel Aldana. Forthcoming. "The other low-carbon protagonists: Poor people's movements and climate politics in São Paulo." In *The City as the Factory: Social Movements in the Age of Neoliberal Urbanism.* Miriam Greenberg and Penny Lewis. eds. Ithaca, NY: Cornell University Press.

Curran, Winifred and Trina Hamilton. 2012. "Just Green Enough: Contesting Environmental Gentrification in Greenpoint, Brooklyn." *Local Environment* 17(9): 1027–1042.

D'Allant, Josephine. 2014. "The UN Wants Sustainable Urban Development, But What Does That Look Like?" *Huffpost Impact.* December 3. Retrieved January 19, 2016 (http://huffingtonpost.com/josephone-dallant/the-un-want-sustainable_b_5926652.html).

DeSena, Judith N. 2009. *Gentrification and Inequality in Brooklyn: The New Kids on the Block.* New York: Lexington Books.

Dot, Esteve, Antonia Casellas and Monserrat Pallares-Barbera. 2010. "Gentrificación Productiva en Barcelona: Effectos del Nuevo Espacio Económico." *IV Jornadas De Geografía Económica.*

Evans, Peter. ed. 2002. *Livable Cities? Urban Struggles for Livelihood and Sustainability.* Berkeley, CA: University of California Press.

Florida, Richard. 2015. "Sorry, London: New York is the World's Most Economically Powerful City." March 3. *The Atlantic Citylab.* (www.citylab.com/work/2015/03/sorry-london-new-york-is-the-worlds-most-economically-powerful-city/386315/).

Friedmann, John. 1986. "The World City Hypothesis." *Development and Change* 17(1): 69–84.

Friedmann, John and Goetz Wolff. 1982. "World City Formation: An Agenda for Research and Action." *International Journal of Urban and Regional Research* 6(3): 309–344.

Gedicks, Al. 2001. *Resource Rebels: Native and Environmental Challenges to Mining and Oil Corporations.* Boston, MA: South End Press.

Goldstein, Jesse. 2013. "Appropriate Technocracies? Green Capitalist Discourses and Post Capitalist Desires." *Capitalism, Nature, Socialism,* 24(1): 26–34.

Gotham, Kevin Fox and Miriam Greenberg. 2014. *Crisis Cities: Disaster and Redevelopment in New York and New Orleans.* New York: Oxford University Press.

Gould, Kenneth A. 1992. "Putting the (W)R.A.P.s on Public Participation: Remedial Action Planning and Working-Class Power in the Great Lakes." *Sociological Practice Review* 3(3): 133–139.

Gould, Kenneth A. 2006. "Promoting Sustainability." In *Public Sociologies Reader.* Judith Blau and Keri Iyall Smith. eds. New York: Rowman and Littlefield, 213–230.

Gould, Kenneth A. and Tammy L. Lewis. 2012. "The Environmental Injustice of Green Gentrification." In *The World in Brooklyn: Gentrification, Immigration, and Ethnic Politics in a Global City.* Judith DeSena and Timothy Shortell. eds. Lanham, MD: Lexington Books, 113–146.

Gould, Kenneth A. and Tammy L. Lewis. 2015. "The Paradoxes of Sustainable Development: Focus on Ecotourism." In *Twenty Lessons in Environmental*

Sociology. Kenneth A. Gould and Tammy L. Lewis. eds. New York: Oxford University Press, 330–351.

Gould, Kenneth A., Tammy L. Lewis and J. Timmons Roberts. 2004. "Blue-Green Coalitions: Constraints and Possibilities in the Post 9-11 Political Environment." *Journal of World Systems Research*. 10(1): 90–116.

Gould, Kenneth A., David Naguib Pellow and Allan Schnaiberg. 2008. *The Treadmill of Production: Injustice and Unsustainability in a Global Economy*. Boulder, CO: Paradigm Press.

Gould, Kenneth A., Allan Schnaiberg and Adam S. Weinberg. 1996. *Local Environmental Struggles: Citizen Activism in the Treadmill of Production*. Cambridge, UK: Cambridge University Press.

Greenberg, Miriam. 2009. *Branding New York: How a City in Crisis Was Sold to the World*. New York: Routledge.

Greenberg, Miriam. 2014. "The Sustainability Edge: Competition, Crisis, and the Rise of Eco-City Branding in New York and New Orleans." In *Sustainability in the Global City: Myth and Practice*. Melissa Checker, Cindy Isenhour and Gary McDonough. eds. Cambridge, UK: Cambridge University Press.

Grist, 2007. "15 Green Cities." Retrieved January 17 (http://grist.org/article/cities3/).

Guha, Ramachandra and Juan Martinez-Alier. 1997. *Varieties of Environmentalism: Essays North and South*. London: Earthscan.

Harvey, David. 2008. "The Right to the City." *New Left Review* 53: 23–40.

Hum, Tarry. 2014. *Brooklyn's Sunset Park: Making a Global Immigrant Neighborhood*. Philadelphia, PA: Temple University Press.

Institute For Transportation and Development Policy. 2014. "New São Paulo Master Plan Promotes Sustainable Growth, Eliminates Parking Minimums Citywide." July 7. Retrieved January 29, 2016 (www.itdp.org/new-sao-paulo-master-plan-promotes-sustainable-growth-eliminates-parking-minimums-citywide-2/).

International Union for the Conservation of Nature. 2013. "Barcelona's quest for a green urban future." December 9. Retrieved January 28, 2016 (http://iucn.org/about/union/secretariat/offices/europe/?14172/Barcelonas-quest-for-a-green-urban-future).

Kallis, Giorgos, Christian Kerschner and Joan Martínez-Alier. 2012. "The Economics of Degrowth." *Ecological Economics* 84: 172–180.

Lewis, Tammy L. 2016. *Ecuador's Environmental Revolutions: Ecoimperialists, Ecodependents, and Ecoresisters*. Cambridge, MA: The MIT Press.

Lindmäe, Maria. 2016. "22@ and the Gentrification of Barcelona's Poblenou Area." Retrieved January 28, 2016 (www.academia.edu/5412123/22_at_and_the_Gentrification_of_Barcelona_s_Poblenou_Area).

Logan, John R. and Harvey L. Molotch. 1987. *Urban Fortunes: The Political Economy of Place*. Berkeley, CA: University of California Press.

Misra, Tanvi. 2015. "Mapping Gentrification and Displacement in San Francisco." August 31. *The Atlantic Citylab*. Retrieved February 3, 2016 (www.citylab.com/housing/2015/08/mapping-gentrification-and-displacement-in-san-francisco/402559/).

Mol, Arthur P.J. and Gert Spaargaren. 2000. "Ecological Modernisation Theory in Debate: A Review." *Environmental Politics* 9(1): 17–49.

Molotch, Harvey. 1976. "The City as a Growth Machine: Toward a Political Economy of Place." *The American Journal of Sociology* 82(2): 309–332.

Montero, Sérgio. 2015. Mobilizing Bogotá: The Local and Transnational Politics of Urban Policy Circulation. Unpublished dissertation. Department of City and Regional Planning, University of California, Berkeley

Obach, Brian. 2004. *Labor and the Environmental Movement: The Quest for Common Ground.* Cambridge, MA: The MIT Press.

O'Neill, Karen M. and Daniel J. Van Abs. eds. 2016. *Taking Chances: The Coast After Hurricane Sandy.* New Brunswick, NJ: Rutgers University Press.

Pantsios, Anastasia. 2014. "Top 10 Greenest Cities in the World." EcoWatch. October 24. Retrieved January 27, 2016 (http://ecowatch.com2014/top-ten-greenest-cities-world/).

Pellow, David Naguib. 2007. *Resisting Global Toxics: Transnational Movements for Environmental Justice.* Cambridge, MA: The MIT Press.

Pellow, David Naguib and Ted Smith. 2006. *Challenging the Chip: Labor Rights and Environmental Justice in the Global Electronics Industry.* Philadelphia, PA: Temple University Press.

Pete, Joseph S. 2016. "Feds Tap Gary for Urban Agriculture Initiative." Retrieved February 6, 2016 (www.nwi.com).

Sassen, Saskia. 2001. *The Global City: New York, London, Tokyo.* New York: Princeton University Press.

Schilling, Joseph and Jonathan Logan. 2008. "Greening the Rust Belt: A Green Infrastructure Model for Right Sizing America's Shrinking Cities." *Journal of the American Planning Association.* 74(4): 451–466.

Schnaiberg, Allan. 1980. *The Environment: From Surplus to Scarcity.* New York: Oxford University Press.

Schnaiberg, Allan and Kenneth A. Gould. 2000. *Environment and Society: The Enduring Conflict.* Caldwell, NJ: Blackburn Press.

Schwartz, Ariel. 2013. "The 10 Cities That Are Leading The Way In Urban Sustainability." September 5. Retrieved January 27, 2016 (http://fastcoexist.com 3016816/the-10-cities-that-are-leading-the-way-in-urban-sustainability).

SF Environment. 2016. "Our Mission." Retrieved February 5, 2016 (http://sfenvironment.org/about).

Shi, Linda, Eric Chu, Isabelle Anguelovski, Alexander Aylett, Jessica Debats, Kian Goh, Todd Schenk, Karen C. Seto, David Dodman, Debra Roberts, J. Timmons Roberts and Stacy D. VanDeveer. 2015. "Roadmap Towards Justice in Urban Climate Adaptation Research." *Nature Climate Change* 6: 131–137.

Smithsimon, Gregory. 2010. "Inside the Empire: Ethnography of a Global Citadel in New York." *Urban Studies* 47(4): 699–724.

SP-Urbanismo. 2012. *Sustainable Urban Development of São Paulo: Challenges and Opportunities.* Miguel Luiz Bucalem Secretary of Urban Development.

Stretton, Hugh. 1976. *Capitalism, Socialism, and the Environment.* Cambridge, UK: Cambridge University Press.

Szasz, Andrew. 2007. *Shopping Our Way to Safety: How We Changed From Protecting the Environment to Protecting Ourselves.* Minneapolis, MN: University of Minnesota Press.

Sze, Julie. 2015. *Fantasy Islands: Chinese Dreams and Ecological Fears in an Age of Climate Crisis.* Oakland, CA: University of California Press.

Taylor, Bron Raymond. ed. 1995. *Ecological Resistance Movements: The Global Emergence of Radical and Popular Environmentalism.* Albany, NY: State University of New York Press.

Taylor, Peter J. 2004. *World City Network: A Global Urban Analysis*. New York: Routledge.

The City Project. 2011. "Environmental Justice, Parks and Health: Department of Interior and National Park Service Plan." December 7. Retrieved January 25, 2016 (www.cityprojectca.org/blog/archives12124).

The City Project. 2012. "California Forever PBS: Urban State Parks." September 6. Retrieved January 22, 2016 (www.cityprojectca.org/blog/archives15463).

The Mayor's Office of Long-Term Planning and Sustainability. The City of New York. 2013. *The Future of PlaNYC: Innovations in Sustainability*. School of International and Public Affairs and The Earth Institute, Columbia University.

Toffa, Tariq. 2014. "Sustainability or Transformation? City Futures in Cape Town and the Global South." September 22. Retrieved January 29, 2016 (www.urb.im/c1409).

Weinberg, Adam S. and Kenneth A. Gould. 1993. "Public Participation in Environmental Regulatory Conflicts: Treading through the Possibilities and Pitfalls." *Law and Policy*. 15(2): 139–167.

Wen, Ming, Xingyou Zhang, Carmen D. Harris, James B. Holt and Janet B. Croft. 2013. "Spatial Disparities in the Distribution of Parks and Green Spaces in the USA." *Annals of Behavioral Medicine* 45(1): S18–S27.

Wolch, Jennifer R., Jason Byrne and Joshua P. Newell. 2014. "Urban Green Space, Public Health, and Environmental Justice: The Challenge of Making Cities 'Just Green Enough'." *Landscape and Urban Planning* 125: 234–244.

Index

Page numbers in italics indicate illustrations, bold indicates a table.

Printed in the United States
by Baker & Taylor Publisher Services